MUNICIPAL BOND FINANCE AND ADMINISTRATION

Municipal Bond Finance and Administration

A Practical Guide to the Analysis
of Tax-Exempt Securities

ALAN RABINOWITZ

WILEY—INTERSCIENCE

A DIVISION OF JOHN WILEY & SONS

New York · London · Sydney · Toronto

Library of Congress Catalogue Card Number: 71-81325

SBN 471 70460 1

Printed in the United States of America

Foreword

by the Editor of *The Weekly Bond Buyer*

Municipal Bond Finance and Administration, by Alan Rabinowitz, is unique in the collection of contemporary literature on the profound crisis which now confronts most of our state and local governments, a crisis whose depth is measured by the serious debate in leading circles in Washington and Wall Street as to whether the financial and political structures of these governments can be sustained entirely in their present form. In magnitude, whether measured in terms of the aggregates of the itemizations of social needs or whether measured in dollar equivalents, there is no parallel to the present challenge; in substance, the threat now to the existing organizational apparatus of our state and local governments and to their relationships to the federal government ranks below only two previous governmental crises in our nation's history.

The nature of the problem and the nature of the setting are well known: The overwhelming urbanization of American life, the depopulation of rural areas, the overpopulation of urban centers, the flight of the middle class to "compounds" and "colonies" created around the periphery of urban centers; the compounding of social miseries which results from the growing gap between the rationalized social demands and the fractional fulfillment of these demands; the social disutility of the breakdown in education; the resources disutility in the breakdown in transportation; the inability of the community to use fully the labor resources of certain sectors of our population; the inability of our organized society to effect an adequate transfer of labor from the oversupplied areas of the unskilled to the scarcely supplied areas of the skilled; the limited reach of community law; the impression creeping upon large areas of our population that they are becoming increasingly immobilized within a society which is becoming increasingly rigid in its stratification; and the gradually less formless impression among many of our political and financial leaders that many of our state and local governments are approaching the effective limits of their taxing powers and effective limits of their abilities to raise money through bond issues at a time when these problems still seem to lie beyond the grasp of solution.

Within this context, the wide range of this present work by Mr. Rabinowitz gives it unique value. It looks at the whole problem as an interrelated, interconnected complex that binds both local government and finance.

But, although Mr. Rabinowitz's work is in many ways about money, it is also very much not about money.

As every treatise on economics does tell us, economics is about the allocation of scarce resources among competing ends. Whether the allocation is done by the price system and the marketplace, or by fiat, or by both in a "mixed economy," the scarce resources, the people (who are the basic asset of any community), are real, and the resource of their production, alone or with machines, is limited; whereas the competing ends are endless, whether they be the brick and mortar of a skyscraper or the cap and gown of a new scientist. As the old saying goes in this country, "Something has to give."

The underlying principle in this book is that the mirror image of a social need is a financial resource. This may be obvious in the abstract, but that it is not so obvious in practice is common knowledge. The landscape of our economy is littered with the wrecks of social programs, inadequately funded in their inception and bankrupt at the end, which, like half-built cities recaptured by the jungle, are nothing but dreams that have run out of money.

It is the virtue of Mr. Rabinowitz's approach that it is, in part, technical, although the technic, unlike that of outer space mathematics, is within easy comprehension of the layman. It is the fault of too many architects of social programs that their sociotechnical ability to assess a priority of social needs and bind them into the most efficient package is not matched by an ability to design a companion funding program that the community which has to finance the program can accommodate. And it is the fault of too many financial specialists that their ability to analyze the contour of financial resources of a community is not matched by insights into the social needs which are to be financed: To some, both the dole and job training are identical in that money is given to anonymous groups of people designated to receive it.

The principle can be extended: The mirror image of a social need is a financial resource, and a financial resource is a claim on a real resource. In any reasonably stable society, money not spent is a deferred, but continuing claim, on a real resource. But, whereas one person may defer a claim on a real resource, there are others who can use that claim on real resources and so they borrow the claim, stipulating to repay it in a given period of time, and while they are using the claim, they pay a price, an interest rate. Thus, Wall Street, which is the blanket term for the nation's money markets, bond markets, and stock markets, is a market in deferred financial claims on real resources. Our state and local governments compete, even-Steven, in this market for deferred financial claims with the federal government, corporations, foreign governments and foreign companies, and individuals. The money, in a general way, goes to the highest bidder.

Of the two financial arms of the state and local governments, there is the taxing power, mainly for current revenues to cover current expenses and to cover "debt service," that is, the repayment of principal and interest on old bond issues, and then there is the power to float bond issues for the financing of longer-term capital projects. It is in the latter that the state and local governments enter the arena to compete in the market for deferred claims. But the two are intertwined, and as the current expenses press upon the practical ceiling of current revenues from taxation, thus narrowing the coverage for debt service, there is the simultaneous development of ever larger longer-term capital projects being developed, to be financed with bond issues which have a relatively narrower base for servicing.

Until recently the marketing of municipal bonds for social projects has been facilitated by the fact that the interest payments on these bonds has been exempt from federal income taxes. Originally, in the early nineteenth century, this exemption was a matter for the Constitutional sphere, and it was not until passage of the presently structured federal income tax in February 1913 that the exemption began to become a marketing factor for state and local bond issues.

But now this too is changing, as all bonds are becoming, in effect, tax-free. Institutions which are already tax-free, such as pension funds and endowment funds (a field which is one of the fastest growing among buyers of securities), now purchase bonds whose interest rates would be taxable to others; and investors who are subject to taxation are buying the tax-exempt bonds. In the "mix" however, the preponderance is with institutions whose income is already tax-free, and among the two dominant groups of taxed investors who are major buyers in the municipal market, the commercial banks are a "sometime factor" and the individuals, disillusioned by a 4 per cent to 5 per cent rate of inflation which reduces their bond interest return to a net of zero, are increasingly turning to equities and real estate.

It would be too much of an overstatement to suggest that state and local governments, in their bond financings, are becoming orphans in the marketplace, but it would be an understatement bordering on delusion to suggest that all is well or that all can continue as in the past.

Mr. Rabinowitz, essentially an optimist, looks upon the crucial financial problems of our state and local governments as a challenge which will be met; others, however, look upon these problems as a crisis that will not be resolved in a meaningful way within the present context of our social programs and social goals.

What this book does is demonstrate with great style the inseparableness of social development and financial resources, and delineate the nature of the market mechanism which translates one into the other. It is, again, the underlying principle: The mirror image of every social need is a financial resource.

The approach of this book is in the sound, old-fashioned tradition of what was once called "political economy," a notion of the mixture of social, political, and financial elements brilliantly depicted once by John Maynard Keynes when he pictured the Middle Ages as a "catastrophic deflation."

The book's author, Alan Rabinowitz, is eminently qualified for the multifaceted task he has undertaken. His work is known to and respected by investment bankers, municipal dealers, banks, social scientists, institutional investors of all types, municipal analysts, municipal finance officers, and financial and political staff specialists in Washington. In his many active financial dealings in Wall Street he is a pragmatic realist; in balancing assessments of projected social needs and financial resources he is a compassionate social scientist; in analyzing the investment quality of municipal bonds for large institutional investors he is conservative and critical; and in research, the nature of his perseverance is well known both on Wall Street and in Washington.

Southport, Connecticut   *Charles Brophy*

Author's Preface

I have had the good fortune to work on both sides of the paper curtain that separates local government in the United States from the investment community. Although each side has a concern for the municipal tax-exempt bond, it cannot be said that there is common understanding about the subject. The extreme of misunderstanding is reflected in the Wall Street stories about the underwriters who think that local governments were created for the sole purpose of issuing bonds and the other stories about state and local officials who honestly believe that underwriters buy new issues for their own investment portfolios.

I had often looked for a book that would tell Wall Street's real story to those who issue tax-exempt bonds. I had also looked for a book that would examine the significance to the municipal bond community of the important changes taking place in local government finance and administration. Finding neither, I set out to write a book to fill both needs and to explore controversial policy questions concerning long-term local public securities. The result is *Municipal Bond Finance and Administration,* which took its final form when the editors, the reviewers, and the writer agreed that four main interests of readers should be covered: (a) market operations; (b) policy problems; (c) bond analysis; and (d) future conditions.

Part 1, *How the Municipal Bond Market Works,* is specially addressed to local officials and others who may have had little direct exposure to the process. We begin with total immersion in the work of underwriters as a particular set of new issues is put up for bid, then bought and distributed to investors. Later chapters consider both the methods by which local communities create a supply of bonds and the nature of investor demand for the bonds.

We agreed further that, having observed the market at work, the reader would be ready to plunge into the politics of the municipal bond field.

Thus Part 2 is concerned with the four *Critical Issues in Tax-Exempt Finance* that have occupied such a prominent place in Congressional hearings and in the financial press. At the risk of making strong enemies but equally strong friends, I was urged to take a position on the evidence in each of these areas. My thoughts on the four questions covered in Chapters 7 through 10 can be summarized as follows.

Should bond ratings be standardized? Improvements to municipal bond rating systems are clearly needed as part of a better decision-making process concerning individual municipal credits, but federal intervention should be discouraged.

Should dealer banks underwrite revenue issues? A strong commercial banking system is essential for the municipal bond market, but it does not seem harmful to maintain the present regulations that do not allow commercial banks to underwrite revenue bonds.

Should industrial revenue bonds be tax-exempt? The arguments that once favored unlimited tax exemption for industrial revenue bond financing now seem to be weaker than those against the practice, but the debate calls attention to the need for overhauling much of the structure of municipal financing for development.

Should any local public securities be tax-exempt? I think tax exemption for municipal bond interest is worth preserving, but I also think that revenue sharing by the federal government and far-reaching structural changes in intergovernmental relations are both essential to make the institutions of local government viable and to relieve the pressures on the limited market for tax exempt securities.

Next we agreed that the reader, especially one burdened with the responsibility for evaluating both individual communities and particular bond issues, should be aware of the forces that are changing urban America and of the ways in which new administrative procedures and research methods might be applied. Thus Part 3 takes up *Problems for the Bond Analyst* who is dealing with a commodity that is shaped, on the one hand, by a market system that so far has defied systematic analysis and, on the other hand, by a set of state regulations and local options in great need of revision.

Finally we agreed to hold consideration of the macroeconomic facts and figures concerning municipal finance for Part 4, *The Next Decade.* Nothing, of course, is riskier with respect to municipal bond finance than projecting the future by extrapolating historical figures or by assuming that resources will be made available in amounts required to satisfy estimates of America's needs for the kind of local public facilities often financed by tax exempt bonds. However, the extensive studies made for Congress' Joint Economic Committee deserved attention, for, if valid, the Committee's published projections imply that the volume of bonds will continue to rise, a situation that, under the existing tax system, would require rising bond yields.

Responsibility for the preparation of the manuscript is mine alone, but encouragement for the writing of the book, and ideas to be developed in it, came from many friends and colleagues over many years. In the realm of urban economics and public administration, I think particularly of Martin Meyerson, Henry Cohen, Lloyd Rodwin, and Jerome Rothenberg. On the Street, I think of long association with Edward Besse, Charles Brophy, Marquette de Bary, Austin Tobin, Jr., and John Thompson. To many others unnamed but well remembered, to the tireless researchers whose work has been cited, and to typists Ann B. Hopkins and Judy Edgett, I am also grateful. By far the greatest help, however, in countless marvelous ways, came from Andrea, Eric, Peter, Marli, and Kate; to them the book is dedicated and for them we struggle to improve America's cities.

Cambridge, Massachusetts   *Alan Rabinowitz*
September 1968

Contents

1

How the Municipal
Bond Market Works

Chapter I The Marketplace

A. OVERVIEW

There was a time when bonds issued by a local government were literally peddled in adjacent towns by salesmen knocking on office doors. What we now refer to as the market is the process by which thousands of governmental agencies each year supply new issues of bonds to underwriters who, in turn, resell them to individuals and institutional investors. Smaller issues are still handled locally, but the larger blocks of bonds are bought and sold in what is known as the general market. Action in the general market is concentrated in a few financial centers, notably Wall Street itself.

The case study that begins in the next section covers only one week in June 1967, but the market has been under similar pressure consistently during the 1960's. It is more than likely that substantially the same problems will face underwriters for many years to come. Although an occasional "up" market comes along (when prices of bonds are steady or gently rising), dealers have become accustomed to depressing headlines in *The Bond Buyer* (and the other sources of market information) as the nation moves through recurrent crises of credit restraint, inflation, trade deficits, and urban unrest. Let us turn the clock back, then, to the familiar conditions that characterized the municipal bond market on June 26, 1967.

The Market's Place in the Federal System

It may be helpful to the reader at this point to consider how the municipal bond market fits into the larger conceptions of local public finance and of welfare economics that cannot be discussed in detail in this book. Figure 1 illustrates the pattern of interactions among the major concepts and factors that are involved. The market mechanisms and the primary supply and demand functions are heavily outlined to reflect our emphasis on (a) the process by which underwriters and dealers purchase the supply of new

3

bonds offered by local governments and reoffer them to investors, and (b) the impact of the political environment and the various interventions by federal and state legislative and regulatory agencies in the market.

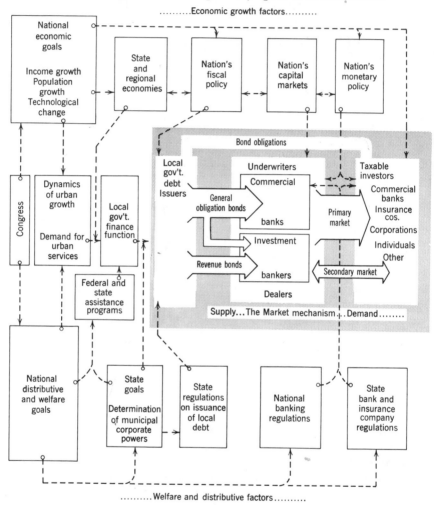

Figure 1 A concept of local public finance and the municipal bond market.

These environmental and interventional factors, and the policy issues we shall consider with respect to them, are responses to competing national goals concerning economic growth and the distribution of net benefits under the federal system. Congress, subject to Constitutional restraints, is the focus of the national debate concerning these goals and has established many of the institutions with which the market must deal. Regional differences in resource endowment may be magnified by the complementary (and sometimes conflicting) sets of institutions and fiscal policies which the several states are privileged to establish within their own jurisdictions. Thus the functions of the bond market and the operations of local public finance are subject to a complex set of national and state influences. Broad national programs affecting the economy and its rates of population growth and technological change are associated with national fiscal and monetary policies and are shown across the top of Figure 1. The arrows indicate that these trends and policies affect the rate of urbanization, the relative health of state and regional economies, the flow of revenues to local governments, and the demand for urban services.

On the welfare or distributive side, shown along the bottom of Figure 1, the factors at work include Constitutional and legislative provisions concerning the forms and powers of local government, the programs of financial assistance being made available to local government, and regulations concerning both issuance of local debt and the operation of banking and investing institutions.

The six chapters of Part 1 are all segments of a single story, beginning with the case history in Chapter I of how underwriters in the general market operated during a representative week. Chapter II provides a closer analysis of the activities of the market professionals, dealers, and underwriters. Then Chapter III steps back to cover fundamental aspects of the supply side of the market, including the types and dollar amounts of bonds sold, and Chapter IV is an evaluation of the normative advice given to local governments concerning the kinds of bond that are acceptable and the way the new issues should be packaged for the underwriters. The demand side of the market is covered in Chapters V and VI, where our attention becomes riveted on the dominant role of commercial banks among the investors in tax-exempt bonds.

B. A CASE STUDY OF THE NEW ISSUE MARKET [1]

The objective of this chapter is to portray the New York municipal bond market as an underwriter might have seen it in the last week of June 1967, finding himself cautious on Monday, determined on Wednesday, and still alive and kicking on Friday.

New bond issues, large and small, are underwritten in many financial centers around the country, but the market in New York dominates the others in size and influence, and thus most of the large banks and investment houses in the nation maintain representatives in New York. The

[1] See references in the bibliographic notes at the end of the book under the heading *Bond Buyer* (a).

market process finds them meeting face to face at information and final-price-setting meetings in the offices of the bidding syndicate managers, and making innumerable telephone calls.

In the last week of June 1967 64 local finance officers headed for the marketplace to see what their wares were worth. A local government offers new bonds to the market rather infrequently, rarely more often than once a year except for the very large general governments and utility districts, and sometimes only once (as might be the case for a turnpike revenue bond). Most of the paperwork is handled by correspondence, and the local finance officer typically is found in his office at City Hall on the day of sale as the bids are made. The financial consultants and bond attorneys who represent the issuers are seen more frequently on the Street.

Notices of Sale

The Bond Buyer's Calendar of Sealed Bid Openings listed offerings by the 64 issuers totaling almost $400 million for sale during that busy but representative week. Since the Calendar lists only issues with face amount of at least $750,000, there must have been two or three smaller issues for sale in regional markets for every one being offered in the general or national market dominated by the bond underwriting firms and banks in New York, Chicago, San Francisco, and a limited number of other major cities.

Of these 64 large issues, more than half (33) had something to do with education, including many forms of school districts and various kinds of college building authorities. One state government and 18 local governments were selling general obligation bonds. The remaining 12 issues were made up of revenue bonds, mostly for community facilities such as water and sewer systems, and only one was identified in the transportation field.

Distributed by day, the list turned out to include 12 issues for which bids would be received on Monday, 30 issues for sale on Tuesday, 14 on Wednesday, and 8 more on Friday. This pattern would please the underwriters. It meant that Monday could be spent setting up for the week's bids, working down last week's inventory of unsold bonds, and observing how the 12 issues posted for Monday's sale were received. Tuesday would see the usual heavy load, tapering off over the following two days. Then would come Friday, with time to pick up the pieces, to think about the Federal Reserve statistics and other general money market indicators that are published in the latter part of the week and that provide the basis for the following week's price level, and to listen to speeches at formal and informal luncheons for which there had been no opportunity during the hectic trading days earlier in the week.

Three-quarters of the 64 issues listed by *The Bond Buyer* had face values less than $5 million. The larger issues were wisely scheduled for sale in midweek rather than on either Monday or Friday. Among them were bond issues for $30 million in the Los Angeles Unified School District, $20 million in the Dallas Independent School District, $32 million in the Georgia Education Authority (Schools State Secured Lease Rental Revenue), all on Tuesday, and, on Wednesday, $75 million in the Chicago City School District, $70 million in the San Francisco Bay Area Rapid Transit District, and $8 million in the Clinton Bridge Commission, Iowa (Revenue).

Table A   *Ratings Available on 64 New Issues, June 26, 1967*

	Rating Agency		Type of Bond	
Number of Issues	Moody's	Standard & Poor's	General Obligation and School	Revenue Issue
1	Aaa	AAA	1	...
1	+	AAA	...	1
4	Aa	AA	3	1
4	Aa	✷	4	...
1	*Aa	AA	1	...
4	+	AA	3	1
2	A	AA	2	...
8	A	A	6	2
3	+	A	2	1
2	*A	A	1	1
1	*A	+	1	...
1	*A	✷	...	1
5	Baa	A	5	...
5	Baa	BBB	4	1
1	*Baa	BBB	1	...
1	+	BBB	1	...
1	NR	BBB	1	...
2	+	BB	1	1
16	+	✷	12	4
2	+	NR	...	2
			49	16

Source: *The Bond Buyer.* Actual total is 65 because one issue was in two parts with separate ratings. The Bond Buyer's symbols are as follows:

[+]   "Provisional rating not yet assigned."
[✷]   "Not yet determined."
[NR]   "Not rated."
[*]   "Provisional ratings are assigned to bonds not yet issued; they are based on available information and are subject to change as new information is received."

Ratings

As for ratings (which are the subject of Chapter VII), Moody's and Standard & Poor's agencies rated the Dallas, Los Angeles, and Georgia bonds as

Aa (Moody's) and AA (S&P). Chicago received an A rating from Moody's
and AA from S&P. The San Francisco Bay Area bonds got Aa from
Moody's, but S&P had not yet assigned its provisional rating, and neither
service had yet rated the Clinton Bridge issue. Such ratings would be used
by some investors as a general guide and, consequently, would influence
underwriters as to the price they would bid for the bonds. Table A shows
the twenty different combinations of rating or lack of rating for the 64
issues that week, further categorized by whether the issues are basically
general obligation and school bonds or revenue bonds.

C. MARKET CONDITIONS, JUNE 26, 1967

The underwriters that week were going to have a difficult time figuring
out how to bid for these issues. A large number of factors concerning the
market and the economy are taken into account as the bids are made; and
the market felt weak on June 26.

Risk of Mispricing

The risks of mispricing are formidable: a bond is priced to yield a certain
return for an investor if held to maturity (or to earliest call date), with the
premium or discount paid over face amount calculated in relation to the
"coupon" or stated rate of interest. Thus 1000 bonds due in 10 years (each
$1000, totaling $1 million) might have a 4 per cent coupon and be priced at
par (yielding 4 per cent). The underwriter, having paid par, might have to
sell the bond to yield the investor 4.05 per cent, a difference of five "basis
points" of yield or $7 of value per bond. If an investor bought each of 1000
bonds for $993, the underwriter would lose $7000. Changes in a single day
of 25 basis points are infrequent but not unknown. Such a dip in the market would cause a loss of $35,000 in the case above. An underwriter is also
aware that a 4 per cent bond at a 4.05 per cent basis may not be as attractive
to an investor as a bond whose coupon rate is the same as the yield rate
because of the capital gains tax levied on the difference between the discounted price and the par value of the bond.

Recent Price Levels

The underwriters would be lucky to have avoided losses during the preceding weeks. As underwriters, they become the owners of the whole bond
issue at the price bid; if they have overpaid for the bonds by overestimating
their ability to sell the bonds at a marked-up profit to investors, they have

no alternative but to clear up their inventory of new bonds by reducing price below cost. Figure 2 shows that the level of the market had fallen in each of the two preceding weeks as measured by *The Bond Buyer* indexes; when average yields go up, average bond prices decline.

Figure 2 contains some of the other information that would have been in the minds of the underwriters that Monday morning, June 26, 1967. The underwriters could only guess how the graphs would change during the coming week (as we, with 20-20 hindsight have shown on the chart).

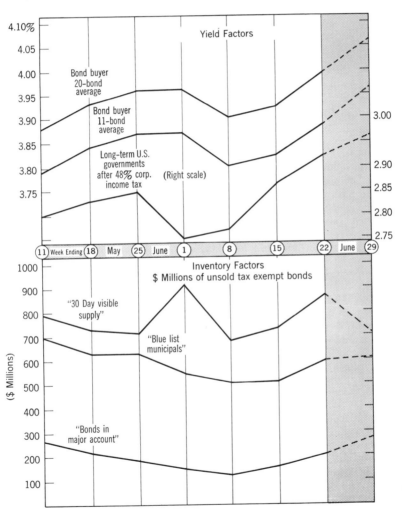

Figure 2   Municipal market factors, yields, and inventories, by weeks in May and June 1967.

Inventories of Unsold Bonds

As shown on Figure 2, there was an inventory of about $200 million in Bonds in Major Accounts, the unsold bonds from new issues of the preceding few weeks which might have to be marked down in the coming week, a factor that would depress price levels and further increase yields. The total amount of bonds for sale advertised in *The Blue List* (a daily listing that includes the bonds in the major syndicate accounts and most of the bonds available in the secondary market) was also increasing, and the 30-day visible supply, the sum of the new issues for sale in the coming weeks as tabulated by *The Bond Buyer,* had climbed to about $860 million. All of these amounts could be considered relatively high. Meanwhile, the yield curve for long-term U.S. Government securities had also been rising. The roundup of the preceding week's events in the capital markets in *The Weekly Bond Buyer* (June 26) was hardly encouraging:

THE FINANCIAL SITUATION: HAPPINESS IS A
6.00 PER CENT YIELD WITH CALL PROTECTION

Time was rolling back to late Summer 1966 in the capital market last week. Top-grade corporate bonds again were available at a 6 per cent yield. Treasury bonds were yielding more than 5 per cent. And average yields on tax-exempts were rising toward the 4 per cent level once more. . . .

Many bond buyers obviously looked backward over the span of financial history, noted that 6 per cent on top-grade corporate debt is available rarely, and decided they would be foolish to pass it up. But there's no law which says rates cannot rise further and some indicators which suggest they might. . . .

Like corporations, State and local governments also are putting pressure on the market. The 30-day visible supply of municipals in late week again was approaching the billion dollar level. It was up to $908.9 million from $798.6 million a week earlier.

It was surprising then that municipal underwriters were able to market as many bonds as they did. Long-term tax-exempts put up for bidding totalled $204.8 million and the placement ratio was a gratifying 68.4 per cent, compared to 59.2 per cent the previous week.

The price paid for this success was yield, of course. *"The Bond Buyer"* yield indexes for both rose six basis points to highs for the year, the 20 bonds at 3.98 per cent and the 11 bonds at 3.88 per cent.

A skein of down days depressed the revenue bond market. *"The Weekly Bond Buyer"* list of dollar bonds showed not a single gain. Thirty bonds were lower and six unchanged.

Another indication of the danger of still higher rates was the failure of the Government bond market to react to the Fed's big purchases of securities. The Fed increased its holdings by $934.5 million to a record level, including purchases of long-term Treasury coupon issues.

But the Treasury coupon market fell heavily again on a rising volume. Declines ranged to more than a point. . . .

There was increasing talk of a tax increase. If it comes, it would help bonds. But it would hurt corporate earnings and, thus, common stock prices.

Last week the stock market paused and buyers nibbled at defensive issues, such as the golds and selected utilities. Some funds were passing up stocks to grab the high yields on bonds, a development long anticipated with the enormous reverse yield spread between stocks and bonds.

By last midweek, this minus gap as measured by two widely-used averages had opened up to 228 basis points, a record spread for the third week in a row.

Preferred stocks went down with the other markets. . . .

D. CHARACTERISTICS OF THE SUCCESSFUL BIDS

Yields

Bearing *The Bond Buyer's* note of caution in mind, the underwriters then looked at their private charts of yields by grade and by year. We have charted in Figure 3 *The Bond Buyer's* weekly average yield index (based

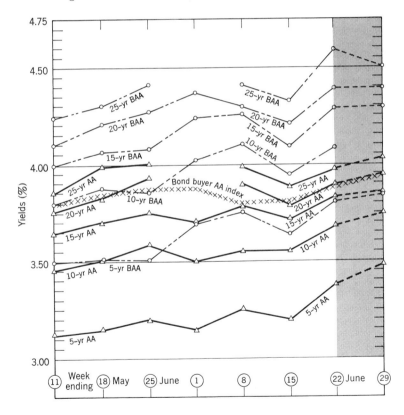

Figure 3 New issue reoffering yield averages, by weeks in May and June 1967, for various maturities and grades of municipal bonds.

on whatever sales happened to be reported during the given week) for AA and BAA tax-exempt securities and the 20-year 11-bond average of AA-type securities. The lowest line of Figure 3 shows that a new-issue bond due in five years and rated AA would have been priced to yield about 3.13 per cent during the week ending May 12 and about 3.38 per cent in the preceding week ending June 23 (a difference in price of about $10 per $1000 bond). For 25-year AA bonds the increase in yield between May 11 and June 23 was 13 basis points, from 3.85 to 3.98 per cent, a dollar change per bond amounting to about $24. Gaps in the trend lines indicate that no major bond issues in that category were sold during that week, according to *The Bond Buyer* records.

Tuesday, June 27
First Sales of the Georgia Bonds

What actually happened in the case of the Georgia Education Authority and the San Francisco Bay Area Rapid Transit issues provides a good illustration of the way the market operates under uncertainty. On Tuesday, June 27, while the Treasury bill market took "one of the sharpest one-day skids in recent memory with 91-day bills rising 21 basis points in yield over Monday's auction rate," the big sale in the municipal bond market was that of the Georgia Education Authority (Schools) with $32,120,000 state-secured lease rental revenue Series A bonds sold to a joint group headed by First National City Bank of New York, Chase Manhattan Bank, The Trust Company of Georgia and Morgan Guaranty, Bankers Trust, First National Bank of Chicago, Continental Illinois Bank, Citizens & Southern Bank, and F.S. Smithers at an average net interest cost of 4.060 per cent. A Halsey, Stuart, John Nuveen, Drexel Harriman Ripley group was a close second bidder with a bid carrying interest of 4.079 per cent. Only two bids were made.

By the end of the first day, $14,830,000 in bonds had been sold (with the 1967, 1968, 1988, and 1989 maturities oversubscribed), leaving a balance of $17,290,000 in inventory. Only $2,205,000 were sold in the balance of the week, indicating that both the buying group and the other bidder probably overpriced the bonds and might have difficulty getting rid of the remaining $15,085,000 balance that was listed in the Bonds in Major Accounts list for July 3, unless the original reoffering prices were lowered. However, having delivered a good-faith check with a bid, the syndicate had three more weeks of selling time before the balance of the money owed the Georgia agency would be due (August 1) and the bonds themselves delivered. Unfortunately in this case, the market did not improve during that period, and the issue was sold out at "down" prices.

Wednesday, June 28
Formation of the BART Syndicates

For the marketing on the following day, Wednesday, of the $70 million San Francisco Bay Area Rapid Transit (BART) District General Obligation Series G bonds, the firms of Halsey, Stuart & Co., Inc., and John Nuveen & Co., Inc., joined forces with some of their erstwhile opponents in the competition for the Georgia bonds (such at the First National Bank of Chicago and F. S. Smithers & Co.) as major participants in a group of 178 potential underwriters to consider a bid for the bonds. The first meeting of the syndicate had been held the day before. Shortly before 1:00 PM (EDT) in New York (or 10:00 AM on the West Coast) on the day of the sale, the members of the syndicate account met at the offices of the senior manager, Halsey, Stuart & Co., Inc., in a "lock-up," a closed meeting in which no one is allowed to leave. The chairman of the meeting, Mr. Barry Rockwell of Halsey, Stuart & Co., Inc., presented the managers' bidding ideas to the group and "polled" the account, reading each member's name for a positive or negative response to the bid. Out-of-town firms were represented by proxy.

After vigorous discussion of alternative interest rates, reoffering yields, indications of institutional buying intentions, and profit potentials, 9 of the 30 underwriters who had each been invited to underwrite $800,000 bonds "dropped from the account." So did 11 of the 24 firms in the $525,000 bracket, 11 of the 32 firms in the $400,000 bracket, 24 of the 62 firms in the $300,000 bracket, and 17 of the 30 firms in the $200,000 bracket. Altogether 72 firms, or 40 per cent of the invited membership, declined to underwrite about $28 million, or 40 per cent, of the $70 million required, because they disliked the price scale, the profit spread, or the amount of unsold bonds overhanging the market in other accounts, or for various other reasons. The members remaining in the account either stayed with their original commitment or increased their participation in the deal. The "net interest cost" on the Halsey, Stuart bid, as calculated by the Investment Bankers Association (IBA) method, was 4.1418 per cent, as shown in Table B.

Meanwhile a group managed by the Bank of America NT & SA, San Francisco, was going through a similar process at a meeting only blocks away in New York. The "B of A" managers coaxed a bid of 4.1503 per cent from its underwriting syndicate, a bid that was only 0.0085 per cent or $5950 less than Halsey, Stuart's winning bid. Minutes before a bid is scheduled to be opened, the "lock-up" is ended and members of the competing groups make informal comparisons of their respective bids. The Street soon knew that the Halsey, Stuart bid had topped "B of A's" by an "0085," and immediately thereafter the winning reoffering scale was telephoned to important investors by eager members of the Halsey, Stuart account.

A sale with a "close cover" (with the second responsible bid very close to the winning bid) is considered a good omen in the market, for it shows that two groups of managers and their compatriots in the syndicates, meeting separately and in secret, have both appraised the market factors of supply, demand, and general capital in a similar fashion. That both groups had been overly optimistic that Wednesday concerning the intensity of non-bank demand for the BART bonds is a fact known only by hindsight.

Midweek Reports

The Daily Bond Buyer for Thursday morning reported:

Market prices for tax-exempt bonds moved sharply lower yesterday under the pressure of a big supply of new issues. Dealers were at a loss to guess just when and where the downward slide would end.

Buyers reacted selectively to the large new offerings, even though lower prices offered investors 10 to 15 basis points higher yields than comparable issues of last week.

By late afternoon, it was still not clear just what the week's two largest issues—$145 million of Chicago and San Francisco bonds—had contributed to a going price level. Both dealers and buyers were extremely cautious and demand for the new high grade offerings tended to cling to the higher-yield bonds. . . .

There was no let-up in the tremendous pressure on prices of short-term maturities in the secondary market yesterday as bonds in big blocks continued to come in for bids.

An announcement by the United States Treasury that it would sell $2 billion of March and $2 billion of April tax anticipation bills on July 5, also served to keep the municipal markets off balance.

About $30 million of the $70 million San Francisco BART bonds were sold the first day and another $3.7 million the second day, leaving finally some $36,935,000 in the account for disposal during the following weeks. By comparison, $55 million of the Chicago School issue was sold on the first day and another $8 million the second day, leaving that $75 million account with a weekend balance of only $12 million. The winning syndicate's advertisement of the BART bonds, reproduced as Figure 4, is a formal notice to investors concerning coupons, maturities, and the reoffering scale. The advertisement lists the members of the account in the upper bracket, with the managers' names at the top.

Scales

The array of yields year by year for serial bonds is known as a scale, and Figure 5 shows how scales for the two issues described above compared with each other and with *The Bond Buyer*'s index of AA-grade bonds. The Georgia bonds on Tuesday were priced to yield somewhat more than the Index compiled at the close of the preceding week, perhaps because of the quality and the size of the issue and the unsettled state of the market.

Interest exempt, in the opinion of counsel, from all present Federal Income Taxation.

$70,000,000

San Francisco Bay Area
Rapid Transit District, California

General Obligation Bonds, Series G

Due serially June 15, 1972 to 1999, inclusive
($5,000 denominations)

Redeemable as a whole or in part in inverse order of maturity (by lot within a maturity) on any date on and after
June 15, 1981 at 103½ and accrued interest if redeemed prior to June 15, 1984 and at decreasing prices thereafter.

These Bonds, in the opinion of Counsel, will constitute general obligations of the San Francisco Bay Area Rapid Transit District
and the full faith and credit of the District are irrevocably pledged for the punctual payment of the principal of and interest
on the Bonds according to their terms. The Board of Directors of the District has power and (unless funds for the payment
of the Bonds are otherwise provided) is obligated to levy ad valorem taxes for the payment of the Bonds and the interest
thereon upon all property within the District subject to taxation by the District without limitation of rate or amount (except
certain intangible personal property which is taxable at limited rates).

Amount	Maturity	Rate	Yield	Amount	Maturity	Rate	Yield or Price	Amount	Maturity	Rate	Price or Yield
$ 675,000	1972	6%	3.60%	$1,325,000	1977	6%	3.85%	$11,750,000	1987-90	4.05%	100
800,000	1973	6	3.65	1,475,000	1978	6	3.90	10,200,000	1991-93	4.10	100
925,000	1974	6	3.70	3,400,000	1979-80	6	3.95	11,400,000	1994-96	4.15	100
1,050,000	1975	6	3.75	1,925,000	1981	4	3.95	8,350,000	1997-98	4.20	100
1,200,000	1976	6	3.80	2,050,000	1982	3.95	100	4,000,000	1999	3	4.50%
				9,475,000	1983-86	4	100				

(accrued interest to be added)

*These bonds are offered when, as and if issued and received by us and subject to approval of legality by counsel, whose opinion will
be furnished upon delivery. The Offering Circular may be obtained in any State in which this announcement is circulated
from only such of the undersigned and other dealers as may lawfully offer these securities in such State.*

HALSEY, STUART & CO. INC.   THE FIRST NATIONAL BANK
                                    OF CHICAGO

CROCKER-CITIZENS NATIONAL BANK   WELLS FARGO BANK   KIDDER, PEABODY & CO.
                                                             INCORPORATED

GLORE FORGAN, WM. R. STAATS INC.   SALOMON BROTHERS & HUTZLER   JOHN NUVEEN & CO.

SECURITY-FIRST NATIONAL BANK   MERCANTILE TRUST COMPANY, N.A.   BEAR, STEARNS & CO.

WERTHEIM & CO.   BACHE & CO.   W. H. MORTON & CO.   LOEB, RHOADES & CO.   ALLEN & COMPANY
                 INCORPORATED   DIVISION OF AMERICAN EXPRESS COMPANY

F. S. SMITHERS & CO.   SCHWABACHER & CO.   THE FIRST NATIONAL BANK   L. F. ROTHSCHILD & CO.
                                              OF MEMPHIS

DOMINICK & DOMINICK,   FRANKLIN NATIONAL BANK   ROBERT GARRETT & SONS
     INCORPORATED   INCORPORATED

NEW YORK HANSEATIC CORPORATION   STATE-PLANTERS BANK OF COMMERCE AND TRUSTS

THE BANK OF VIRGINIA   W. E. HUTTON & CO.   COOLEY & COMPANY   G. H. WALKER & CO.

ADAMS, McENTEE & CO., INC.   BANK OF THE COMMONWEALTH   BARR BROTHERS & CO.

THE CHICAGO CORPORATION   ESTABROOK & CO.   STERN BROTHERS & CO.   WOOD, STRUTHERS & WINTHROP

KING, QUIRK & CO.   DEMPSEY-TEGELER & CO., INC.   RAND & CO., INC.   AUSTIN TOBIN & CO.
                                                                          INCORPORATED

June 30, 1967.

Figure 4 $70 million San Francisco Bay Area Rapid Transit District, California, General Obligation Bonds, Series G: newspaper announcement by winning syndicate, June 28, 1967.

Coming the next day, the San Francisco BART issue, roughly comparable in rating as a general obligation to the Georgia issue, was priced generally lower, with yields slightly higher than the Georgia bonds, except for the bonds due in the late 1980's. Perhaps the price set for these longer-term bonds reflected the demand for 20-year paper evidenced by the sell-out on Tuesday of the 1988 and 1989 Georgia bonds. By the week's end (June 30), the Index had shifted up in yield.

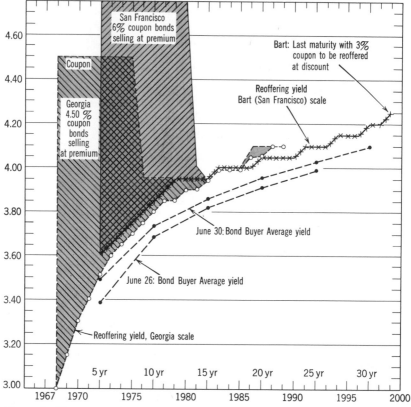

Figure 5 Tax-exempt bond yield scales and coupons, with *Bond Buyer* averages, for selected weeks and selected new issues sold June 27 and 28, 1967.

Coupons and the Bid Calculations

Also shown in Figure 5 are the coupon rates for the various maturities offered in the two issues. Both the BART and the Georgia issues had high coupons for the near-term maturities, which meant that those bonds would be reoffered at a substantial premium: the ten-year (1977) maturity in the San Francisco BART issue, with a 6 per cent coupon to sell at a 3.85 per cent yield, would have a price of $1,177.10 per $1000 bond; conversely the 1999 maturity, with a 3 per cent coupon and a 4.50 per cent yield over the thirty-two-year term, would sell for $743.40. The bidding calculations for the winning BART bid are shown in Table B.

One reason the Halsey, Stuart group won the issue was a variation in the coupon rates to be applied to the bonds of different maturities: the Halsey, Stuart group sequentially used coupons of 6, 4, 3.95, 4, 4.05, 4.10, 4.15, 4.20

and 3 per cent; Bank of America used a combination of 6, 5, 3.90, 4, 4.10, 4.20, and 3 per cent coupons.

When all the premium, par, and discount bonds are added up at the selling price set by the underwriters, the total produced is $70,842,377.50, which the reader can find at the bottom of column 9 in Table B. This "production" would be distributed as follows: first $70,007,000 would go to BART (because the final bid as reported was 100.01 for the whole issue or $7000 over the face amount of the issue); then the direct expenses of the syndicate would be deducted; and finally the "spread" of about $10 a bond to be available to the members of the syndicate on a pro-rata basis according to the number of bonds each one agreed to underwrite represents the remainder. It is clear that a slight miscalculation in the order of a fraction of 1 per cent of the face amount of the issue would be sufficient to wipe out the entire margin of profit or "spread" anticipated. As it happened, market conditions impelled the syndicate to mark down some of the prices and increase the yield offered, and thus most of the hoped-for profit from the BART underwriting was never made.

The Net Interest Cost Calculation

The BART issue was to be awarded to the bidder who provided the lowest "net interest cost" to the issuer, as calculated by the standard (or Investment Bankers Association) method. The winning bid by the Halsey-Stuart account produced a "net interest cost" of 4.141 per cent, representing the weighted average interest rate on a weighted average amount of bonds outstanding. The procedure as outlined below is widely used, although issuers might be able to obtain more advantageous bids if the calculations were based on discounting future flows of funds to "present value," a method that is discussed further in Chapter 4 and in books by Robinson and Ott-Meltzer (see Bibliography).

The "net interest cost" on the winning BART bid was figured by inserting the proper values into the following equation:

$$\text{"net interest cost"} = \frac{\text{(gross interest cost over the life of the bond issue) less (premium)}}{\text{total number of "bond years"}}.$$

The total number of "bond years" is the sum of separate calculations for each of the years in which bonds mature. The number of "bond years" represented by the 675 BART bonds (each $1000 face amount) maturing in 1972 (or 5 years after issuance) is calculated by multiplying 5 (years) by 675 (bonds). The total number of "bond years" for the BART issue is found by summing the entries in column 5 of Table B.

The "gross interest cost" is also the sum of separate calculations for each

Table B The Underwriters' Calculation of "Net Interest Cost" and "Production": $70 Million San Francisco Bay Area Rapid Transit District General Obligation Bonds, Series G, June 28, 1967.

Basic Characteristics				Net Interest Cost Calculations		"Production" Calculations		
(1)	(2)	(3)	(4)	(5)	(6)	(7)	(8)	(9)
Years to Maturity	Year Due	Amount Being Offered ($000)	Coupon Rate^a (%)	"Bond Years": [Col. 1 × Col. 3]	"Interest Cost": [Col. 4 × Col. 5] ($)	Reoffering Price [Yield] (%) or (100=PAR)	Reoffering Price per Bond. ($)	"Production" [Col. 3 × Col. 8] ($)
5	1972	675	6.00	3,375	20,250	3.60	1,108.90	748,507.50
6	73	800	6.00	4,800	28,800	3.65	1,125.60	900,480.00
7	74	925	6.00	6,475	38,850	3.70	1,140.70	1,055,147.50
8	75	1,050	6.00	8,400	50,400	3.75	1,154.30	1,212,015.00
9	76	1,200	6.00	10,800	64,800	3.80	1,166.40	1,399,680.00
10	1977	1,325	6.00	13,250	79,500	3.85	1,177.10	1,559,657.50
11	78	1,475	6.00	16,225	97,350	3.90	1,186.40	1,749,940.00
12	79	1,625	6.00	19,500	117,000	3.95	1,194.40	1,940,900.00
13	80	1,775	6.00	23,075	138,450	3.95	1,206.90	2,142,247.50
14	81	1,925	4.00	26,950	107,800	3.95	1,005.30	1,935,202.50
15	1982	2,050	3.95	30,750	121,462.50	100	1,000.00	2,050,000.00
16	83	2,175	4.00	34,800	139,200	100	1,000.00	2,175,000.00

18

17	84	2,300	4.00	39,100	156,400	100	1,000.00	2,300,000.00
18	85	2,425	4.00	43,650	174,600	100	1,000.00	2,425,000.00
19	86	2,575	4.00	48,925	195,700	100	1,000.00	2,575,000.00
20	1987	2,700	4.05	54,000	218,700	100	1,000.00	2,700,000.00
21	88	2,850	4.05	59,850	242,392.50	100	1,000.00	2,850,000.00
22	89	3,025	4.05	66,550	269,527.50	100	1,000.00	3,025,000.00
23	90	3,175	4.05	73,025	295,751.25	100	1,000.00	3,175,000.00
24	91	3,275	4.10	78,600	322,260	100	1,000.00	3,275,000.00
25	1992	3,400	4.10	85,000	348,500	100	1,000.00	3,400,000.00
26	93	3,525	4.10	91,650	375,765	100	1,000.00	3,525,000.00
27	94	3,650	4.15	98,550	408,982.50	100	1,000.00	3,650,000.00
28	95	3,800	4.15	106,400	441,560	100	1,000.00	3,800,000.00
29	96	3,950	4.15	114,550	475,382.50	100	1,000.00	3,950,000.00
30	1997	4,100	4.20	123,000	516,600	100	1,000.00	4,100,000.00
31	98	4,250	4.20	131,750	553,350	100	1,000.00	4,250,000.00
32	1999	4,000	3.00	128,000	384,000	4.50	743.40	2,973,600.00
		70,000		1,541,000	$6,383,333.75			

Maximum "production" at posted prices less: $70,842,377.50

Par amount for issue, plus premium equals: 70,007,000.00

Amount available as "spread" or gross syndicate profit before expenses, allowances for syndicate members, etc. $ 835,377.50

Source: Calculated from the winning syndicate's advertisement, Figure 4.

a Rate set by bidder within limits specified by issuer.

19

of the years to show the amount of coupon interest to be paid on the bonds outstanding in any maturity. Interest will be paid at 6 per cent for 5 years on the 675 bonds due in 1972. The calculated amount of interest for that first maturity is, therefore, $675,000 times 5 years times 6 per cent, or $20,-250. This figure can be found in column 6 of Table B. For the BART issue as a whole, "gross interest cost" amounts to $6,383,333.75. The number of separate calculations can be reduced by multiplying the coupon rate by all the bond years for maturities with the same coupon.

When the data from Table B are inserted into the equation above, the "net interest cost" can be calculated:

$$4.14123\% = \frac{\$6,383,334 \text{ (from column 6, Table B)} - \$7000 \text{ premium}}{1,541,000 \text{ "bond years" (from column 5, Table B)}}$$

This calculation, in fact, differs slightly from the reported rate of 4.1418 per cent, but has been checked by market professionals. The error might be typographical or might have arisen from use of data other than those published. It might also represent the result of one of the myriad alternative calculations made by a computer for the guidance of the syndicate managers, as they explore the effect of possible combinations of coupons and yields in order to find the bidding scale that syndicate members will agree is both marketable and acceptable to the issuer at that time.

Farewell to BART

It was not the computer's fault, however, that the underwriting of the $70 million BART issue was less profitable than expected. The San Francisco Area Rapid Transit District got its money, but the underwriters lost part of their anticipated profit on the deal because the bonds were slightly overpriced at the time of bid. Day after day, while the Halsey-Stuart account continued to post the original prices, other bond issues were being sold at relatively higher and more attractive yields. Every dealer on the Street and every potential institutional buyer knew that a cut in price for the BART bonds still held under the syndicate agreement was inevitable unless the market unexpectedly reversed its downward course.

Finally, after twenty-one days, the syndicate account was "broken up," and the bonds remaining unsold were distributed to the members of the bidding syndicate in proportion to their share of the underwriting liability. Whatever syndicate profits had been credited to the individual members' accounts on sales of $33 million in the first week, sales of 6 million in the second week, and some further sales in the third week, would be offset by the below-list and perhaps below-cost prices they would receive in the free market that would ensue after syndicate restrictions had been removed.

An issue such as BART becomes a matter of market history as the account is broken up. During the first few days of the free market that follows, dealers and brokers engage in a flurry of transactions to clear the market. Some of the syndicate members take their losses, but other dealers (including some members of the former syndicate) stockpile blocks of such bonds at the lower price level. Moreover, bargain-hunting institutional and other permanent investors come into the market at that time and are thus rewarded for having foregone the opportunity to put in orders on the day of sale at the posted price level. In any case, after a few months most of the bonds end up in institutional or bank portfolios, although on almost any day, for such a large issue, some of the bonds may be found in the offering sheets of the secondary market. Since the BART issue is a fine example of how the municipal bond issue works, we shall meet it again from time to time in the next few chapters as we go deeper into the subject.

Chapter II   Underwriting and
Trading Municipal Bonds

A. DEALER ORGANIZATION AND INVENTORY FINANCING

The sad history of the $70 million BART issue that highlighted the first chapter served as an introduction to the work of underwriters and dealers. This chapter provides more information about the nature of competition in the market.

An underwriter deals in new issues (or very large blocks of bonds coming out of portfolio). Thus he can be called an investment banker if he is not connected with a commercial bank, but a more inclusive term is "dealer," one who not only underwrites new issues but buys and sells blocks of bonds in the secondary market. Some of the major commercial banks are known as dealer banks. Dealers as a class also act as financial consultants and, on rare occasions, as brokers earning a fee for arranging a given transaction. A handful of firms, extremely important to the operation of the market, operate exclusively as brokers, never taking a "position" of ownership in the bonds they handle.

Dealers Own the Bonds

Unlike the corporate securities market, the municipal underwriters rarely promise their "best efforts" as agents for the seller, and there are few "private placements." Almost always, the nervewracking function of the underwriter (or of a group of underwriters acting as a syndicate) is to buy the issue as a whole from a state or local government (with cash on the barrelhead due as payment in approximately thirty days) in the expectation of selling the bonds piecemeal to investors, sometimes at a profit.

Despite the risk involved in holding bonds when the price level is more than likely to sag and yields to rise, the underwriter must carry the bonds that remain in the bidding syndicate's account until it is terminated. In addition, the underwriter will typically have an inventory of other bonds, some of them leftovers from unsuccessful syndicate accounts and some of them issues in which he has taken a position both as speculation and as a service to customers. It takes money to finance such an inventory.

Financing Inventories

Municipal bond inventories are large, in relation to inventories of other securities. Irwin Friend's studies of investment banking and the new-issues market (done at Wharton School, University of Pennsylvania, and based on broker-dealer inventory practices for the first quarter of 1962) show the following averages (with great variations among individual firms) for the ratio between securities in inventory and securities actually sold: (a) for new issues, the ratio

averaged 4 per cent for common stock, 9 per cent for corporate bonds, and 29 per cent for municipal bonds; (b) for outstanding issues, the figures were 8 per cent for common stock, 11 per cent for U.S. Governments, 24 per cent for corporate bonds, and 30 per cent for municipals.[1]

The dealers finance these essential inventories of municipal bonds by using as little of their own capital as possible and by borrowing as much as the banks will allow, usually 90–95 per cent of the price paid. Dealers also sometimes enter into repurchase agreements.

Investment bankers, however, cannot deduct interest charges on short-term commercial bank loans incurred for the purpose of carrying inventories. In the example in the IBA's study for the Joint Economic Committee, a firm will thus find itself paying bank-loan interest of 6 per cent in after-tax funds to carry bonds which are yielding tax-free (and hence after-tax) income of only 4 per cent, a continuing loss at the rate of 2 per cent.

This 2 per cent loss, however, may represent more than a third of the firm's own capital investment in the inventoried bonds. Holding bonds in a slow market thus has a built-in loss potential. The typical response by the firm is avoidance of slow-moving issues whenever possible and "unloading" bonds at no profit or at a small loss in preference to holding them for possible profits at an uncertain time in the future.

The risk of holding bonds in the falling markets of recent years has been particularly high and has virtually eliminated use of the once popular repurchase agreement. Repurchase agreements enable the investment banker to sell his bonds to a short-term investor with an agreement to repurchase them within a specified time at the same price. The purpose of such an agreement is to provide the investor with a short-term tax-exempt investment and to minimize the dealer's use of capital in carrying inventory. Unfortunately, the call to repurchase may come as the market falls,

[1] JEC—*Financing* (a).

forcing the dealer to buy back his then-overpriced bonds which he must then sell at a loss just when his needs for capital are at a peak.

Commercial versus Investment Bankers

Although commercial bankers and the nonbank investment bankers work closely together, they are essentially adversaries, for two very cogent reasons, expressed below in the words of Roland Robinson:

> Commercial banks, being investors as well as underwriters, do not have to fret about the financing of their dealer inventories to the same extent that nonbank dealers do.

> *   *   *

> Commercial banks which are members of the Federal Reserve System would very much like to have the present statutes, which limit them to the underwriting of state and local government general obligations, liberalized. The volume of revenue financing is large and the profit margins are higher than those on general obligations. Commercial banks would like to have access to this new sector of the market.[2]

Risks in Holding Inventory

This competition from banks is the subject of Chapter VIII. As profit margins have declined and interest rates increased for various reasons, the risk element for the *nonbank* dealer has measurably increased, for a deal that is not an almost immediate sell-out and that requires him to borrow funds to hold inventories of slow-moving bonds can lead to financial catastrophe; for example, a repurchase agreement which specifies the price and time for the dealer to reacquire the bonds, with the market taking a turn for the worse in the interval, may force the dealer to pay last month's high price for a bond worth less today and further complicate his life by requiring him to visit his friendly commercial banker for an inventory loan at a higher interest rate than he will receive on the tax-exempt bonds he is repurchasing. In such situations, nonbank dealers are under special pressure to take their losses by selling the bonds through brokers or other dealers for whatever amount the market will pay, in preference to carrying the bonds indefinitely in inventory with no assurance that the market will rise sufficiently to cancel their accumulating losses.

Secondary Market

As soon as bonds leave the syndicate account, they find themselves in the secondary market, where dealers trade with each other both directly and through brokers until a dealer finds a final investor. "Because transactions

[2] Robinson, pp. 104–105.

in this market are shrouded in secrecy, the size and character of this market is not known except in a fragmentary way," said Roland Robinson, whose judgments were based on Irwin Friend's study of the over-the-counter market and data from *The Blue List,* a daily listing of offerings of bonds by dealers in and out of syndicate.[3]

Lack of data is still a characteristic of the market, even for its professionals. In the opinion of the dean of municipal bond brokers, John J. Kenny, however, the secondary market is working well as a medium for trading large and small blocks of municipal bonds. Kenny reports that "recently, in a period of steadily rising interest rates and no great cessation of new issues coupled with really substantial selling by larger holders it has absorbed this selling in orderly fashion." [4]

B. SYNDICATE BIDS AND SPREADS

The average number of bids for a new issue has been increasing steadily as a number of dealer banks became more active in the early 1960's. In general, however, independent underwriting firms are consolidating (as in the rest of the securities business), partly because of the narrowing spreads between the price paid to an issuer and the reoffering price to investors.[5]

These factors are highly related and tell much about the organization of the industry. What seems to have been happening is that syndicate managers (particularly when the manager is a dealer bank or a prominent securities firm) feel that greater profits can be made by limiting the number of firms in the syndicate, so long as they are confident of being able to approach enough investors to "distribute" the bonds in the event their bids are successful.

Syndicates

A most spirited and still accurate account of how bidding syndicates are put together for an underwriting can be found in Robinson's book (his Chapter 4). Somewhat similar accounts can be found in the Investment Bankers Association primer (chapter 5) and in the chapter contributed by the research director of the IBA, John E. Walker, for the Joint Economic Committee study.[6]

Little has changed over the years regarding syndicates; the methods of compensating syndicate members remain substantially unchanged; firms

[3] Robinson, p. 139.
[4] JEC—*Financing* (b).
[5] JEC—*Financing* (a), pp. 178–185.
[6] Robinson, Chapter 4; IBA (a); JEC—*Financing* (a).

still jockey for major participations or managerships of good deals, and loyalties among syndicate members bidding for the bonds of a given issuer still tend to keep it together to bid on the next offering by the same issuer. Increasingly, however, firms that are not able to produce investors are given smaller shares of the underwriting or are quietly dropped from the syndicate when it must be recreated for another bid, and the competition between and among dealer banks and investment bankers has on occasion led to the formation of two syndicates where there was one before; this increases competition and adds one more factor to decrease the all-important spread. A major contribution made by the IBA to the Joint Economic Committee study has been its collection and analysis of data concerning bidding and profits, information that was not available to Robinson.

Spreads

Underwriting spread is the expected difference between the bid price and the price set for the bond when "reoffered" to the investor. The IBA found that spreads have declined significantly since data began to be collected in 1958. Spreads (expressed as dollars per $1000 bond) averaged about $10–$11 per bond in 1965, without allowance for the frequent downward adjustments in selling price; the average spread was slightly higher for smaller and/or lower quality issues. Although the process may have abated in the last few years, the cost of underwriting to the issuer—another way of looking at the spread—had therefore probably declined about 30 per cent, according to the IBA, between 1958 and 1965.[7]

C. BIDDING TRENDS BY TYPE OF ISSUE

The IBA had also set about to determine how different kinds of issues were being underwritten. Between 1957 and 1965, IBA collected information on every successful bid brought to its attention, noting the type of bond (general obligation or revenue), the size of the issue, whether it was a competitive or negotiated deal, and whether the manager of the successful syndicate was (a) one of the ten most important dealer banks in that year, (b) one of the ten most important nonbank underwriters in that year, (c) some other bank, or (d) some other underwriter.[8]

These data are unique and of great importance; the seven tables prepared by the IBA, covering total, general obligation, and revenue bonds, are reproduced in this book as Appendix A. (The many charts showing the

[7] JEC—*Financing* (a), p. 197.
[8] JEC—*Financing* (a), pp. 200–203.

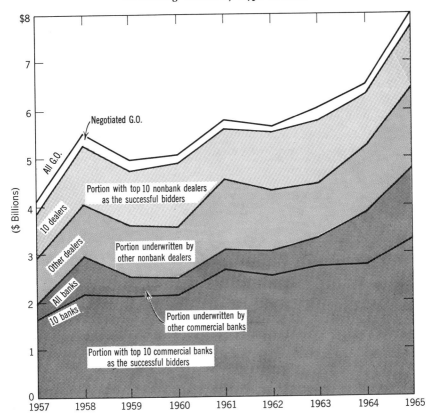

Figure 6 Distribution of amount of all new general obligation bond issues, by type of underwriting and type of underwriter, by year, 1957–1965.

same data on percentage distributions can be found in *Public Facility Financing.*) Some of the trends they suggest are summarized:

1. The total volume of general obligations offerings continues to be far greater than the volume of revenue issues (Figures 6 and 7).

2. The volume of negotiated general obligation issues is typically small (around $200 million), whereas the proportions of negotiated revenue bonds and their value are substantially greater.

Bank and Non-bank Competition

3. The banks' share of managership is predominant in the general obligation field and negligible (but not nonexistent) in the revenue bond field for the years covered.

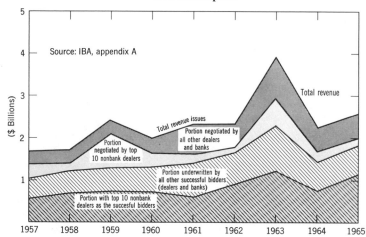

Figure 7 Distribution of amount of all new revenue bond issues, by type of underwriting and type of underwriter, by year, 1957–1965.

4. The group of ten major dealer banks managed the lion's share of all the general obligation bonds sold competitively.

5. The nonbank underwriters maintained a fairly steady rate of underwriting of general obligations sold by competitive bid, in the face of rising competition from the commercial bank-managed groups. The business was split fairly evenly among the ten major and the other nonbank underwriters.

6. The ten major nonbank underwriters in an average year also appear to split the business of underwriting revenue bonds fairly evenly with the other nonbank underwriters, but the graph in Figure 7 suggests that in years characterized by a surge in the volume of either negotiated or competitive deals the ten major houses become the managers of the extra volume. In 1959 the number of negotiated revenue issues was actually smaller than in either 1958 or 1960, evidence that the size of the individual issues was particularly great; the surge in the value of 1963 negotiated revenue deals came as the number of deals more than doubled. The year 1963 also saw a substantial increase in both the number and the value of competitive revenue underwritings.

Syndicate Patterns

Life among the underwriters of municipal bonds can be dramatic, in a way that rarely makes the headlines except for *The Bond Buyer*. The splitting up of a traditional syndicate into two competitive groups can send a thrill through the market. The courage of one syndicate in submitting a strong bid in a panicky market can elicit profound admiration, sometimes followed by even more profound sympathy. The bond community will not soon forget the foolhardiness of an individual firm that bid against the dealer bank syndicate that for years had submitted the only bid for bonds issued by the State of California. The surprise when that small firm won the issue and earned a magnificent profit turned into a wordless farewell when the same firm drastically overpriced a winning bid on an equally large issue some months later, a mistake compounded by use of a repurchase agreement in a falling market that quickly forced the firm to liquidate itself. Thus the game of underwriting changes; in this case, multiple competitive bids began to be received for the immense issues of California bonds, substantially reducing the spread the underwriters had enjoyed in the days of the single bid. Similar and largely unchronicled drama attends the introduction of any new type of bond or of bonds for new definitions of public purposes. Above all, it is an industry marked by close personal friendships and excellent working relationships in the midst of fierce but honorable competition among giant banking and investment institutions.

Chapter III   Creating Different
Types of Municipal Bonds

A. INTRODUCTION: LOCAL PUBLIC FINANCE AND
BOND APPROVALS

The San Francisco Bay Area Rapid Transit District (BART), which sold
the $70 million issue discussed in Chapter I, was created in 1957 by act of
the California legislature. BART was charged with the responsibility of
planning and constructing (and then operating) a new major high-speed transit system to provide service to a number of communities in the Bay Area.
To finance its work the District was authorized to sell $792 million in bonds,
which, having been approved by a squeaky margin over the required 60 per
cent of the voters, became general obligations of the participating communities. The Series G bonds were the seventh group sold. BART was also
empowered to sell revenue and other limited obligation bonds.

Transit, of course, is only one of many reasons why bonds are sold, special districts like BART are only one of many types of government authorized to sell them, and general obligation bonds are only one of the forms
these bonds can take. It is time, then, to define "bond," to consider important questions concerning why and how bonds are issued, and to explore
the different types, purposes, amounts, and conditions of long-term local
financial obligations. Discussion of these aspects of the supply side of the
market will be followed, in Chapter IV, with an evaluation of the kind of
advice given to local financial officers by market professionals with respect
to the design of a particular issue for presentation to the underwriters.

As a citizen, the reader is familiar with the annual or biennial battles in
the states and their political subdivisions concerning budgets, taxes, and
the need to sell long-term securities to raise funds for capital improvements
and certain other welfare programs. What we seek here is a more helpful
explanation of why some communities sell bonds and others do not and
why a given community elects to sell bonds for some purposes and not for
others. Currently, predictions about future offerings of bonds are only in-

formed political guesses based on general characteristics of relevant urban and suburban populations, whereas very few communities show how a given bond issue relates to an economic appraisal of net benefits or a particular process of planning, programming, and budget-making. In the meantime, the market is open to any of the approximately 80,000 autonomous local governments at any time, and each of these potential issuers has at least some latitude with respect to the type, amount, and timing of bonds issued.

The Political Context

A meaningful approach is to see an individual community's handling of local public finance as a set of strategies, more or less rational. We might then hypothesize that bonds are created:

1. When there exists some workable political compromise within the community between (a) the conservatives who would forego expansion of public facilities for ideological reasons and in order to minimize tax-supported expenditures and (b) those who will be benefited by a proposed improvement or program;

2. When there is general agreement (supported as much by hope as by analysis) that future budgets can support the financial costs being incurred for the expected benefits;

3. When it would be political suicide for politicians to oppose the bond issue; and

4. When no higher level of government can be induced to provide the long-term funds desired.

By this reasoning concerning the strategy of decision-making, a municipal bond issue is the financial consequence of a political process, as well as one of the means of implementing a public policy derived by a more formal consideration of growth and distributive goals. Some of the many-faceted attempts to understand and rationalize decisions with respect to local public finance, especially in terms of "the metropolitan problem," are treated elsewhere in this book, and since a substantial portion of municipal bond issues require voter approval as a prior condition to their sale, we shall also be concerned with the work of political scientists interested in the reactions of voters to proposed bond issues.

Figure 8, based on data collected by *The Bond Buyer* over the past forty years, shows the degree to which voters have authorized the issues presented for their approval at the polls. In almost every year, with the exception of a few toward the end of the 1930's and during World War II, approvals exceeded defeats by a substantial margin, and one can see that generally higher percentages of approvals have been obtained in recent years. It is

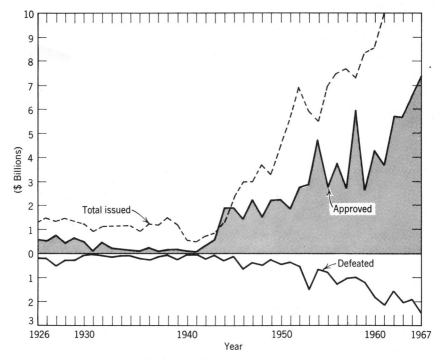

Figure 8 State and municipal bond election results and long-term new issues sold, by year, 1926–1967.

also apparent that defeats mount in recession periods such as the late 1950's, and perhaps one can say that the voters are somewhat less inclined to incur debt currently than they were in the immediate postwar years. That large amounts of bonds (typically revenue bonds) are sold by agencies who do not need voter authorization is shown by the extent to which actual sales of new issues of long-term bonds have exceeded the amounts authorized by voters in the same or the preceding year.

B. BOND CHARACTERISTICS

Basic Types

A *bond,* "municipal" or otherwise, is a promise to pay back the borrowed money at a specified date or under other specified conditions, plus the promise to pay interest at specified times and in specified amounts as long as the bond is outstanding. The face amount of the bond is typically $5000, smaller denominations becoming less frequent.

A *municipal bond issue* is composed of all the bonds issued by a particular local government at one time to raise funds for a stated set of purposes. The term "municipal bond" ordinarily refers to obligations sold by any local government, from a state to the smallest incorporated village or special-purpose district, so long as the interest on its indebtedness is considered exempt from federal income taxation.

A *general obligation bond* is backed by the full faith and credit of the issuer. In a most important recent decision, Judge Holtzoff wrote that the "generic term, 'general obligations,' has been customarily used in the field of government finance as referring to promises of payment by a government entity that possesses general powers of taxation and that are sustained by the full faith and credit of the promisor." [1] The issuer has pledged himself to raise funds by whatever means are required, including a tax increase or sale of property, in order to honor its full faith and credit. (For further discussion of this case, see Chapter VIII.)

A *revenue bond* is the pledge of revenue from a specified income-generating facility such as a toll road or an electric power utility (and, increasingly, from rentals of industrial plants). The issues are not ordinarily guaranteed, but typically a system of sinking funds and operating controls is set up to assure investors that the financial affairs of the facility will be maintained in good order and all commitments honored.

Form of Bond

General obligation municipal bonds are not generally issued under the terms of a deed of trust or bond indenture. Instead each bond bears upon its face a reference to the statutes and ordinances authorizing the obligation and the statement that all "acts, conditions, and things required to be done, precedent to and in the issuance of this bond, have been properly done, happened and been performed in the regular and due form as required by law." If the bond has been signed by a qualified municipal official, the city cannot deny its validity (under the doctrine of Dillon's Estoppel Clause), and every bond holder has the individual right to act singly and without the knowledge and cooperation of the other holders to protect his rights and privileges.[2] Revenue and limited obligation bonds, and many general obligations, however, are covered by indentures and administered by trustees for the bondholders.

"Dillon's rule" to the effect that local governments are subject to the strictest interpretation by the courts with respect to their powers has been

[1] *Bond Buyer*, December 12, 1966, p. 13.
[2] Readings (a).

shown to be one of the significant factors in the analysis of the debt-issuing powers of local governments. When implied powers in the Constitution have enabled the federal government to expand its capacities for action, strict interpretation has kept municipal corporations dependent upon state legislative and constitutional bodies, for the doctrine provides that a local government can do little without explicit and unambiguous enabling authority. In a larger sense it has been a major factor in the weakening of local government generally, a condition that has been variously interpreted, sometimes to suggest that local governments have "abdicated" their responsibilities, sometimes as an argument for giving them broader powers to raise revenue. The rule is an obvious restraint on the types and purposes of bonds issuable by a given general or special-purpose government.

Municipal bonds are ordinarily sold in what is known as coupon form, so that any person holding the bond in his possession can clip the coupon in order to get the interest and to turn the bond in at the proper time for repayment. Tracing or establishing the ownership of such bonds is extremely difficult, and this is one of the factors that has limited our knowledge of the ownership of municipal bonds. In recent years, however, some municipal bonds and/or coupons have been issued in registered form, whereby notice is given to the issuer or its paying agent that payments of principal and/or interest can be made only to the registered party.

C. DEFINITIONS USED IN THE MARKET

Serial, Term, and Dollar Bonds

A *serial bond* is part of an issue of bonds due in a series of consecutive years; for instance, a city may sell bonds for building a sewer in 1967 with some of the bonds earmarked for repayment in 1976, another portion in 1977, a third portion in 1978, and so on through the series of years specified. Different amounts ("irregular serials") can be due in any year.

Term bonds are all or a major part of an issue to be repaid in any one year, usually the last year of the progression, comparable to the balloon maturity of a mortgage. An issue may be composed of both term and serial bonds, with serial bonds for the intermediate years and term bonds due as much as forty or fifty years in the future.

Dollar bonds are revenue issues composed of very large amounts of term loans and are traded in the market in a fashion that closely resembles the trading in corporate bonds, with prices expressed in dollars rather than rate of yield. Where an ordinary bond price quotation includes the coupon rate, yield rate, and date of maturity, a dollar bond's quotation will be given as "98½" or "102," referring to dollars per $100 face amount.

Call Provisions

Investors, hence the dealers, are particularly concerned with the financial characteristics and the security underlying a bond. Among the important financial characteristics are the *provisions for "call"* or early retirement of a bond. These are fully as important as a bond's maturity date for the investor trying to manage a portfolio. Woe betide the trader who confuses "yield to maturity" with "yield to earliest call date," for a bond callable before maturity at a premium price is bought and sold on a different basis from a bond without such calls, or from a bond with some protection against call for a different number of years from the first, even though all three bonds are of the same credit quality and have identical coupon rates and final maturity dates.

Bond Quality

Finally, bonds are described in terms of the credit quality of the issue as well as in terms of the market quality created by the technical features of coupon rate, call provisions, and the terms. Part 3 of this book is an exploration of the difficulties faced by the bond analyst responsive to the investor's intense concern for the security underlying the issuer's promise to pay interest and principal.

The several rating agencies publish their alpha-numeric or descriptive ratings for some but not all of the specific issues and, more generally, for all the debt securities outstanding against the credit of the issuing community. The bond analyst, in any case, tends to look beyond the issue itself to the aggregated local economy and its burden of debt. He is interested in the "debt capacity" of the issuer (the maximum amount of debt that can legally be issued by the governmental unit) and in the untapped margin of debt capacity still available. (The term "fiscal capacity" is a more complex term referring to the larger amount of expenditure and debt that the local economy could reasonably be expected to support under an idealized fiscal structure.) The analyst is also interested in a quantification of "indirect debt," composed of bond issues for which the issuer may be a guarantor, and "overlapping debt," the sum of all debt issued by all local governments in an area. Usually expressed in per capita terms, overlapping debt includes the individual citizen's proportionate share of city, county, school district, and other special district debts outstanding.

The time distribution of the issuer's debt, including the relative amounts of short-term (due in one year or less) and long-term debt, the purposes for which debt has been issued, the record of the issuer in meeting his obligations without default or repudiation, and the reputation of the

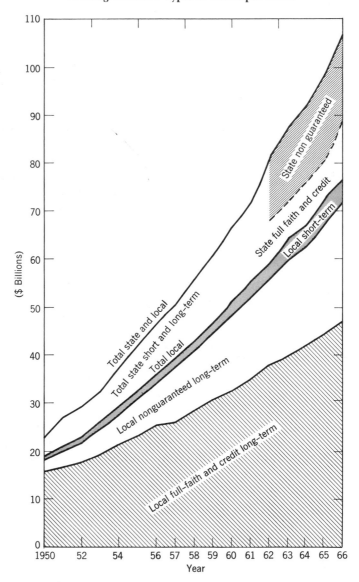

Figure 9 State and local obligations outstanding, by term and nature of security, by year, 1950–1966.

political administration—these are some of the other inputs into credit analysis that affect the description of bond quality. Most prized among descriptive terms is "double-barreled," indicating that there are two independent ultimate sources for repayment. Although almost all state bonds must be implemented by appropriations from a legislature at some future conditional time, a local bond with the same conditional guarantee is viewed with considerable apprehension.

New Forms of Obligation in the Market

Any bond type, however named, that is clearly backed by the full faith and credit of a government with taxing powers can be considered a general obligation of the issuer. The diminished role of general obligation bonds and the growth of other types (illustrated in Figure 9) have been described as follows:

Nonguaranteed Bonds

By far the most striking change in the composition of local government debt during recent years (and which has also involved State Government debt) concerns the *type of liability incurred*. There is an increased proportion of nonguaranteed bonds, as distinguished from bonds backed by full faith and credit of the issuing governments.

Nonguaranteed debt, as defined for Census Bureau reporting on governmental finances, is debt "payable solely from pledged specific sources—e.g., from earning of revenue producing activities . . . , from special assessments, or from specific nonproperty taxes." In the bond issue data reported regularly in the *Statistical Bulletin* of the Investment Bankers Association, "revenue bonds" are similarly defined, except that public housing authority bonds (not guaranteed by the issuing unit, but backed by the Federal Government), and any nonguaranteed bonds purchased by the Federal Government are excluded from this broad category, and are separately reported. . . .

Nonguaranteed debt originally developed to finance utility-type operations of local governments, such as water supply. It was later broadened (with Federal backing) to provide for local public housing projects. As recently as 1957, the bulk of all local nonguaranteed debt outstanding had been incurred for these two kinds of purposes. But the past few years have witnessed a rapid extension of the so-called "revenue bond" device to finance types of project traditionally financed by full faith and credit borrowing, e.g., public schools and office buildings, with debt service paid from "rentals" derived from taxes or other general government revenue; and various projects with debt service payable from the yield of earmarked nonproperty taxes or other specific revenue sources.[3]

Other Limited Obligations

A limited obligation bond can be in any one of many forms and may carry a variety of names, requiring the bond analyst to read the small print of the prospectus to ascertain the precise security that underlies the issue. The Investment Bankers Association makes further distinctions between "special tax" bonds (where the issuer's taxing power is limited to a specified maximum tax rate) and "special assessment" bonds (a form of special tax

[3] ACIR (a), pp. 24–25.

bonds supported by revenues from those who benefit from the facility).[4] Where contingent guarantees are added, the credit rating and hence the market value of the bond issue may be improved, except perhaps where the local or state legislative body would have to meet to appropriate funds to honor the guarantee, should the specific primary source of revenue fail.

D. THE NUMBER OF BONDS SOLD BY TYPE AND PURPOSE

On the supply side of the market, we are also interested in the relationship between the type of issuer and the type and purpose of bonds sold in recent years and in the reasons for the relative increase in popularity of revenue bonds in the postwar period and the policy issues that have resulted from it.

The purposes for which bonds are issued are described in rather broad categories in the aggregate data covering the tax-exempt market. Although finer breakdowns are available for certain categories such as toll highways, college housing, and other special programs, the data are ordinarily grouped by such terms as "education" and "transportation." Since the mid-1950's, the Investment Bankers Association and *The Bond Buyer* have been the two primary sources for such data; comprehensive data for earlier years appear to be unavailable.

The IBA tabulations for the 1957–1965 period, cross-classified by type, purpose, issuer, population size, region, maturity, and other characteristics, are to be found in Appendix A. Historical and economic perspectives of total bond sales in relation to total revenues and expenditures of state and local governments are discussed in Part 4.

The distribution of bond sales by purpose and type of issuer provides an index to the preferences of the American voter with respect to the activities to be performed by his local government. As Figures 8, 9, and 10 showed, the volume of new issues sold has increased dramatically in the postwar years, almost doubling in the 1957–1965 period covered by the IBA data. Bonds for educational facilities, generally considered to be worthy of top priority on any list of local government projects, have represented a relatively steady proportion of the rising totals throughout the past decade, but bonds for other purposes have tended to fluctuate in popularity.

With reference to Figure 10, the IBA noted in its report to the Joint Economic Committee that many of the major turnpike and toll highway projects had been financed in the early 1950's, so that the transportation category was taking a smaller proportion of the total by the early 1960's; the low interest rates prevailing in 1962 and 1963, however, represented a

[4] IBA (a), p. 3.

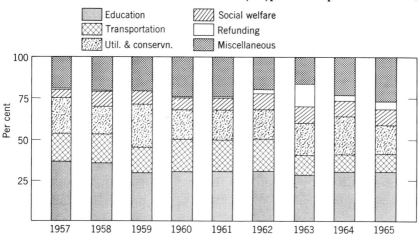

Figure 10 The percentage distribution, by use of proceeds, of the value of all tax-exempt bonds issues, for each year from 1957 to 1965.

favorable time for converting high interest debt into lower interest debt by means of refunding issues, a practice that is still the subject of vigorous debate. The IBA noted further that the increase in miscellaneous issues reflected the trend toward consolidated and general-purpose issues and away from issues that could be clearly identified as to purpose.

To some extent a counter-trend with respect to the specificity of bond issues can be seen in Figure 11, where the bars represent amounts of bonds sold rather than proportions and the categories represent the type of issuer rather than the purpose of the financing. Here the growth of the market

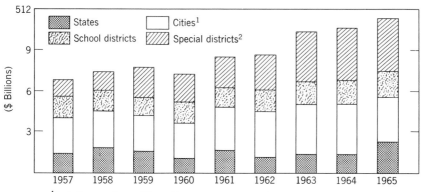

[1]Includes counties and townships
[2]Includes statutory authorities

Figure 11 Value of all tax-exempt bonds issued, by type of issuer, each year from 1957 to 1965.

can be traced to increased sales by special districts, the special-purpose authorities and commissions that operate on a metropolitan or county-wide
basis. Many of the 40-odd types of special district governments are in the
transportation or utilities field, but the others can be assumed to have specific purposes represented by some of the bond issues in the miscellaneous
category above.

The data accumulated by *The Bond Buyer* and graphed in Figure 12 are
distributed into categories generally similar to those employed by the IBA,

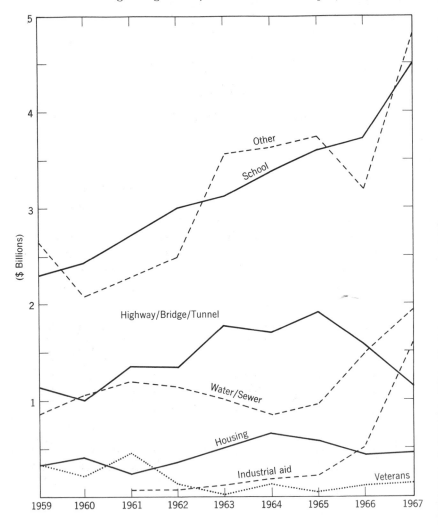

Figure 12 Dollar volume of new tax exempt issues, by purpose, by year, 1959–
1967.

but "housing" is included in the IBA's "social welfare" group, "water/ sewer" is in the IBA "utilities," and its "industrial aid" data come from other IBA sources.

These data indicate that the overwhelming majority of tax-exempt bonds are issued to finance traditional forms of local government activity. Unfortunately, the data do not show the extent to which revenue bonds are used within any of the categories of purpose and are not particularly useful for making predictions about the future so long as a given bond issue remains as the final product of a political process designed to generate alternative means of financing from higher levels of government. Thus the bond markets of the future will reflect the fiscal legislation of the future concerning traditional purposes in regard to educational, transportation, and utilities facilities and the more controversial fields of social welfare, housing, and industrial development financing (the last being the subject of Chapter IX).

E. THE IMPACT OF REVENUE BOND ISSUES [5]

The story of the rise to prominence of the revenue bond form of financing is, in fact, the story of American local government in the postwar years. Since the turn of the century, when there was a strong movement toward the establishment of municipally owned electric and water systems in preference to the granting of franchises to private companies, revenue bonds have represented at least a fifth of all municipal bond issues.

As the urban communities began to invest in new facilities both within older cities and in the suburban hinterlands after the hiatus of depression and war, the proportion of revenue bonds has come to represent at least a third and sometimes as much as 45 per cent of all tax-exempt bonds issued in a given year. The reasons for the shift are many and highly interconnected; the impact of the shift has yet to be closely analyzed, but the framework of such a study may be found in the commentary that follows

Special Districts Become Acceptable

As one of the leading municipal bond attorneys has pointed out, the way was cleared for an expansion of revenue bond financing by the series of decisions and regulations involving the Port of New York Authority and the Triborough Bridge Authority in the early 1940's. Not only was it established that such public enterprises were political subdivisions entitled to exemption from federal income taxation on bond interest, but it was also clear that similar special district governments with wide functional and

[5] JEC—*Financing* (c) and (d).

territorial jurisdictions could play a vital role in the development of intra-metropolitan and intercity facilities needed in the postwar age.

Thus the courts began to accept the arguments, legal and economic, that justified these revenue-financed enterprises. Meanwhile the technical features of sinking funds, reserves, and the whole financial structure of these authorities had been improved to make the bonds acceptable to investors and the markets, and tax rates remained high enough to induce continued investor interest for the purchase of substantial quantities of tax-exempt bonds, particularly since revenue bonds were sold at slightly higher yields than general obligation bonds. From the point of view of municipal managers, revenue-financed enterprises often bypassed both the requirement for authorization by the voters and the debt limits of the issuing community. In addition, it was possible to finance construction without raising taxes, even though in some cases the new authority's bonds might carry a contingent guarantee from the local government it served.

Revenue bond financing and the special-district form of government have, however, raised a host of philosophical questions which are still contentious. Among them, and beyond the scope of this book, are the differences of opinion concerning (a) the extent to which the authority form of government should be responsive to the electorate, and (b) the range of activities for public enterprises that can be held to be in the public interest. At any rate, revenue bonds have financed highways, power plants, industrial plants, recreation facilities, airports, parking facilities, mass transit facilities, dormitories, school buildings, and a host of more or less important projects, all of them found at the time to be within the definitions of public purpose allowed by the respective state courts that interpret the enabling acts. The extraordinary growth of a particular form of revenue bond financing for the construction of industrial plants under long-term leases to private companies receives special coverage in Chapter IX, because of the impact this form of financing is having on the market itself.

One other effect on the market that should be mentioned is the problem that revenue bonds in general present to the municipal bond credit analyst, for the analysis requires far more sophistication in approach than for general obligations and the data are far more unavailable and speculative than those for similar corporate issues. The possible speculative nature of the revenue bond, suggested by the current defaults on $250 million worth of bonds issued by various turnpike and bridge commissions, is one of the major arguments advanced by the investment bankers in their fight against commercial bank underwriting of revenue issues (a struggle that is the subject of Chapter VIII).[6]

[6] Hearings (a).

Chapter IV   The Market's Advice to the Issuers

The local finance officer needs to know (a) what kinds of bonds he should sell and (b) how to prepare a bond issue for the market. The ill-favored BART issue we have encountered in earlier chapters was beautifully prepared for the market, and its troubles stemmed from the over-optimistic pricing by the winning syndicate. Its financial advisers had shaped the issue to conform to conservative estimates of future revenues and expenditures. A brochure that described in detail the operation of the District and the terms of the bond obligations had been distributed to institutional investors and prospective underwriters throughout the country, and the District had promised to provide a qualifying legal opinion without cost to the successful bidder. In due course a series of advertisements were placed in trade publications announcing the forthcoming sale and specifying the bidding procedure to be followed. Higher interest costs are the penalty imposed by the market on less well-known and less diligent issuers.

The market's advice, however, is far too general to please the inexperienced issuer, and because of the heterogeneity of local governments, the underwriters have acquired monopsonist powers, setting prices and terms in a market with many sellers and few buyers. The underwriters are not only free to pick and choose among the bonds offered to them; they are impelled to do so to minimize the risk of holding bonds that are unattractive to the investors. Thus the advice comes in the form of one-way communications from investor to underwriter to issuer; we have no record of admonitions sent from local governments to the financial community.

A. ON THE PROPER FUNCTIONS OF LOCAL GOVERNMENT

A local government has relatively wide latitude in its practice of the art of local financial management, so long as state regulations are complied with, especially with regard to the amount and type of debt obligations sold for various purposes. In this section we are concerned with the market's preferences on this score.

As a practical matter, almost any bond issue that is in proper technical form (that is, approved by the voters, certified as to enabling legislation, and so forth) can be sold at any time, but the market's opinions are reflected, directly or indirectly, when its terms (amount, maturity, extent of security for its repayment and, above all, the interest rate) are set. Whether a particular offering thereafter meets favor with underwriters and investors at the date of sale depends upon the congruence of many factors (notably, as further discussed in Part 4, the relationship between bond quality ratings and the interest to be paid in the context of prevailing conditions in the financial markets).

Theory of Public Expenditure

There is substantial agreement in the United States regarding certain kinds of municipal services that ought to be available. These "collective goods," described in pure theories of public expenditure, include the functions of local government from which no private entrepreneur could make a profit, for which prices would not reflect real value in use, and for which costs do not rise as one extra member of the public partakes of the service. Thus streets, public health services, educational services, and fire and police protection are universally accepted among the functions of local government.

The theories of local public finance deal with the questions how costs and benefits of municipal services should be apportioned and how the jurisdictional boundaries of local governments affect the efficiency with which various functions are performed. In addition, they consider what level of government should provide the necessary funds and what portion of total expenditure should be considered operating costs.

The local finance officer, however, deals with the political realities of the state, metropolis, and community he serves. The decision whether a particular service is to be offered is rarely up to him. His job is to match available revenues with a formidable list of voter-approved projects. He deals with such questions as these: Should renovation of the hospital or fire station be an operating cost or a capital project? What will be the effect of a toll-free interstate highway link on the revenues of a toll bridge? If parks are open to the public, can one charge admission to a public swimming pool and, if so, can such charges support a bond issue with "recreation facility" as its purpose?

Financing "Public" Enterprise

Almost all the sticky problems with respect to purpose, in fact, concern public enterprises performing functions and offering services for which prices can be set. Is it proper for municipalities to compete with private industry in selling water, gas, electricity? Should garbage removal and pollution control be paid for by assessments on those creating the effluents or by the community as a whole? Should not private companies build and operate parking garages, swimming pools, nursing homes, college dormitories, industrial parks, and other new forms of public activity? Men can honestly bring different political philosophies to bear on these questions, but some conservative investors are known to avoid bond issues whose purposes they believe are beyond the proper scope of local government and whose financial burdens might be repudiated in periods of local financial distress.

A good example of the interplay between political philosophy and practical finance can be illustrated by consideration of the role of public utilities. Basically, water supply and electric power are necessary ingredients for a community's growth. At the turn of the century many electric and water supply systems were financed by municipalities themselves when the enterprises were too small and speculative to attract investor interest. In other larger places the municipality often gave a franchise to a private concern. One of the interesting controversies at the present time of municipal impoverishment is whether rates for municipally owned utility services should be set "at cost" or at a level to generate "profits" for the municipality. Another form of question is whether private utility firms should be acquired and refinanced at the lower interest costs prevailing for tax-exempt bonds in order to either (a) lower rates to consumers, (b) generate "profits" for the municipality, or (c) accomplish some combination of the two.

As the long-term franchises given to private companies expire (after 50-60-70 years as agreed on at the beginning of the twentieth century), more municipalities may discover the joy of selling low-interest bond issues to acquire the private companies and of maintaining service at the same utility rates in order to generate useful surpluses.[1]

The city of Gainesville, Florida, for instance, in 1965 derived 23.2 per cent of its general funds from transfers from the earned surplus of its electric utility operation; 35.2 per cent from *ad valorem* property taxes and 41.6 per cent from all other sources that year. In the preceding decade the tax rate had been lowered by about one-third by virtue of such transfers and,

[1] Spiegel.

with growth expected in the suburbs to which it also sold electricity and water, the city expected such revenues to increase substantially. Widespread opposition to this practice existed in the past, however:

> . . . Private utilities fighting against the growth of municipally owned utilities . . . maintained that the lower yields available to state and local governments encouraged "uneconomic" borrowing and misallocated resources from the private to the public sector. Loose versions of this argument charged that state and local governments engaged in "wasteful" and unnecessary projects, leading toward more socialism, under the stimulus of lower borrowing costs. This particular argument has not received much attention in recent years.[2]

The Ott-Meltzer comment referred to the conflict between public and private utilities in the 1920's, a struggle that continues and that may become more intense as Gainesville's example is followed. Such utilities can make handsome contributions by maintaining rates equivalent to those that would be charged by private utilities, a point of view in direct contrast to that presented to the Municipal Finance Officers Association to the effect that "municipally owned utilities . . . are created by the people to furnish service to them at cost." [3]

B. ON PRINCIPLES OF DEBT MANAGEMENT

Once over the hurdle of determining whether the purpose of a given bond issue is "proper," the local finance officer is confronted with the problem of fitting the quantity of bonds to be sold into the financial structure of the municipal corporation. Although absolute criteria are lacking, for this is a question for the exercise of judgment, he will find the opinions of the financial community reflected in the bond ratings set for the issue and in the manuals and pamphlets that deal with administrative aspects of municipal fiscal policy and that warn the prospective borrower of "dangerous and undesirable" practices.[4]

Purpose and Time of Borrowing

From the viewpoint of the International City Managers' Association, for instance, borrowing is not really a source of revenue, for the loans must be repaid with interest; however, the capital costs of self-supporting enterprises, such as water and power systems, may justifiably be met by borrowing so long as the debt is to be paid off before the facility becomes obsolete. ICMA recognizes that difficult policy and economic questions arise when

[2] Ott-Meltzer, p. 14.
[3] MFOA (a).
[4] ICMA (a), pp. 120–122.

the community desires to subsidize a particular project by maintaining a low level of service charges, and they assume that revenues will ordinarily be set to cover the operating and financial service costs.

ICMA condones, with reservations, (a) borrowing to smooth out wide fluctuations in the annual budget (especially when large, nonrevenue projects such as a city hall or a school building are required) and (b) borrowing in anticipation of larger assessment bases in the future (as a community expands rapidly and is encouraged to put street and utility lines in place for expected use by industries and large residential subdivisions), but they urge cities to be extremely cautious in their estimates of probable growth: "A large part of the financial difficulties that encumbered many cities during the depression resulted from overoptimism with respect to population increase." [5]

A community is well advised, they continue, to reserve debt capacity for periods of depression when revenues from property taxation may be curtailed, and they discuss in some detail the advantages of a modified pay-as-you-go plan which increases taxes so that substantial portions of capital expenditures can be paid for out of current revenues in good years. However, in shifting to a pay-as-you-go basis, in the context on a long-term capital budget, ICMA warns against both "debt equalization" borrowing to provide equal annual debt service over a period of years and "cyclical borrowing," whereby debt is incurred only in "good years." [6]

The conservative investor, almost by definition, is more concerned about economic cycles and balanced financial structures than other actors in the municipal bond field, if for no other reason than that his institution expects to hold the bonds until maturity a generation later, when a new group of voters and a new finance officer will be in charge. In the interim he does not want to see the market value of his portfolio depreciated by a drop in the credit ratings given the issuers represented therein.

The problem with the abstract propositions expounded by such organizations as the ICMA and the Municipal Finance Officers Association is not their validity (which is hard to test) or their call for symmetry and moderation. It is rather the inapplicability of some of these precepts at a time (a) of vast intermetropolitan and intrametropolitan upheaval, evidenced by migrations of persons and industries among cities and from central cities to outlying areas, and (b) of expansion in the scope of governmental projects.

In spite of the four additional ICMA policy statements quoted below, for instance, a rapidly growing suburban community has present needs for capital projects that continually increase debt service and push the dates for final repayment farther into the future. Today's municipalities find debt service on outstanding debt constantly decreasing as a percentage of

[5] ICMA (a), p. 121.
[6] ICMA (a), p. 121.

total expenditures; it is the ability to repay that is of concern, not the interim payments of interest. Pending changes in the flow of funds from higher to lower levels of government under programs for restructuring intergovernmental relationships, and pending reconsideration of existing state restrictions on local governments, municipalities have had little choice but to think up strategies for establishing special authorities and for avoiding debt limits. The ICMA excerpts follow.

Choice of Debt Structure. The totality of a municipality's borrowing for tax-supported purposes should be so arranged, (1) that there will be no pronounced irregularities in debt service from year to year to cause gyrations in the tax levy, and (2) that there will be a progressively downward trend in annual requirements which will make room for new borrowings without pyramiding debt service costs. When new borrowing is undertaken it should be so fitted into the existing structure that no irregularities, actual or potential, will result. The use of straight serials normally will tend to facilitate such a program, but no general rule can be laid down as the planning of debt structure often has years of no planning at all as a background. An irregular structure is likely to take some years to correct, may involve some unconventional scheduling of a new borrowing, and sometimes necessitates the judicious refunding of some maturities before past mistakes can be rectified.

*   *   *

Use of Callable Bonds. Municipal bonds are sometimes issued with the provision that they can be called for payment at the option of the debtor in advance of the maturity date. Such bonds are known as "callable" or "optional" bonds. The call provision may be used with serial as well as with term bonds. It takes a wide variety of forms.

At some times and under some conditions the call feature has definite advantages. When the interest rate at which the optional bonds are issued is normal or high, there is always the possibility that the bonds can be called and refunded at a lower interest rate at some time during the term for which they are to run. This may be because of a period of low interest rates or because a municipality has been able to improve its credit standing. In considering the desirability of making bonds callable, however, it must be borne in mind that this feature ordinarily makes bonds less attractive to investors and tends to increase the original rate at which they can be sold. For this reason there is likely to be little financial advantage and possibly a financial loss, in making bonds callable when sold in periods of low interest rates. Some of the objection can be removed, however, if the time when bonds become callable is set several years from the date of issue and a reasonable premium is required for calling. The call feature also may have a proper place in a revenue bond issue since earning estimates at the time of issuance may have been ultraconservative.

Special Assessment Financing. Special assessment bonds offer, in theory, an admirable means of assessing the cost of improvements of localized benefit upon the direct recipients, and of permitting the property owners of a limited area to secure and pay for a type or quality of improvement superior to that which the city generally can afford. In actual practice, however, special assessment bonds have often been used to dodge borrowing limits, to avoid popular referendums on bond issues, to give undue stimulus to the flow of construction contracts, and to furnish capital to real estate promoters to develop new subdivisions.

*   *   *

Appropriate Uses of Revenue Bonds. Laws of the several states vary as to the use of revenue bonds. It should be remembered that the legal availability of such bonds does not justify their indiscriminate use. They should not be employed to evade sound and reasonable debt limits or to engage in speculative ventures. When a municipality has adequate general borrowing power at its disposal, due consideration should be given to which type of bond can be sold at the lower cost. Usually, general obligation bonds sell at a lower interest cost than can be obtained on a revenue bond issue sold by the same municipality. Revenue bonds, however, have certain advantages. They are an aid to municipalities wishing to undertake revenue-producing enterprises which have been held back by unduly restrictive general borrowing provisions; they tend to encourage the businesslike management of such enterprises; and they permit the financing of basically essential utilities by municipalities which are seriously limited as to general credit and taxing power; and they assign the cost of added improvements to those who will benefit from the availability of such new improvements.[7]

The ICMA text then notes that constitutional and statutory provisions restricting the issuance of debt are written in fairly general terms which leave the timing and, to a considerable degree, the amount of financing to the local decision makers. If the city's past borrowing policy has been improvident, the text says, an emergency may find it without a market for its bonds. As an independent fiscal entity, the municipality must bear all the responsibility for rationing its borrowing capacity and its reserve funds among the many forms of competing demands for money. As we shall see in many places in this book, these decisions are interesting mixtures of economic, political, and social policy.

C. THE WORK OF FINANCE OFFICERS, ATTORNEYS, AND CONSULTANTS

About 10,000 new issues are brought to market each year, and only a few issuers offer more than one. The process of preparing an issue is the step that links all the thinking about local finance with all the activities that take place in the many worlds of finance.

Life Cycle of a Bond Issue

Big or small, the coming to market of an issue of tax-exempt securities represents a halfway point in the cyclic nature of the municipal bond system. In the first half, each issuer has had to appraise his position as a viable economic and social entity caught up in the turmoil affecting the federalist system of government in the United States and often manifest in the metropolitan complex of which the issuer may well be part. Political dialogues are the ultimate source of decisions within a community, but the final prospectus for a particular bond issue may have involved the professional skills

[7] ICMA (a), pp. 251–253.

of economists and planners, perhaps through the work of independent consultants employed by the issuer. Authority for the issue had to come from a political body, struggling with the budgetary concepts being developed by the professional administrators and operating within the framework of state constitutional and statutory restrictions on the issuance of long-term obligations.

The second half of the municipal bond cycle is played in various parts of the market itself. It begins with a sheaf of documents, evidence that the bond is, indeed, a binding obligation of the issuer, who promises to pay the money back at a certain time and to pay interest for the use of the money in the intervening years. The character of the issuer and the particular climate in the capital market at the time of sale—plus the attributes of the bond itself in terms of interest rate, type of revenues tapped for its repayment, term of years, and so forth—are all vital considerations as the bond becomes a commodity, a money market instrument, as it is called, that can be bought and sold until the day comes when its little life is extinguished in the process of being repaid at maturity or refunded.

The finance officer is caught in the middle, pressured on the one hand by uncertainty as to the political and economic structure of his community, and burdened on the other hand by uncertainty as to the treatment he will receive when he comes to a marketplace he cannot fully comprehend. In the marketplace itself, he must never forget that underwriters do not expect to hold bonds for their own account; the *underwriter* is interested only in bonds he can resell immediately to permanent investors!

Guidelines for Finance Officers

Noting the lack of a practical, down-to-earth basic guide for the municipal finance officer in both the general and the specific aspects of bond financing, *The Bond Buyer* put together a manual "to assist busy, public officials in the orderly, efficient consideration of the many decisions that must be made in preparing a bond offering for the market." [8]

This pamphlet begins by observing that tax-exempt bonds were once comparatively rare jewels, but since the recent multiplicity of tax-exempt issues dulled their luster, the harassed staffs of the underwriters and credit rating agencies are not willing to waste time on "a sloppily prepared offering, unless, of course, there is a prospect of obtaining a bargain." As the day for selling the issue approaches, says *The Bond Buyer*, the evaluation of the project itself plays an important role:

From the initial enabling resolution to the actual issuance of bonds, the creation of a debt by one group of people and acquisition by another group of people must be in the

[8] *Bond Buyer* (c).

form of a definite contract stripped of all ambiguities and free of all illusory promises. There is no gainsaying the fact that in a vibrant, expanding Nation the contagion of growth is irrepressible. Consequently, as communities vie with each other for the means to grow, it is understandable that at times the very nature of competition may produce excesses of ambition and desire insupportable by fact or performance.

In times such as these, very human temptations will arise to embrace some community undertaking which, by more prudent judgment, might be better left untried. Or at other times, a merely "good" project might find itself magically transformed into a many-splendored thing adorned with promises a cynical future might disapprove.

In addition to making the best possible case for the uses to which the funds are to be put, the issuer must pay strict attention to the technical details of the offering. This process is described by *The Bond Buyer:*

> Making an offering acceptable in the market resolves itself into two separate, but closely related problems; one is to attract the attention of several underwriters so that there will be active competition to handle the bonds; two, is to make the bonds so attractive credit-wise that investors will want to buy them, and put them away in their lock boxes more or less permanently.
>
> Each is very important. In the short run, meeting the requirements of the underwriters tends to be uppermost in the minds of officials preparing the new issue. This is proper, for there are no unimportant details in preparing the bond offering; but it should not be forgotten, in the pressures to get the issue out, that the maintenance of credit quality is basic. A low grade bond can be sweetened up, in fact it may be necessary to do so to sell it; but when this is done the astute analysts will be acutely aware of what it is—a bond of poor credit quality dressed up for the market.

Role of Attorneys and Consultants

Dressed up or not, the bond issue that emerges from this process of creation has often been wet-nursed by financial consultants, bond counsel, and consulting engineers, sometimes for years, before it is presented to society. *Public Facility Financing,* one of the most comprehensive collections of materials about the municipal securities market ever assembled, includes separate essays on each of these professional adjuncts to the work of the finance officer. It is a sign of grace when all of the various officials, financiers, and independent contractors manage to work together during the municipal bond life cycle.

Practically any competent registered engineering consulting firm may qualify for such work, and the range of project types allows for some specialization among them, but the Joint Economic Committee's authors estimate that there are no more than 128 law firms, 6 financial consultants, 30 investment banking firms, and a handful of commercial banks that are regularly engaging in consulting activities. Their comment about the legal advisor also applies to the two other groups: "The principal qualification of bond counsel is an established reputation in the municipal bond market," an attribute that takes years of effective service to obtain.

Role of the Attorney

The scope of counsel's contribution, since it became common practice some years ago to secure a written legal opinion and even to have that opinion printed on the back of the bond itself, is suggested by the following few paragraphs excerpted from the detailed descriptions of approaches that lawyers might take to different kinds of bonding situations.

Specifically, the duties of bond counsel are broad as necessary to establish to his satisfaction the legality of the bonds when they are issued and delivered. He is expected to examine the applicable law and to review the bond proceedings, resolutions, ordinances, election documents, if any, and other documents to determine whether he can render an approving opinion as to the validity of the bonds. . . .

However, the role of bond counsel in connection with many bond issues, particularly revenue bond issues, is far more extensive. . . . The challenge of coping with such demands (for better and more extensive public facilities) has called forth the specialized knowledge and experience of bond attorneys to develop new, or to adapt old, legal concepts and techniques of public financing. In cooperation with legislators, public officials, underwriters, investors, engineers, and others, bond attorneys have engaged in drafting legislation, even constitutional amendments, devising new methods of financing, creating new public instrumentalities and preparing trust indentures, resolutions, ordinances, contracts, and other documents that have contributed to the acceptance by the investing public of an increasing volume of municipal bonds. . . .

A trust indenture of over 150 printed pages is not unusual in revenue bond financing. Its length, often facetiously attributed to the verbosity of lawyers, is essential for the proper delineation of the security for the bonds and for the protection of the interests of the public agency issuing the bonds, the purchasers of the bonds and the trustee administering the trust. . . .

With respect to general obligation bonds payable from ad valorem taxes, the work of bond counsel generally is not as time consuming as that for revenue bonds. The forms of legal instruments therefor are not subject to the degree of continual revisions typical for revenue bond issues and, moreover, general obligation bonds, unlike revenue bonds, offer little basis for discussions and agreements as to the security and other matters. Trust indentures usually are not involved.[9]

Role of Financial Consultants

Although some commercial banks, notably in New England, provide package services to municipalities (for a fee and in consideration of obtaining compensating balances from the municipality and of arranging short-term and other financing), rarely are the functions of counsel and financial consultant commingled in any one person. National banks under existing statutes may not underwrite revenue bonds, and so their services are ordinarily concentrated on the more routine aspects of municipal

[9] JEC—*Financing* (e).

finance. Investment banking firms, which are struggling to retain an exclusive franchise on the handling of revenue issues, often supply financial consulting services for a fee to a prospective issuer; one of the questions is whether the issuer should have a negotiated sale or engage in competitive bidding. The financial consultant who is in daily contact with the market, whether or not he is an independent operator, can play an important role; as summarized for the Joint Economic Committee, he:

(a) Surveys issuer's debt structure and financial resources to determine borrowing capacity for future capital financing requirements.

(b) Gathers all pertinent financial statistics and economic data such as debt retirement schedule, tax rates, overlapping debt, etc., that would affect or reflect on the issuer's ability and willingness to repay its obligations.

(c) Advises on the time and method of marketing; terms of bond issues; including maturity schedule, interest payment dates, call features and bidding limitations.

(d) Prepares an overall financing plan detailing the recommended approach and probable timetable.

(e) Prepares, in cooperation with bond counsel, an official statement, notice of sale, and bid form and distributes same to all prospective underwriters and investors.

(f) Assists the issuer in getting local public assistance and support of the proposed financing.

(g) Keeps in constant contact with the rating services to insure that they have all the information and data they require to properly evaluate the credit.

(h) Is present when sealed bids are opened and stands ready to advise on the acceptability of bids.

(i) Supervises the printing, signing, and delivery of the bonds.

(j) Advises on investment of bond proceeds.[10]

The functions of a financial consultant are the responsibility of the local finance official. With regard to the background material and the maintenance of contacts with the rating agencies, some of the larger issuers make pilgrimages to the major financial centers on a regular basis to acquaint prospective underwriters and investors with the local program, even though the financing itself may not take place for months or years thereafter.

D. DESIGNING THE BOND ISSUE

One of the hardest jobs of all is the technical design of both the bond indenture (typically only for revenue bonds) and the bidding terms. With respect to revenue bond indentures, the problem is to anticipate the time when revenues begin to flow into a completed project and to set forth precisely the flow of revenues into operating and sinking funds, with appropriate guarantees by sponsoring agencies if revenues fall below expectations.

[10] JEC—*Financing* (f).

The call provisions, with *The Bond Buyer*'s discussion similar to ICMA's in the preceding section, are of special importance in the case of projects for which future revenues are hard to estimate. The provision for call is relatively unnecessary in years of low interest rates. Under prevailing high-interest conditions, inclusion of a call provision may lead the finance officer to accept an unattractive bid in the hope of refunding at lower interest rates in the future. A call provision may be particularly useful should unexpectedly high revenues constitute additional security for the bond holder and hence justify lower interest rates if the issue were refunded.

Coupon Rates

Although call provisions are complications for the bidders, the coupon rates (which are ordinarily set by the underwriters within limits set by the issuer) and the decision whether to accept competitive or negotiated bids constitute particularly subtle problems. First, on the subject of coupons. *The Bond Buyer* stated:

> *Coupon Rates.* The following points should be covered explicitly: (1) Statutory requirements concerning the coupon rate (the rate of interest specified on the interest coupons attached to the bonds). (2) Whether or not the successful bidder will be allowed to name the coupon rate. (This is ordinarily desirable.) If so: (a) The multiples that will be acceptable—¼, ⅛ or ⅒ of 1%, for example; (b) If there is a limit on the number of coupons this should be explained; (c) If all the bonds of one maturity date must carry the same coupon, this should be stated. (Ordinarily it is not wise to allow more than one coupon rate for the same maturity); (d) It should be stated whether or not supplemental or B coupons will be accepted. If such coupons are acceptable the limits, if any, should be stated. This is very important so that all of the bids will be on the same basis; (e) If trick coupons, such as high coupons on the early maturities, and very low coupons on the late maturities, are not acceptable this should be indicated. (There is considerable question if, under most circumstances, such devices work to the advantage of the issuer.) . . .[11]

The Bond Buyer pamphlet, however, does not deal with the logic of couponing to obtain the highest bid for the bonds at the lowest real interest cost. The usual procedure (as standardized by the Investment Bankers Association) has been for state and local governments to accept the bid with the lowest "net interest cost" calculated, in Robinson's terms, as "a simple ratio of coupons to principal weighted by the period the principal is outstanding" and illustrated in Table B. As Robinson has shown in his Appendix, "Results of Conventional (Nonaccrual) Method of Computing Interest Cost which Prevails in Competitive Bidding for State and Local Government Issues," the issuer pays a substantial penalty by not employing one of several "present value" methods for calculating time interest costs to be incurred. Computers and desk calculators now widely available have demolished the remaining arguments against use of the slightly more

---

[11] *Bond Buyer* (c), p. 25.

complicated but far more rational method of discounting future interest, but, at this writing, the process of "accepting the worst bid," as some call the conventional method, persists, surprisingly even in the more tailored forms of negotiated bids.

Bid Specifications

The pros and cons of bidding form are frequently debated, with many underwriters convinced that issuers get better bids at lower gross spreads by negotiated rather than competitive sales. *The Bond Buyer* expresses some of the normative judgments well in the following quotation.

Competitive Bidding Versus a Negotiated Deal. A decision must be made rather early on whether to use competitive bidding or a negotiated deal. Competitive bidding has become so much the accepted practice for the sale of new offerings that exceptions call for an explanation. The chief advantage of competitive bidding from the viewpoint of local officials is that if the sale is properly advertised and conducted they are shielded from the criticism of favoritism in the selection of an underwriter. Also the gross spread may be less when there is competitive bidding than when a deal is negotiated, but this may not be a real economy since the underwriter very often performs additional services in the case of a negotiated deal.

If a bond issue must be sold when money is tight a negotiated deal may be the best solution. Also in the cases of offerings that require special study and the development of new markets, a negotiated deal may be indicated. It is sometimes difficult to sell an extremely large issue or a special situation except as a negotiated deal. An unknown issuer coming to the market with a large offering might well consider the possibilities of a negotiated deal. Since it is so generally recognized that a negotiated sale opens the door for serious abuses, there is a possibility that the fear of criticism may cause public officials to shy away from this form of sale in certain instances where it could be used to advantage.

In this connection it seems well to repeat that the "dealing at arms length" involved in competitive bidding places the responsibility for tailoring the offering to the wishes of the market and for building investor acceptance squarely upon the issuer. Underwriters depend for their profit upon rapid turnover, and only in a limited way are they in a position to build a demand for the bonds of a given issuer. Dealers are very conscious of the fact that the next offering may be handled by a competing syndicate.

The middle ground between competitive bidding and a negotiated deal is very treacherous. Allowing a bond house to bid for an issue which it assisted in preparing, except in most unusual cases, results in a conflict of loyalties for its employees which is not fair either to the issuer or to the house. One of the poorest methods of selling a new issue is to go through the motions of a public sale while informing only a few favored houses.[12]

The subject of competitive versus negotiated bids deserves more attention than it has received in the market (and in this book). It can be argued that very large issuers of general obligation bonds, such as New York City, might do well to issue debt securities day by day on the basis of negotiated sales, as some of the larger commercial credit and finance companies do. Moreover, proponents of the negotiated route point out that the under-

[12] *Bond Buyer* (c), p. 12.

writers for negotiated sales come to know a great deal more about the strengths of the community or agency issuing the bonds than do the underwriters of an issue bought in a flurry of competitive bid meetings, that the negotiating underwriters go to more trouble to inform potential investors about the proposed issue, even to the point of giving the prospective buyers a tour of the area, and that the investor can properly have greater confidence in the merits of a negotiated deal than in the more perfunctory credit and price factors of a competitive sale. There is too much diversity among issues to support generalizations about relative prices received for similar issues under different bidding conditions.

Calling the Underwriter

The concern of the issuer for proper arrangements and procedures begins long before an underwriter is called into the picture and really ends only when the bonds are finally called for redemption, and not even then if some act of commission or omission has stuck in the long memories of investors. In competitive bidding, the issuer has extra responsibilities with respect to advertising for bids, setting the time and place for the opening of bids, and describing the precise terms of the bid itself, before he calls the underwriters to bid. As for the time and place for the bid, the "old China hands" at the game of underwriting are full of stories of midnight rides over dirt roads to empty rural town halls because the announcement of bid specified 10:00 AM Eastern time for an issuer in the Far West; woe betide such issuer if no one is there to greet the young men from the underwriting firms bearing the bids. In later life some of these men have been known to urge state governments to establish a convenient facility for the opening of all bids on bonds being sold by local governments, and in fact, centralized bidding using discounted present values is a real possibility for the future.

Chapter V Investor Demand for Tax-Exempt Bonds

Underwriters and dealers are in business to sell their inventories of new issue and secondary market bonds to various institutional and individual investors. By the end of 1967, large blocks of the $70 million BART Series G issue showed up in the portfolios of fire and casualty insurance companies and of commercial banks. The balance was in the hands of smaller institutional and individual investors, except for some bonds in the hands of dealers (or given to them to sell) and listed among the offerings in the *Blue List*.

No data are available, however, to show how many trades among dealers and short-term investors were executed on the passage from the original underwriting syndicate into these portfolios or how the losses were apportioned between dealers and investors as the original offering prices fell over the period. Since the market value of an average 20-year bond dropped about $50 as the *Bond Buyer* index of yields rose from 4.06 per cent on June 29, 1967, to 4.44 per cent at year's end, we can assume with a fair degree of confidence that many dealers in the secondary market took short-term inventory losses and that investors were showing proportionate book losses on their balance sheets.

Investor interest in the securities offered by state and local governments is determined in large measure by fundamental economic and fiscal factors, and the differential response to changes in those underlying factors, while slow, is apparently inexorable. This chapter is a report on how the pattern of demand and the relation between yields on tax-exempt and corporate bonds may react to the continuing increase in the volume of bonds offered in the market; prices and yields for tax-exempt bonds are dealt with in greater detail in Part 4.

The reader will find below our interpretation of a number of treatises on the emerging patterns of demand, with special attention given to the com-

57

prehensive study prepared for the Subcommittee of the Joint Economic Committee of the Congress in 1966. We begin with an analysis of the different investment responses over time on the part of commercial banks and life insurance companies, followed by a closer look at the investment record of twelve groups of investors that have been identified, with a running commentary concerning the impact of the tax laws.

A. GENERAL PATTERNS

Projections of Demand

The projections of demand made for the Joint Economic Committee occupy center stage in the discussion, and an introductory word is in order concerning the method by which these projections were fashioned.[1] In the first part of the Committee's study, the requirements for state and local public facilities were projected in relation to projections of GNP, internal migration, construction costs, and changes in demand for municipal services of all kinds. These projections were converted into amounts of tax-exempt securities to be issued and outstanding by year in the 1966–1975 period, assuming a smoothed rate for such financings. Thus by 1975 the outstanding debt was projected in the amount of $198.8 billion. Matched to these projections of bond offerings was a projection of estimated net demands for municipal securities by the twelve different investor groups that reflected expected growth patterns of their assets and the proportions to be invested in municipal securities, on the assumption that the existing yield structure of the market would be maintained over the decade.

Under these assumptions, demand by commercial banks for their portfolios accounts for 60 per cent of the net expansion in outstanding debt, and, although the Committee projects total demand for tax-exempt securities at the prevailing price level in excess of projected offerings, recognition is given to the possibility (which we think is a probability) that a shortage of credit resources might develop if commercial banks are unwilling to invest the projected amounts. The Committee then assumes that the commercial banks could be induced to invest the amounts required by decreasing the yield differential between taxable and nontaxable securities, a policy which has been shown to diminish further the savings in interest cost currently available to the local government issuers.

Institutional Responses over Time

Investment patterns change slowly in the municipal bond market, but, once a trend in the pattern sets in as a response to the underlying tax fac-

[1] See JEC—*Needs and Financing.*

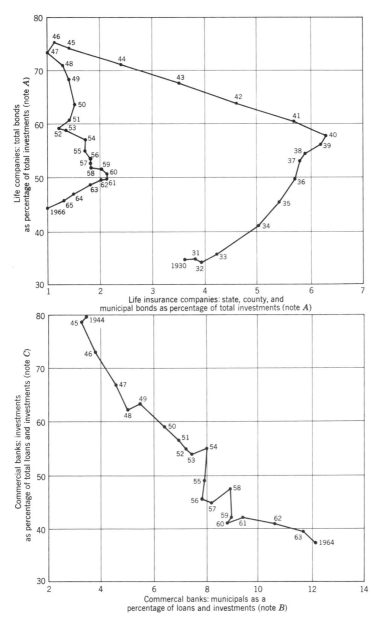

Figure 13 Relative rates of growth in tax exempt portfolios.
(*a*) Total bonds as a percentage of total investments in life insurance companies' portfolios, 1930–1966.
(*b*) Investments as percentage of total loans and investments in commercial banks' portfolios, 1944–1964.

tors, it tends to be maintained over a substantial period, barely reflecting short-term movements in tax interest rates. Within a given type of investing group, a change in policy is often implemented by allowing bonds that mature to be replaced by some other kind of investment or by gradually increasing the bond portfolio by selective buying over a long period.

The slow steady pace of change for two types of institutions as they follow separate investment policies can be seen in Figure 13.

Between 1944 and 1964 commercial banks increased their investments in municipal bonds as a proportion of total loans and investments, and bank investments came to represent a smaller percentage of bank assets than loans; the relationship is almost a straight line on the correlation graph over the 20-year progression.

Over a somewhat longer period, the correlation graph for the life insurance companies reveals three phases of fairly long duration: (a) between 1930 and 1940 tax-exempt bonds were a steadily increasing proportion of total investment portfolios, in which bonds were increasingly represented; (b) during the war the bond portfolios continued to increase, but a decision had been reached to decrease tax-exempts as a percentage of total investments; (c) in the two postwar decades the life companies have allowed their total holdings of bonds to decrease as a percentage of total investments but maintained tax-exempts as a minor percentage of total investments.

Benefits from Tax Exemption in the Postwar Market

An important insight into the reluctant quality of demand as it existed in the first postwar decade (a condition that has held true in the second postwar decade and as projected to 1975) was expressed by Roland Robinson as part of his discussion of whether tax exemption benefited the issuer as much as it did the investor:

State governments and governmental units at lower levels have unquestionably benefitted in some measure from the privilege of selling securities that offer the investor exemption from federal income taxes. But this advantage has also had a clear counterpart: the market for state and local obligations has had to be found among investors exposed to income taxation. Investors who are tax exempt per se—pension funds, most savings and loan associations and mutual savings banks, and nonprofit foundations, for example— are not interested in such a market. Those who have limited tax liabilities—life insurance companies and lower income individuals, for example—have only a mild interest in this market. If, as some feel, the future direction of institutional investment is toward those institutions with limited tax liabilities or none at all, this forecasts a further discounting of the value of the privilege of borrowing on a tax-exempt basis.

Furthermore, state and local government securities are not the first preference of any important group of investors. Commercial banks prefer loans. Individuals, and fire and casualty companies, mutual savings banks, and life insurance companies all prefer mortgages. State and local government obligations are the second choice of many investors, the first choice of very few.

This must account for some of the jerky quality to the market for state and local government obligations and to their price instability. When banks can find all the loans they want, they do not buy tax exempts; when fire and casualty companies think equity prices are reasonable, they do not buy tax exempts. And, as a class, individuals do not seem to have a true preference for tax-exempt obligations. They require a fairly clear price advantage to be enticed into the market. They will not pay out most of the value of tax exemption in buying as the commercial banks seem to do in periods of easy money. It is true that commercial banks and individuals have tended to put funds into this market at somewhat different phases of the yield cycle, a fact that tends to have a steadying influence. But unfortunately it has not been a strong enough influence to offset other unstabilizing influences.

All of this argues that the borrowing advantage of tax exemption becomes seriously depreciated except when the volume of market offerings is small.[2]

Benefits Greater for Investors than Issuers. Robinson goes on to show that most of the benefits of tax exemption accrue to investors rather than to the issuers when yields increase in order to attract investment by individuals. As he reports the findings of economists Gurley and Shaw concerning bank investment activities, this increase in rates tends to happen when banks (financial intermediaries) withdraw from the market, and the market is forced to induce individuals to increase the proportion of their assets invested in tax-exempt securities by shifting the yield curve upwards.

Thus a major public issue emerges. As the interest rate for issuers goes up, the differential narrows between what they pay with tax exemption and what they would pay if their bonds were like corporate securities. And the higher the yields become on tax-exempt bonds, the greater the benefit becomes for the investor. Municipal savings shrink as investor gains increase.

B. THE TWELVE INVESTOR GROUPS

Twelve groups of investors are said to furnish the demand for tax-exempt securities. Most of this section is concerned with a promising lot of five: commercial banks, fire and casualty companies, municipal bond investment funds, personal trust funds, and individuals and others.

Seven other groups are "also-rans," largely because of special tax legislation that lowers or eliminates their exposure to income taxes and thereby cancels the advantages that tax-exempt securities can bring to their portfolios. Two of these "also-rans"—state and local retirement funds and state and local governments themselves—were net buyers in their traditional way in the first postwar decade but became enlightened or emboldened thereafter and have turned into net sellers out of their portfolios. Five other groups are decreasing in importance: mutual savings banks, life insurance companies, "other financial institutions" (fraternal orders,

[2] Robinson, pp. 99–100.

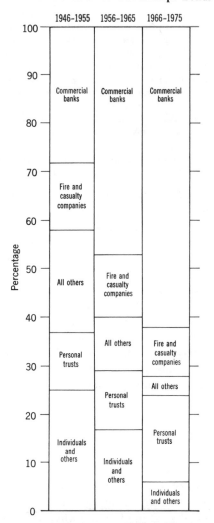

Figure 14 Percentage distribution of
tax-exempt bonds outstanding, by type
of investor, by decade, 1946–1975.

brokers and dealers, American Express Company, and certain other investment loan enterprises), "other corporations" (of a nonfinancial character),
and federal credit agencies.

The two state and local government types of holders added $2.8 billion
to their portfolios after the war, sold $0.5 billion between 1956 and 1965,
and are expected to divest themselves of another $3.1 billion bonds be-
tween 1966 and 1975.

The five other "also-ran" groups, largely represented by the "other corporations" and the federal credit agencies, altogether added $2.3 billion in the first postwar decade and $6.4 billion in the second decade, thus representing a market for about 11 per cent of all the bonds issued during that 20-year period. In the present 1966–1975 decade, they are expected to add only $6 billion to their portfolios, representing only 5 per cent of the supply of bonds.

The methods employed by the Joint Economic Committee staff in analyzing the past and projecting future demand for tax-exempts is described

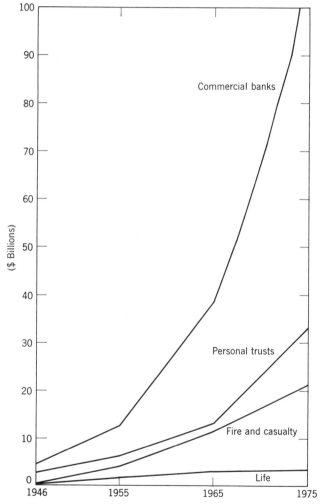

Figure 15 Holdings of state and local obligations, dollar amounts, by type of investor, end of year, 1946–1975.

in Section A of Chapter XIV. Its projections are summarized in Table C (net flows of funds into holdings of state and local government obligations by twelve investor groups during the 1946–1975 period). Additional data are found in Figure 14 (share of offerings estimated for major investor groups by decade during the 1946–1975 period) and in Figure 15 (a graph of data from which Table C was derived and which shows the basic demand year by year by the various investor groups).

Table C   Net Flows in State and Local Government Obligations by Investor Groups, 1946–1975

(Dollar Amounts in Billions)

Investor Group	1946–1955 Amount	1946–1955 Per Cent	1955–1965 Amount	1955–1965 Per Cent	1965–1975 Amount	1965–1975 Per Cent
1. Commercial banks	$ 8.3	28	$26.0	47	$68.8	62 [a]
2. Mutual savings banks	0.6	2	(−0.3)	(−1)	0.1	
3. Life insurance companies	1.4	5	1.5	3	0.3	[a]
4. Fire and casualty insurance companies	4.0	14	7.2	13	10.0	10
5. State and local retirement funds	1.9	7	(−0.1)	[b]	(−2.1)	(−2)
6. State and local governments	0.9	3	(−0.4)	(−1)	(−1.0)	(−1)
7. Municipal bond investment funds			[c] 0.2	[a]	2.4	2
8. Personal trust funds	3.6	12	6.5	12	19.8	18
9. Other financial institutions	0.1	[a]	.7	1	0.6	1
10. Other corporations	0.9	3	2.4	4	2.4	2
11. Federal credit agencies	0.3	1	2.1	4	2.6	2
12. Individuals and others	7.2	25	9.4	17	7.1	6
Total [d]	29.2	100	55.2	100	111.0	100

Source: JEC—*Financing*, p. 18.

[a] Under 1 per cent.

[b] Between 0 and −1 per cent.

[c] Municipal bond investment funds began to operate in 1961.

[d] Total may not equal sum of figures due to rounding.

The Committee's systematic study of the size and structure of each of these twelve investor groups, the sources of their investable funds, the way they invest, and present and future composition of their portfolios (under present tax and other ground rules) has been reported in Chapters 21–30 of *Public Facility Financing*. Excerpts from the findings of that study, found in Appendix B, set forth the critical factors affecting the major bank, insurance, and individual investor types.

C. IMPACT OF THE TAX CODE

Tax-exempt bonds are bought by those whose income is taxable. Corporate bonds, U.S. Government Securities, mortgages, and many other types of securities whose taxable yields may be higher are bought in great quantity by pension funds, foundations, and other nonprofit entities already exempt from income taxation. It is a curious circumstance that the removal of federal tax exemption from state and local government securities would apparently (a) tend to increase the interest cost for the issuers and the yield for investors, and (b) provide nontaxable investors with a fresh supply of high-yield securities on which the federal government would still not be levying a tax.

The Treasury's Interpretations

The tax consequences of investment in municipals are therefore paramount considerations throughout the system. The Treasury Department provided a summary of the tax statutes and regulations applicable to the various investor groups for the benefit of the Joint Economic Committee's study as its Chapter 19, "Relative Tax Advantages to Different Investor Groups in Acquiring or Holding Municipal Securities."

The general intent of the tax laws is to maintain the annual interest income exempt to at least one holder, a relatively familiar proposition for those dealing with trusts, corporations, and other forms of investments; the more complicated regulations affecting institutions such as banks and insurance companies are based upon the following sentiment as expressed by the Treasury: "In order to prevent recipients of tax-exempt income from being doubly benefitted, the Internal Revenue Code provides several restrictions on the deductibility of expenses connected with earning exempt income."

This concept is especially applicable to interest on loans incurred to carry inventories of bonds. Special provisions apply to banks regarding capital gains and losses taken in any given year, and insurance companies are subject to special regulations with respect to reserves for the benefit of policy holders. One hardly need add that changes in tax regulations and changes in the level of taxation create ripples of excitement throughout the municipal bond system.

Tables of Taxable Equivalents

Every municipal bond dealer has available for distribution a supply of tables or charts with more or less of the detail shown in Figure 16, so that a person in a given income bracket can determine how much annual return

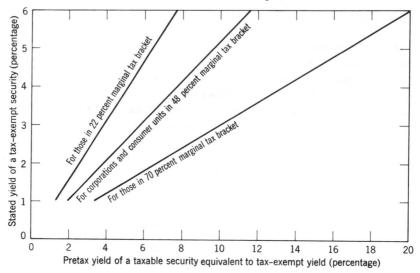

Figure 16   Pretax equivalents of tax exempt yields, by income tax bracket.

from a fully taxable investment he would have to receive to be as well off as he would be with a municipal security exempt from federal income taxation. The 1962 Federal Reserve Survey of Financial Characteristics of Consumers has become the source of most of our information concerning how individuals actually do invest in tax-exempts.[3]

Investment by Individuals

As reported by the Joint Economic Committee, the Federal Reserve found for 1962 that about 95 per cent of the 57,930,000 consumer spending units (or families) in the United States had incomes below $15,000; the average unit held a financial portfolio of $3994 with an average investment in tax-exempt securities of $18.

For the 2,020,000 units with incomes between $15,000 and $24,999, marginal tax rates were overwhelmingly (84.3 per cent) at the 34 per cent level or lower, and the average portfolio of $21,826 contained only $262 tax-exempt bonds.

For consumer units with even higher incomes, municipal bonds are more attractive in terms of after-tax yields. The Federal Reserve found that 530,000 units with incomes between $25,000 and $49,999 had average portfolios of $94,961 including tax-exempts amounting to $3701; that 160,000 units had incomes between $50,000 and $99,999 with portfolios averaging $270,270 and tax-exempts amounting to $34,722; and, lastly, that 40,000

[3] JEC—*Financing*, Chapter 30, Table 2A, p. 446; see also Readings (b).

consumer units had incomes over $100,000, average portfolios of $1,104,-971, and average holding of tax-exempts in the amount of $87,997. The financial life of the very rich, it was noted, varies according to age and ambition, so that generalizations about the appeal of tax-exempts for them are particularly hazardous, but, as Figure 14 shows, they are expected to favor investment through personal trusts rather than as individuals.

Chapter VI Implications for the Commercial Banking System

A. INTRODUCTION

In the previous chapter we saw how the Joint Economic Committee study assumes a continuation of national fiscal policy that makes tax-exempt bonds attractive to tax-paying investors and identifies the commercial banking system as the demander for the larger share (62 per cent) of tax-exempt bonds to be issued and outstanding in the 1966–1975 decade. The projection implies that commercial banks would hold these bonds in their investment portfolios, over and above bonds in trust or dealer accounts, and in spite of short-term fluctuations in money market conditions or long-term trends in monetary policy which, by affecting yields and spreads, might change both the amounts supplied by local governments and the amounts demanded by investors.

Of course, all such projections assume that the demand for local capital projects would continue to increase with no appreciable change in the sources of capital available to local communities. Under existing conditions, however, it was not surprising that 22 dealer banks had been invited into the winning BART syndicate. Four of the larger of these banks had been designated as comanagers with Halsey, Stuart, for the bonds were general obligations eligible both for bank underwriting and for bank portfolios. Banks that drop from such accounts before the final bid, and dealer banks in unsuccessful bidding syndicates, can satisfy their requirements for bonds at other times.

There is a certain ironic note in the fact that the Joint Economic Committee report went to the printer as commercial banks began dumping their holdings of municipal bonds onto a market desperately short of money. Yields soared, and the many resources of the federal government were thrown into the battle to lower interest rates and stabilize credit conditions. Examination of the market in the months following that summer of 1966 has provided exceptionally good insights into the policies of the commercial banks under pressure. Based on the experience during that tight-money period, a number of reforms for the banking system have been instituted or proposed, and extra attention will be directed to the flow of funds through the 13,500 commercial banks, almost half of which are members of the Federal Reserve System, but the greatest amount of concern will be devoted to the "100 largest banks," a group that, as of December 31, 1964, included 79 banks with over 43 per cent of total deposits.[1]

Nature of the Policy Issues

Although Robinson, in his postwar study of the municipal bond market, hardly foresaw the onslaught of local government spending and the revision of Regulation Q which would permit commercial banks to borrow relatively short-term money at fairly high rates and to invest the proceeds in relatively longer-term tax-exempt securities, the events of the past few years in the world of commercial banking have not changed the relevance of his perceptions of the basic nature of bank demand for municipal bonds. The dealer banks (which operate as underwriters as well as investors in tax-exempt bonds) remain as important determinants of commercial bank demand, especially for high-coupon short-term securities. Better data were available to the Joint Economic Committee than to Robinson, but it appears to have been true then as well as now that commercial bank investments are largely in upper-grade bonds (to the extent rated) with maturities concentrated in the 1–10 year group.

In short, although the analysis of commercial bank demand is an urgent daily occupation for the market, the fundamental relationships within the commercial bank sector and between it and the other sectors of demand have changed somewhat in degree but hardly in substance. It follows that if the commercial banking system is either unable or unwilling to absorb the $69 billion in tax-exempt bonds that will make the Joint Economic Committee's projections turn into realities, then the yields on tax-exempt issues will have to rise sufficiently to attract buyers from among the other institutions and individual investors for whatever bonds state and local governments feel impelled to sell at the higher interest cost. And no one is willing to predict to what extent tax dollars collected by the federal government will provide financing of local public facilities as a major alternative to the sale of new issues from state and local governments. If it turns out that state and local governments can get neither a good market for their new issues (with much of the demand coming from commercial banks) nor larger amounts of funds from federal tax sources, we may face the other alternative: fewer new public facilities and perhaps lower standards for some existing public activities.

[1] JEC—*Financing,* p. 298.

B. EXAMINATION OF BANK RESPONSE TO MONETARY CONDITIONS

As the money market tightened up during the summer of 1966, high demand for regular bank loans impelled commercial banks to switch from profitable investments in municipal bonds to even more profitable and far more basic loan investments. The result, as described by Federal Reserve economist William F. Staats, was a surprisingly large increase in average yields to the highest level in 30 years, followed by a return to former levels over the succeeding quarters. His concise explanation of the process follows.

Although many forces have been at work, the contribution of the investment policies of commercial banks perhaps has the most far-ranging implications—for banks, for the municipal bond market and for monetary policy.

Commercial banks' behavior has had a two-pronged effect on yields of tax-exempt bonds. First, banks substantially reduced acquisitions of new municipals in 1966. In contrast with 1965 when commercial banks bought about 75 per cent of new state and local government bonds, in 1966 banks absorbed less than 33 per cent. Second, some banks did not replace maturing municipals while others dumped large amounts of municipals in the secondary market in order to satisfy business loan demand. . . .

The leveling-off of bank holdings of state and local government bonds during 1966 followed five years of uninterrupted rapid acquisition of such bonds by a reserve-rich banking system. . . .

Experience of the past six years suggests a shift in the nature of bank municipal investments. Traditionally, banks purchased state and local government bonds with the intention of holding them to maturity, counting on U.S. Government securities as a rather temporary repository of funds not needed for loans. When loan demand built up, banks simply quit adding to their small stock of municipals. Now, however, many banks are beginning to view municipals as somewhat more cyclical investments and not only stop acquiring new issues but sell some of their holdings when lending opportunities increase.

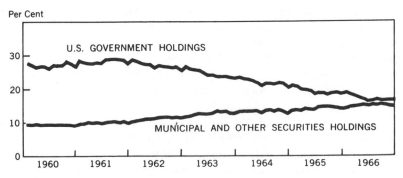

Figure 17 Municipal and other securities and U.S. government securities as a proportion of total deposits, commercial banks, 1960–1966.

[Figure 17] indicates the extent of the substitution of municipal and other securities for Government securities which has occurred in bank portfolios over the past six years. What does this policy shift mean to the market for municipals? . . .

The increasing importance of state and local government obligations in bank portfolios, coupled with bank willingness to liquidate the bonds in periods of intense loan demands, points to greater fluctuations of municipal bond yields over the business cycle. Commercial bank liquidation of municipal obligation in periods of restrictive monetary policy tends to push yields on tax-exempt securities up faster than they would have risen in the past. Conversely, during periods of expansionary (or less restrictive) monetary policy, heavy purchases of municipals by banks tend to push rates down more rapidly than they would have dropped before extensive bank activity in the market.[2]

Staats suggests in his conclusion that commercial bank practice with respect to investment in tax-exempt bonds affects monetary policy in at least three ways:

1. The banks' willingness to take capital losses as high as 12 per cent on their tax-exempt portfolios to obtain loan funds makes it more difficult to control expansion of credit.

2. The higher yield curves that result transfer the burden of credit restrictiveness to local governments that cannot afford to borrow.

3. The amplitude of price fluctuations in the capital market is increased.

The extent to which certain commercial banks during the 1966 crisis were dumping large blocks of municipal bonds on the secondary market (always a fairly thin if usually reliable resource for sellers of seasoned tax-exempt bonds) led the Federal Reserve in September 1966 to send a letter to all its member commercial banks urging them to apply for loans secured by municipals at District Banks' discount windows instead of selling securities in ways that "could contribute to disorderly conditions in other credit markets." With the question of a repeat performance of the credit squeeze of mid-1966 apparent in the market's collective mind throughout the spring of 1967, legislative proposals were advanced to make the discounting of municipal bonds at the Federal Reserve substantially easier than it had been in the past by upgrading the status of state and local bonds as acceptable collateral, and by confirming some of the other actions taken by the Federal Reserve in the crisis of the preceding summer.

Expectations Regarding Bank Performance

We must view the crucial role of the commercial banks as a permanent phenomenon, part of a problem of the money supply, on the one hand, and of the relative prominence of bank buyers versus "yield buyers" (individuals and fire and casualty insurance companies, for instance), on the other. Although more attention is being given to the system's mechanics and to

[2] Staats.

methods of facilitating investment by banks and others in tax-exempts, there will probably remain important incentives for bank investment policies that interfere with the smooth operation of the municipal market.

For example, as F. E. Gynt observed in *The Bond Buyer,* much of the expansion in bank investments in tax-exempts over the past few years has been at the expense of federal government securities, which have been consistently sold on balance and which do not provide as much "mileage" as do tax-exempts. As he shows below, the risks are no more and the rewards greater for a commercial bank that builds up its tax-exempt portfolio.

What is going on at the present time is sale by banks of Government issues of intermediate term and investment of the proceeds in shorter-term municipals, where the yield is the same or better and the prospects of loss not so great. The portfolio is shortened and the average yield is much the same or greater. What can a bank lose?

But even if it loses, as is so often the case on U.S. Government securities, the loss is not a major consideration. There are years in which banks make profits on bond investments and years in which they lose. A fat year off-sets a lean one and vice versa. Furthermore, losses and gains are carried directly through capital accounts and do not affect operating earnings reported to shareholders, and out of which dividends are paid.[3]

What can be done to moderate the short-term effects of commercial bank investments and to fortify their interest in tax-exempts? Gynt looked to enlargement of access to the Federal Reserve discount window as a standard alternative to distress selling of tax-exempt securities, and, as a far more fundamental change for which legislation had been proposed, to "100 per cent Federal Deposit Insurance for public deposits—Government, State and political subdivisions—in place of the age old system of pledging Government and other securities." He calculated that such insurance might free some $46 billion of bank assets, increase bank liquidity, and enable banks to divest themselves of U.S. government securities in favor of the higher yielding tax-exempts.

The short-run and long-run influences of the commercial banks on the municipal bond market are dominant factors in any analysis of the market. On the one hand, the need for sustaining demand requires increasing incentives for commercial banks by making tax-exempt bonds more liquid and more profitable. On the other hand, the need for financing governmental deficits and for stabilizing money market conditions suggests federal fiscal and monetary policies that dampen bank interest in tax-exempts at the expense of Treasury paper. These conflicting pressures will not be reconciled quickly and thus represent important qualifying conditions to projections of demand made from time to time by such agencies as the Joint Economic Committee and by the money market institutions themselves.

[3] *Bond Buyer,* June 19, 1967.

2

Critical Issues in Tax-Exempt Finance

Chapter VII Should Bond Ratings Be Standardized?

No one involved in the municipal bond field questions the fact that the present system of giving quality ratings to bonds needs to be improved. Ratings stand high as a critical issue, for they are powerful influences on the market and, in the past few years, have been the subject of vigorous public debate.

In this chapter, we conclude that ratings should be improved but not standardized, if standardization implies tagging an objective measure of quality onto the bonds of every state and local government in the country. In the pages below we discuss (a) what ratings are and how they are created, (b) recent conditions in the field, (c) proposals for improving ratings, and (d) the purpose and effect of standardization.

A. WHAT RATINGS ARE AND HOW THEY ARE CREATED

Bond ratings, it is said, appraise two basic risk factors: (a) the risk that bond quality will be diluted by an inordinate increase in debt, and (b) the risk that ability to meet maturing bond principal and interest may be impaired under depressed business conditions. The first risk involves activities within control of the issuing government and its electorate; the second risk is related to the impact of general economic conditions on the given locality. As described by the Joint Economic Committee,

These bond ratings are a graduated listing of bond issues according to an appraisal of investment quality and reflect the considered opinions of the bond rating services regarding the ability of an issue to withstand default and capital loss over long periods of time. Two of the bond advisory services use letter symbols to measure bond quality, with the highest grade assigned a rating of Aaa, and the third makes qualitative judgments on principal economic and financial factors affecting credit worthiness.[1]

[1] JEC—*Financing*, p. 10.

Rating Agency Problems

The ratings published by the two bond rating services, Moody's and Standard & Poor's, are based upon periodic evaluations by a small team of analysts of data that have been assembled, supplemented by occasional visits. As critics of this procedure have pointed out, a small number of analysts, working without computers, can hardly do justice to the large number of local governmental units whose general obligation bonds are to be rated, in a market where a lower rating means a higher interest cost. This situation was described in the Committee report as follows:

> One of the two bond rating services employs 13 people in its municipal bond department and the other employs 12. Of necessity, both rating services limit their efforts to issuers with substantial bonded debt, at least $600,000 for one service and $1 million for the other.
>
> Of the approximately 92,000 issuers of municipal bonds, ratings have been assigned to about 20,000, leaving many issuers (generally small) in the nonrated category. A survey of General Obligation bonds sold during 1957–61 found that rated bonds accounted for 85 per cent of their value, but only 43 per cent of the number of issues. Approximately 70 per cent of the issues rated by the two services have similar ratings, but the other 30 per cent have different ratings. The difference of a notch in a rating, or between similar bonds, one rated and the other unrated, is reflected frequently by 25 to 50 basis points in the interest payable by the public borrower.[2]

In January 1968, Standard & Poor's announced a change in its policy that would enable it to expand staff and make a profit on rating services. No longer would it "voluntarily" rate new or outstanding issues. Instead it would provide a confidential rating report under contract to any person or firm willing to pay a fee ranging from several hundred to several thousand dollars. The purchaser of the rating could publish it, and it was expected that prospective issuers and underwriters would do so. The rating itself, prepared by the same method as before but with help from a computer, would be considered valid for one year or until the same issuer came into the market again, whichever time was shorter. The effect of this change cannot yet be measured, but one can expect that most major new issues and many smaller ones will be found to carry the purchased S & P ratings.

Municipal Credit Reports

The third advisory service, Dun & Bradstreet, Inc., which does not rate municipal bonds as such, has for many years issued a series of credit surveys of major issuers of tax-secured bonds and, more recently, of revenue-secured bonds. The credit quality of the issuer is shown as "above average," "favorable," "fair," "poor," and so on, and information is supplied to allow the

[2] JEC—*Financing*, p. 10.

investor to draw his own conclusions as to the overall situation. The credit quality of the BART $70 million Series G bonds, for example, was given as "better good grade." As Dun & Bradstreet's chief analyst, Wade S. Smith, describes the work,

> In our municipal credit reports we organize and test the relevant information under four broad subject-areas. The economic factors have to do with the economic dependency of the debtor, extent and kind of wealth, and stability.
>
> Debt factors relate to the amount, purpose, and kind of debt, the repayment arrangements, and the relative debt burden, while financial factors have to do with the system of fiscal support, the solvency of funds, and the array of features relating to the adequacy and stability of governmental operations.
>
> Administration and legal factors have to do with the governmental structure and organization, the legal framework as it is relevant to the creditor, features of financial housekeeping arrangements, and management. And in the process of reviewing these materials, the experienced and perceptive analyst is able to identify evidences of effective and orderly planning for economic, financial, and physical development, or lack of such planning.[3]

Effectiveness of the Rating System

One could hardly ask for more in terms of the scope of bond analysis, but translating the wish for competent treatment of the enumerated factors into reality is a magnificently challenging job. The problems facing the bond analyst, described in detail in Part 3 in this book, suggests how little is truly known by state officials, credit analysts, budget-makers, politicians, political scientists, economists, and planners about our complex urbanizing environment and the conditions under which local government can best be operated. What is known is rarely subject to administrative control and, in all cases, is subject to revision in an era of rapid change in many dimensions. It has also become clear that a rating system designed to advise a few investors concerning major bond issues is ill adapted to serve the needs of local government generally, a point to be discussed further in this chapter. The excessive burden placed on the existing rating system makes its present deficiencies, as summarized by the Joint Economic Committee, incontrovertible:

(1) The undue dependence by financial institutions upon ratings in determining municipal bond investments;

(2) The higher interest costs to borrowing municipalities because of a lowered rating or the absence of a rating;

(3) The lack of verified information to support ratings (resulting from a lack of a uniform financial reporting system among the States, reliance upon the issuers to supply their periodic financial data, and inadequate staff to ascertain completeness or biases); and

(4) Possible conflicts of interest wherein the bond rating services also function as advisors to investors and as consultants to governmental bodies.[4]

[3] *Bond Buyer,* May 24, 1967.
[4] JEC—*Financing,* p. 11.

Defaults

The risk of default for a general obligation bond backed by the full faith and credit of a developed locality is almost neglible, to the extent that some borrowers claim that all such ratings should be the same. Investors, however, reply that other factors than mere risk of default account for the difference in quality. As Dun & Bradstreet's Smith writes,

> In the literature, evaluation of debt securities is assumed to be primarily or exclusively concerned with identification of the risk of default. Actually, this is a relatively minor problem for reasonably competent portfolio managers cognizant of the significant indicators bearing on this eventuality. Default-prone municipal bond situations, at least, are not inherently difficult to identify. Rather, the problem is one of estimating the added protection in a given situation . . . relative to other available securities.[5]

The risk of default, however, continues to figure in policy regarding municipal bonds. In several recent sets of Congressional hearings (for example, the one on bank underwriting of revenue bonds and others before the Joint Economic Committee), presentations have been made on the subject, frequently by the National League of Cities, using data drawn from *The Bond Buyer* files and from the Depression-period writings of A. M. Hillhouse.[6]

Over the years, more general obligation bonds than revenue bonds have been in default, but most of the general obligation bond defaults were before World War II and included multitudes of speculative land development schemes. However, according to the League's testimony, the best estimate of the prewar experience showed that 144 cities and towns of over 10,000 population (by 1930 census) defaulted, most of which were rated Aaa or Aa at the time.

Thus, although concern over general obligation defaults is still warranted, attention has shifted to the postwar revenue-secured issues. The record shows only two large defaults in the postwar period: the $133 million West Virginia Turnpike and the $101 million Chicago Calumet Skyway. Small investor losses on other revenue or limited liability municipal bond issues resulted, according to the Joint Economic Committee, from "faulty governing legislation and poor planning," although "the post-war experience stands to be marred further by recent marginal financing and others being planned."

A federal guarantee against investor loss, or any similar act to narrow the spread of the rating scale and to cover issues currently unrated, would not

[5] *Bond Buyer*, May 24, 1967.
[6] Readings (c).

only drive certain classes of investors out of the market, as we shall see, but would also remove from the market those investors seeking to make money by calculating the possibilities for a change in an individual rating. Such sophisticated long-range investors scorn use of ratings as reassurance for bank examiners and investment committees.

Making Money by Playing the Ratings

Consider the activities of a portfolio manager whose responsibility is to maximize the investment return of funds entrusted to him, with the risk of default only one of many that make one bond a better investment for him than another might be. "As one old-time manager put it," wrote Wade Smith, "pigeon-holing techniques will keep you out of trouble, but won't make the extra profit the owners want from professional management. Individualized selection techniques are more trouble (and more expensive) but they are also more profitable."

The capital value of a portfolio is enhanced when a bond is upgraded, so that the sophisticated investor seeks bonds with the highest possibility of moving from a lower quality rating to a higher one and avoids bonds which might be downgraded, for downgrading decreases capital value in the market as extra punishment during a period with a persistent general rise in the level of municipal yields.

And the market has a way of downgrading (or upgrading) a bond even before the rating agencies get around to reviewing the underlying factors, as a kind of testimony to the freedom of investors to come to their own conclusions about quality, even though it is easy to demonstrate the generally close conformance of ratings to actual prices in the market. As the manager of Standard & Poor's municipal bond division said in reply to questions about the reclassification of New York City's credit from A to Baa (along with Moody's and Dun & Bradstreet), the going prices of the public market had downgraded New York City's credit standing long before the services took action.

This writer has been privileged to work for a number of years as an independent consultant to major investors in municipal bonds who have been willing to take the trouble to set up their own systems of identifying those bonds of high intrinsic quality that have equally high possibility of being either upgraded or downgraded. It is a terrible chore to handle the incredible mass of statistics concerning the "objective" facts concerning municipal finance and urban development; the statistics themselves are often obsolete, aggregated in difficult ways, and incomplete, reflecting the diversity of our federal system and the neglect of urban research in the past, but the dollar rewards of an improved intuition concerning how the rating services may rate or reclassify certain types of communities, given certain changes in underlying characteristics of the local economy and its populace, can be substantial.

What federal or national rating agency would like the responsibility of changing an issuer's rating under these circumstances? The municipal bond system is probably better off with ratings prepared by privately supported enterprises that collect and disseminate a modest quantum of data and opinion for modest fees, leaving the investor free to place his own bets. The availability of better data, however, is a quite different topic from the manufacture of ratings, and also is more fundamental.

B. RECENT CONDITIONS

The basic conditions in the municipal field that have contributed to the deficiencies attributed to the rating system, and which must be changed as improvements are made, include lack of funds for sustained substantive research that would generate a theory of urban credit, the fear induced in bank officials by the examiners, and the increasing concentration of credit information in the hands of service agencies that are also investment counselors.

Ratings as Private Property

Not only are the rating agencies privately owned and working primarily for the account of subscribers willing to pay only relatively small amounts for contract ratings and/or comprehensive manuals with ratings that affect portfolios valued at millions and sometimes billions of dollars, but the field has narrowed dramatically in recent years. Dun & Bradstreet Corporation purchased the Moody's organization. McGraw-Hill Publishing Company purchased first Standard & Poor's organization and later acquired both White's Market Rating Service (which publishes an index of comparative market prices for 20-year bonds by individual issuer) and that essential journal of the secondary market, *The Blue List* (which lists outstanding bonds for sale plus inventories of new issues in dealer hands). The Fitch organization now provides ratings only upon special request. Several fledgling credit organizations exist but have far to go before they obtain market acceptance. A few very large financial institutions and investment organizations have begun to provide staff resources and time on computers to their municipal bond investment departments so that available "objective" information can be processed in an effort to develop "in-house" private-brand ratings (which may someday be satisfactory to the bank examiners).

The problems with which the critics of the rating system struggle, however, are quite often symptoms of much deeper causes; for instance, the question whether the rating system discriminates against small cities has been the subject of several Congressional hearings, but although there seems to be some evidence that the interest paid by smaller issuers tends to be higher than for larger communities, there is little to indicate that the range of ratings for the small localities is significantly different from that for the larger localities, and there has been little discussion of the relationship between ratings and characteristics particularly affecting certain smaller communities such as rate of recent growth, dependence on a single industry, and uncertain levels of personal income over a future period.

Rating Large Cities

The ratings of the larger cities, if indeed it can be shown that they are also discriminated against, would be found to involve the deeper problems of the urban crisis. One dimension, which has not been quantified to this writer's knowledge, is suggested by the headline of a *New York Times* article during the long hot summer of 1967 which read, "Will the Riots Hurt Municipal Bond Sales?" and included the statement that "in recent years, the major bond-rating services have downgraded the bonds of many cities, often partly because of the urban problems. Ghettos are not viewed as good risks."

In search of a story on the subject, *The Bond Buyer* compiled Moody's ratings for the nation's 50 largest cities for selected years during the 1940–1967 period. From observation of these data, the conclusion was reached that, although some ratings have been recently downgraded and although the analysts believed there would be a general bias toward downgrading over the next several years, a large number of cities had gained improved ratings during World War II, following the aftermath of the Depression and the suppression of local spending during the war years, and had managed to maintain or improve them. As one can see in the record printed in Table D, half the cities, including Chicago, Los Angeles, Philadelphia, and Cleveland, had better ratings in 1967 than in 1940, whereas notable among those that were downgraded in the more recent 1955–1967 period were New York, Detroit, Baltimore, Cleveland (which slipped back a notch), and Boston.

The New York City problem, although significant in terms of its magnitude, is basically no different from that of any other major city and only a little more complicated than that of any other issuer of bonds. Its resources are enormous, its problems are staggering, and its bond rating is as meaningful or meaningless as anyone else's. (How other major cities have fared in terms of ratings to date can be seen in Table D.) The rating services

Table D   Rating Saga of the 50 Largest Cities

The bond rating saga of the nation's 50 largest cities, running from the prewar period, through World War II, and into the postwar period, is shown in the table below, using Moody's bond ratings. To the extent that there is any discernible pattern other than the deterioration in ratings which has now begun to set in (see accompanying story), it seems that a number of cities gained improved ratings during World War II, following the aftermath of the depression and the suppression of local spending during the war years. In the postwar period, some cities managed to retain or improve their ratings up until now, while others are beginning to lose ground. Analysts at the bond rating services suggest that the trend for ratings for large cities over the next several years may be weighted even more toward a downgrading of credits.

City	Selected Years				
	1940	1945	1955	1965	1967
1. New York	A	A	A	Baa	Baa
2. Chicago	Baa	A	A	A	A
3. Los Angeles	A	Aa	Aa	Aa	Aa
4. Philadelphia	Baa	A	A	A	A
5. Detroit	Baa	A	A	Baa	Baa
6. Baltimore	Aaa	Aaa	Aa	A	A
7. Houston	A	Baa	A	A	A
8. Cleveland	Baa	A	Aa	Aa	A
9. Washington	...	...	...	...	...
10. St. Louis	Aa	Aa	Aa	Aa	Aa
11. Milwaukee	Aa	Aaa	Aaa	Aaa	Aaa
12. San Francisco	Aa	Aa	Aa	Aa	Aa
13. Boston	A	A	A	Baa	Baa
14. Dallas	A	A	A	Aa	Aa
15. New Orleans	A	A	A	A	A
16. Pittsburgh	A	A	A	A	A
17. San Antonio	Baa	Baa	Baa	A	A
18. San Diego	A	A	A	A	A
19. Seattle	Baa	A	A	A	A
20. Buffalo	A	A	Aaa	Aa	Aa
21. Cincinnati	Aa	Aaa	Aaa	Aa	Aa
22. Memphis	A	Aa	Aa	Aa	Aa
23. Denver	Aa	Aa	Aa	Aa	Aa
24. Atlanta	Aa	Aa	Aa	Aa	Aa
25. Minneapolis	Aa	A	Aa	Aaa	Aaa
26. Indianapolis	Aa	Aaa	Aaa	Aa	Aa
27. Kansas City, Mo.	A	A	Aa	Aa	Aa
28. Columbus, Ohio	A	A	Aa	Aa	Aa
29. Phoenix	Baa	A	A	A	A
30. Newark	Baa	Baa	Baa	A	Baa
31. Louisville	Aa	Aa	Aa	Aa	Aa
32. Portland, Ore.	A	A	Aa	Aa	Aa
33. Oakland	Aa	Aa	Aa	Aa	Aa
34. Fort Worth	Baa	Baa	A	A	Aa
35. Long Beach, Calif.	A	A	Aa	Aa	Aa
36. Birmingham	Baa	Baa	A	A	A

Table D (Continued)

City	Selected Years				
	1940	1945	1955	1965	1967
37. Oklahoma City	A	Aa	A	A	A
38. Rochester, N. Y.	Aa	Aa	Aaa	Aaa	Aaa
39. Toledo	Baa	A	Aa	Aa	Aa
40. St. Paul	A	Aa	Aa	Aa	Aa
41. Norfolk	Baa	Baa	A	Aa	Aa
42. Omaha	Aa	Aaa	Aaa	Aaa	Aaa
43. Honolulu	A	Aa	A	A	A
44. Miami	Baa	A	A	A	A
45. Akron	Ba	Baa	A	A	A
46. El Paso	Baa	Baa	Baa	A	A
47. Jersey City	Ba	Baa	Baa	Baa	Baa
48. Tampa	Ba	Baa	A	A	A
49. Dayton	A	A	Aaa	Aa	Aa
50. Tulsa	A	Aa	A	A	A

Source: *The Bond Buyer.*

might fail to spend sufficient time evaluating the nuances of life in a small town in Colorado or Mississippi, but they cannot be charged with lack of diligence in their attempts to assign a rating to the largest municipal issuer in the country, the one that houses their own main offices.

It would be an interesting diversion in this chapter, to explore the New York City situation in detail, but it is beyond our scope. In fact, a small book could be put together if all the articles that appeared between January and June 1967 in *The Bond Buyer* were clipped together. The story line is indicated by the 13 headlines cited:

1. "New York City's Cost Averages 4.1815%/Comptroller Accepts Merged Account Bid; Moody's Calls For End To Brinkmanship," January 28, 1967, p. 1.

2. "New York City Budget-Deficit Financing Approved/Court of Appeals Upholds the Legality of 'Borrow Now, Pay Later' Financing," February 25, 1967, p. 1.

3. "New York City's Current Fiscal Crisis: A Study of the Roots and Responsibilities," by Noel Buckley, March 21, 1967 and March 28, 1967, p. 1.

4. "New York (State) $2.5 Bil. Transits Get Bearish Reaction From Rating Agencies," by Fred Golden, April 17, 1967, p. 1.

5. NYC "Budget Tops Record," April 18, 1967, p. 1.

6. "NYC Official Hits Private Bond Ratings, Urges Federal Reserve to Take Over Job," April 25, 1967, p. 1.

7. Mayor Lindsay's hopes for New York as "A Happy Middle Class City," April 28, 1967, p. 1.

8. Editorial, May 1, 1967.

9. "Washington Scans Bond Rating Battle; The Agencies React," by Paul Heffernan, May 9, 1967.

10. "Baa and BBB New York City Ratings To Stand for May 23 Housing Bonds," May 12, 1967, p. 1.

11. "Dun & Bradstreet Studies Bond Analysis Function," by Wade S. Smith, D & B, May 24, 1967, pp. 1, 23, and 24.

12. "NYC Fiscal Trends Still Worry Moody's; Baa Rating Stands," May 22, 1967, p. 1.

13. "Text of Goodman Statement In defense of NYC Credit," by Roy M. Goodman, Finance Commissioner of New York City, May 2, 1967, pp. 18–19.

In the year following the opening of the campaign by New York City against its Baa rating, a number of concrete suggestions were made in Congressional hearings and other forums and the federal government was urged to intervene. The chairman of the Federal Deposit Insurance Corporation said, "We concur in the concern about the inadequacies of the municipal bond rating system and we are already doing some field study in the area," and two governors of the Federal Reserve Board chimed in, "The Board has a deep concern with the rating problem because of its supervisory responsibilities and would have sympathy with the idea of a study by a reputable concern to gain an understanding of the problem and its broad impact on the economy." In addition, a number of agencies outside government, notably the Brookings Institution, undertook long-range studies of the problem and its cure.[7] In the next two sections we review some of the proposals to improve ratings and we consider further the implications of intervention in the system.

C. PROPOSALS FOR IMPROVING RATINGS

According to James Reilly, one of the market's staunchest critics, efforts have been made to place the rating system on a firm, theoretically sound, and empirically practical basis ever since the 1930's, "when events caused so many issues to be devalued and rating agencies to adopt their lingering conservative attitudes." These efforts came even before the banks and insurance companies began to over-comply with the rulings of the Comptroller of the Currency and cause "embarrassment to the rating agencies for, unwittingly, they have come to be looked upon by banks as well as by the public at large as 'official agencies' serving a public rather than a private purpose." Reilly reported further:

[7] *Bond Buyer*, May 9, 1967.

Moody's began rating municipal bonds in 1919; Standard & Poor's not until 1950. Until the great depression, Moody's rated most issues Aaa or Aa. Large numbers of defaults during the 1930's caused Moody's to reevaluate its standards and adopt a more conservative approach. . . . The art of municipal bond analysis has come a long way since the pre-depression days when the rule of thumb was the number of railroads passing through a town. One railroad called for a single A, two for Aa and so forth. Today, a determination of ability to pay involves analysis of a host of economic, social, political, and historic factors tempered in large measure by the analyst's own subjective, or even intuitive assessment.[8]

The McCabe Study

The problem is to obtain a reliable rating system to measure both the "objective" and the "subjective" factors uppermost in the minds of participants in the municipal bond investment community. One of the earliest attempts appears to be the project organized by an academician, James E. McCabe of the Maxwell School of Syracuse University and reported by him in a preliminary memorandum dated 1941 entitled "A Municipal Credit Rating Scale," excerpts of which appear below.

This project was undertaken that it might prove of some practical value to those actually engaged in the analysis of municipal credit. Its aim was to discover the relative significance of the many factors affecting the credit position of a municipality. The method used was to secure the professional judgment of a highly selected group of men with a rich practical experience. As the study progressed, such sharp agreement was apparent among the men in the field that a rating scale was developed, consisting of those factors considered most significant by the practitioners. . . .

This project directly attacks the major problem of the lack of uniform, accurately weighted universally accepted standards for credit appraisal purposes. Basically, the aim has been to measure the relative importance of the multitude of disuniform factors which are currently used in analyzing municipal credit. It employs a new approach to the problem of credit rating, suggested by the late John F. O'Hara in a thesis written at Syracuse University in 1934. Rather than relying on the subjective opinion of a single individual, the aim has been to utilize the collective judgment of the men most qualified to evaluate the significance of many of the credit factors now in use. Accordingly, an extended list of these was presented to a highly selected group of experts familiar with municipal credit and finance. They were requested to record their judgment of the effect of each factor listed on the soundness or unsoundness of the finances of any municipality. When the judgments of these raters were recorded and summarized, it was hoped that out of the excess number of factors presented, a smaller number of the more highly significant ones could be extracted and given a weight, determined by the professional judgment of the men working daily in the field. Finally, if a sufficient number of representative factors could be so derived and evaluated, the possibility of creating a rating scale composed of these expertly selected factors was considered.[9]

McCabe's panel consisted of almost 50 individuals, many of whom are still prominent in municipal bond affairs. The panel's criteria were ap-

[8] JEC—*Financing* (g).
[9] Ratings (a).

plied to a random selection of 25 cities and compared with Moody's ratings for the same places, with "a correlation of +.899 ±.03, a strikingly high correlation for most social data." Twenty-five years later (1966) I found that 11 of those 1941 Moody's ratings had been raised, 3 lowered, and 11 kept the same.

McCabe and his panel considered debt factors, tax data, quality of administration, economic and social stability of the community, and its current operations. Diligent search in major libraries has not succeeded in uncovering any more sophisticated or revealing study in the ensuing quarter century. Except for a proposed use of computers and a proposed allocation of specific weights for given credit factors, the prize-winning method advanced by a California banker in 1966 is no more advanced in concept than the 1941 McCabe study.

Since New York City received its Baa rating, Moody's has agreed to provide special A and Baa ratings, known as A-1 and Baa-1 grades, to indicate that these bonds have "the strongest investment attributes." New York City was among a long list of communities originally put into the new Baa-1 category. Moody's also began to provide provisional ratings for certain large revenue issues which had previously been left unrated until after the capital investment had been completed and the facility was in operation, but otherwise the services have remained silent on the subject of new methods of analysis.[10] There seems to be little disagreement concerning the need for better data on every dimension of the urban situation and the need for analysis of such data by computer, but no guidelines have really been set forth regarding the nature of a revamped rating system. We now address ourselves to this problem.

D. THE PURPOSE AND EFFECT OF STANDARDIZATION

The goal of a rating system that had been nationalized and/or standardized would presumably have something to do with the general welfare—but whose? The national interest per se lies both in strengthening democratic government at the local level and in supporting the efforts of the economic system in providing for the income and financial security of the populace. Thus a rating system that helped local governments secure long-term funds from investors at lower interest rates would be worth creating, for it would help restore the value of tax exemption for the benefited local government rather than, as at present, maintaining high interest rates that are of primary advantage for the relatively few investor groups that pay high taxes and therefore seek the shelter of tax-exempt income.

On the other hand, the national interest could equally well be found in a

[10] Ratings (b).

rating system that would ensure that investment in the securities of state and local government was sound, thus protecting the widows, orphans, depositors, policy-holders, and stockholders of insurance companies, banks, trusts, and other repositories of individual savings.

However, in the pursuit of efficiency and the enhancement of real national income by federal control over the allocation of investible funds among risky local situations, a centralized local credit agency might deprive local governments of a measure of their fiscal independence, even though simultaneously enhancing the security available to the widows and orphans.

Effect of Federal Intervention

As the rating system now operates, it is a creature of the investment community, owned and managed for the benefit of investors who subscribe to the rating services. Let us explore for a moment whether the federal government, directly or indirectly, could as a practical matter advance the general welfare by control of, setting standards for, subsidizing, or otherwise participating in the operation of the rating system.

As discussed in many different contexts in this book, the relations between the federal government and the flock of state and local governments are full of paradoxes and delicate balances between powers and resources. The Advisory Commission on Intergovernmental Relations (ACIR) has assumed leadership in the effort to upgrade the activities of the states and their subdivisions with respect to revisions of restrictions on local financial practices, to amalgamation and coordination of governmental operations at the metropolitan level, and to improvement of state-operated facilities that can assist local governments in the performance of their duties. A federal stamp of approval on a local government's bond rating might have the vitiating effect of transferring responsibility for improvement of that credit to the federal government; the local governments might say to the federal government: "If you are going to allow our ratings to remain low, then you must provide the funds necessary to compensate for the higher interest and other penalties we shall incur. . . ."

This line of reasoning has led to contemplation of a federal guarantee, protecting investors against loss on investment in state and local obligations. The findings of the Joint Economic Committee as to investor reactions to the suggestion of a federal guarantee, in addition to or in lieu of tax exemption, are reviewed in greater detail in Chapter X. The Committee found that investors generally would avoid investment in the lower-yielding securities that the guarantee would generate, thus effectively frustrating the federal goal of expanding the market for states and local obligations.

It is also questionable whether the federal government could do much more than it already does to protect depositors of banks or beneficiaries of insurance companies and investment trusts. The effect of banking regulations has been to place the burden of proof of value for investment squarely on the shoulders of bank directors in accordance with the requirements of the several regulatory authorities that work in close cooperation with one another, especially the Comptroller of the Currency (with jurisdiction over national and state banks that are members of the Federal Reserve System and the Federal Deposit Insurance Corporation) and the various state banking departments, and it is generally believed that examiners, and hence the bank investment officers, rely heavily on the opinion of the rating agencies. Fiduciaries, such as trust departments and insurance companies, undoubtedly also rely on the existing ratings, with further control being exercised by the lists of bonds deemed suitable for acquisition by fiduciaries as published by the supervisory authorities of the leading states, such as New York and Massachusetts.

With the major components of the federal interest already served by the concept of creative federalism with respect to the states and their rural and metropolitan governments, and by the bank examiners and the several fiscal and deposit insurance instrumentalities that connect the federal government to the world of investors, it is appropriate to ask how the federal government (or its proxy) could act to alter or expand or improve the essential nature of bond ratings themselves.

Future Prospects and Federal Activities

If the rating problem is to be solved at all, progress might be accelerated with the addition of small amounts of money and effort. Although a set of official ratings would probably create an even worse set of problems than we now have, the federal government could make a number of contributions on a continuing basis. Among them might be:

1. Expansion of the activities of the Bureau of the Census, the Office of Regional Economics, and the Division of Construction Statistics, all in the Department of Commerce, in a sustained effort to make available to the municipal bond analysts working for the rating services, and in other parts of the investment and academic world, the sort of data that can be used to explore relationships between fiscal, social, and economic trends at the local level;

2. Sustaining a research program by offering grants-in-aid to the universities and professional associations (such as the Municipal Finance Officers Association or the American Society of Planning Officials) for the pursuit

of knowledge about local behavior and the development of norms or criteria which bond analysts could use;

3. Compiling and publishing for every issuer a one-page abstract (perhaps in a computer-readable form) of the data collected by the Department of Commerce and the relative standing of the issuer in terms of the statistical norms developed by the researchers.

Federal activity of the kind just described might have substantial impact. The information already received by the federal government, if properly packaged, would put into the hands of any investor a similar but even more up-to-date review of basic facts than he now receives from some but not all of the rating agencies. This data, if provided to the rating agencies on the same basis as to the public, would lighten their burden of data preparation and enable them (and some new competitors) to spend more time analyzing credit, especially with respect to revenue issues, for their subscribers.

Thus drastic solutions are not in order. A few more data, a little more research, a little more competition, a little slackening of the pressure from bank examiners, a little more understanding that the present rating services are more like private investment counselors than they are public servants, a little more effort on the part of states to collect and process local government data on a current basis—all these small steps put together can make a big difference in the rating field. Many of these steps are already being taken, and more are coming.

The more one considers the rating problems, the more one realizes how intimately connected it is with our inability to date as a nation to come to grips with the "urban problem" or to define adequately a "good city." Intervention by the federal government in the rating picture is not the answer, nor could any other national organization do much better. Since nationalization of ratings is unwarranted, since ratings reflect more than create our concern, the solution may have to be found as the sum of all the small improvements that can be made at all levels of government and within all types of institutions concerned with the municipal performance.

Chapter VIII   Should Dealer Banks
Underwrite Revenue Issues?

This chapter is devoted to a grand and glorious controversy that has involved every branch of government and an imposing array of financial institutions. The roots of the struggle lie in the 1933 Glass-Steagall Act, which, among other improvements to the banking system, prohibited commercial banks from underwriting nongovernmental securities and led to the establishment of an independent investment banking industry.

At this writing, Congress has not yet passed S.1306, Senator Proxmire's bill to remove all restrictions on underwriting and dealing in state and local governments by national banks. The material in this chapter will remain as a guide to the appraisal of the effect of the decision, whether the law is changed or not. The chapter begins with an outline of the issues, provides the reader with a short chronology over the 35-year period between 1933 and 1968, and ends with commentary on the testimony submitted during the summer of 1967.

A. BACKGROUND

In 1933 Congress decided that commercial banks should no longer be allowed to underwrite speculative securities, such as corporate bonds and municipal securities, that were not general obligations of the issuers. General obligation bonds were exempted from these banking restrictions because the legislators felt that the banks were in a position to render an important service to their communities and because the purchasers of local government bonds were largely sophisticated investors and fiduciaries. Banks were allowed to invest in but not underwrite limited obligation and revenue bonds. Change was in the air when a new Comptroller of the Currency took over in 1961:

At the outset of his five-year tenure, Mr. Saxon was confronted with the task of energizing and modernizing an industry that was generally regarded as moribund. Except for a handful of progressively-minded banks, nearly all of the 4,800 nationally chartered institutions were out of tune with the times, and certainly ill-equipped to cope with the problems or opportunities in a fast-expanding economy and a rapidly changing nation.

In his campaign for a freer and more competitive national banking system, the free-swinging Mr. Saxon left in his wake the tattered remnants of his fights with the Federal Reserve System, the Securities and Exchange Commission, the Bureau of the Budget, the Justice Department, investment bankers, State-chartered banks and the official and unofficial friends of all these.

By his own estimates, Mr. Saxon brought about nearly 6000 changes in previously existing Federal bank regulations, chartered more than 500 new national banks, permitted existing banks to open up some 3000 branches, approved such new practices as permitting banks to raise money by issuing debentures and promissory notes, engage in a variety of new practices ranging from equipment leasing to issuing consumer credit cards— and in all these activities, got himself involved in about 40 major lawsuits.[1]

Since 1933 the volume of revenue bonds has vastly increased in response to the changing needs and resources of local governments. The commercial banks, as we have seen in Part 1 of this book, have become the dominant force in the municipal bond market and chief underwriters of general obligation bonds, where the profit margins have been relatively low since 1961 but which the banks can easily finance. The investment bankers do not appreciate the efforts of the commercial banks to join them in the underwriting of revenue bonds; the investment bankers would like to retain that corner of the market for themselves, applying to it their special talents for designing and distributing a class of securities that might be described as more speculative than unlimited general obligation bonds.

So the commercial banks and the investment bankers clash on this issue, and some banks feel so strongly that they will not invite an investment banker to join a syndicate bidding for a general obligation bond; and some investment bankers feel so strongly that they will not invite commercial banks into their syndicates. Nevertheless, the investment bankers must look to the commercial banks for loans to carry their inventories of bonds and as customers for revenue bonds they have underwritten, and relationships between individual investment bankers and individual commercial banks remain cordial enough for the market economy to function. Meanwhile the issue is contested on other fronts.

Related Issues

Some of the issuers of revenue bonds, notably the Port of New York Authority, maintain that the market for their bonds would be expanded and the net interest cost they have to pay lowered if the commercial banks were entitled to underwrite revenue bonds. The Comptroller of the Cur-

[1] *Bond Buyer* (John Gerrity), 1/23/67.

rency, representing the Treasury and responsible for the examination of the investment portfolios of national and state banks that are members of the Federal Reserve System, finally came around to the view (in 1963) that the commercial banks under his wing were really entitled to underwrite those revenue bonds that the Comptroller felt were just about as good as general obligations with unlimited access to taxable resources and buttressed by the pledge of the full faith and credit of the issuing governmental unit. The number of issues so qualified by the Comptroller created quite a stir in the market—the commercial banks gleefully began to underwrite them, the Federal Reserve System found itself again on the other side of the fence from a representative of the U.S. Treasury, and the investment bankers girded for battle. When a federal judge finally ruled that a general obligation bond is a general obligation bond and not something almost as good, the investment bankers won the battle, but it is up to the Congress to say who won the war.

There are many muted themes in the debate. One concerns the survival of the investment bankers over the long run if their independent functions, more or less stabilized in concept since the banking acts were passed, should be truncated by having the commercial banks able to underwrite revenue bonds and maybe ultimately corporate securities as well, as was the practice during the 1920's. Another muted theme has to do with the lingering suspicion that revenue bonds for turnpikes, industrial development, housing projects, and a host of other purposes may in fact turn out to be more speculative than they appear at the time of sale. Still others have to do with the extent to which municipal bonds—currently a most unregulated affair with no watchdog organizations such as the Securities and Exchange Commission or the National Association of Securities Dealers—would begin to be subject to rules and regulations imposed by banking authorities. All of these issues were raised in the testimony which is evaluated at the end of this chapter.

B. CHRONOLOGY LEADING TO THE INVESTMENT BANKERS' SUIT, 1933–1966

The chronology begins with the banking acts and continues through June 1967, at which time the Congress was still conducting hearings on the Proxmire bill. The entries through January 18, 1966, compiled by *The Bond Buyer,* include most of the actions mentioned in the briefs for the litigation that was beginning. The balance of the chronology was compiled by us from later issues of that newspaper.

June 16, 1933. President Franklin D. Roosevelt signed into law the Glass-Steagall Act, which permitted banks to underwrite and deal in U.S. Government securities and "general obligations" of the states and their political subdivisions, backed by the "full faith and credit" and "general taxing powers" of the issuer.

November 21, 1934. In a letter sent to the National City Bank of New York, Comptroller of the Currency J. F. T. O'Conner ruled that Port of New York Authority bonds qualify under the law for bank underwriting as being general obligations of a state or political subdivision.

March 14, 1941. The U.S. Treasury initiated litigation seeking an end to the Constitutional immunity of all state and local government obligations from federal income taxation, using bonds issued by the Port of New York Authority as the basis for this test case.

July 15, 1941. In a letter sent to the National City Bank of New York, Deputy Comptroller of the Currency A. J. Mulroney said, "Our position is that neither the bonds of the Port of New York Authority nor the bonds of the Triborough Bridge Authority of New York represent general obligations of a political subdivision . . . that the term 'political subdivision . . . includes only such units of a state as have the sovereign's power of taxation or powers derived therefrom . . .' "

January 2, 1945. The U.S. Supreme Court refused to review the case of "Commissioner vs. Shamberg's Estate," 323 U.S. 792, thereby upholding a lower court decision that "Port of Authority bonds were exempt obligations of a state or a political subdivision thereof" under the Internal Revenue Acts.

June 22, 1955. A bill to permit bank underwriting and dealing in tax-exempt revenue bonds was jointly introduced in the Senate by Senators John Bricker of Ohio and Homer Capehart of Indiana. No action was taken on the bill S.2290.

October 19, 1962. Comptroller Saxon ruled in the so-called "Georgia State Authorities" instance that revenue bonds issued by public authorities, created by special acts of the Georgia Legislature, are eligible for bank underwriting. The amended state constitution authorized the state to contract "for long-term use" of facilities to be built by the authorities, and rental revenues under those contracts were pledged to secure the revenue bonds.

April 24, 1963. Representative Fernand J. St. Germain, Democrat of Rhode Island, introduced in first session of 88th Congress H.R.5845 amending the Glass-Steagall Act to permit commercial banks to underwrite and deal in tax-exempt revenue bonds.

August 6, 1963. Comptroller Saxon ruled that $35.7 million of Public Building Bonds Series D and Public School Plant Facilities Bonds Series C are eligible for bank underwriting and dealing.

September 4, 1963. The Federal Reserve Board ruled that state member banks of the system could not underwrite and deal in $35.7 million of School Building Bonds and Public School Plant Facilities Bonds, issued by the state of Washington.

September 12, 1963. A revised "securities investment regulation" published by Comptroller of the Currency James J. Saxon in the Federal Register, permitting bank underwriting and dealing in revenue bonds, went into effect.

September 23, 1963. The House Banking and Currency Committee began hearings on H.R.5845, the St. Germain bill. The hearings continued through December 13 sporadically, with the committee taking testimony on eighteen days during that period.

September 24, 1963. Federal Reserve Board Chairman William McChesney Martin testifying before the House Banking Committee, asserted that in the judgment of the board of governors, Comptroller Saxon "had exceeded his statutory powers" in issuing his revised securities investment regulation on September 12, 1963. Mr. Martin opposed the St. Germain bill. The chairman appeared again on December 13, the final day of his series of hearings.

March 18, 1964. President Johnson named Secretary of the Treasury C. Douglas Dillon as chairman of the "Coordinating Committee on Bank Regulation," with instructions to act as arbiter on disagreements between the Comptroller and the Federal Reserve on interpretations of federal bank statutes.

April 15, 1965. Congressman St. Germain introduced a revised bank underwriting bill, which was referred to the House Banking and Currency Committee.

April 26, 1965. The House Banking and Currency Committee began hearings on the revised St. Germain proposal. Federal Reserve Board Vice-Chairman C. Canby Balderston, accompanied by Counsel David Hester, testified against the revised bill and proposed a new definition of general obligation bonds. According to Federal Reserve thinking, a general obligation of local government is one that is backed by an unconditional pledge of a legislative body with jurisdiction to appropriate the full amount of money needed to pay interest on the bonds, and to pay them off when due.

June 29, 1965. A House Banking and Currency Committee staff study was released by Committee Chairman Wright Patman, alleging that Mr. Saxon's revised securities investment regulation was unlawful. The study charged Mr. Saxon with 28 other violations of federal bank statutes.

July 6, 1965. President Johnson named Secretary of the Treasury Henry H. Fowler chairman of the "Coordinating Committee on Bank Regulation." This committee, successor to the previous Dillon committee, was broadened to include as a member John H. Horne, chairman of the Federal Home Loan Bank Board.

August 12, 1965. Congressman St. Germain introduced a third version of his bank underwriting bill, which was referred to the House Banking and Currency Committee. This version provided restraints on amounts banks could underwrite and on underwriting banks' relations with correspondent banks. It is still pending.

August 23, 1965. Comptroller Saxon answered the charge of the staff of the House Banking Committee that the Comptroller's securities investment regulation is unlawful. The Comptroller's rebuttal was that it was "within his statutory authority" to issue the revised investment regulation. He denied that bonds, to be eligible for bank underwriting, must be backed by the general powers of taxation.

November 1, 1965. Comptroller Saxon ruled that $25 million in bonds issued by the Port of New York Authority were eligible for bank underwriting and dealing.

November 12, 1965. The Committee for Study of Revenue Bond Financing, an association of 476 investment banking firms, protested Mr. Saxon's bank investment regulations and rulings, particularly the Port of New York Authority ruling, and asked him to "cease and desist" issuing such rulings.

December 13, 1965. Comptroller Saxon told the complaining investment banking firms he would "review the validity" of his bank investment regulation. But he promised no relief to their complaint.

January 14–17, 1966. A declaratory judgment by the U.S. District Court of the District of Columbia, stating Mr. Saxon's bank investment ruling is unlawful and setting it aside, was sought by 97 investment banking firms. A motion was filed seeking a court order to require Mr. Saxon to produce rulings by the Comptroller's office on bank underwriting dating back to before enactment of the Glass-Steagall act in 1933.

C. CHRONOLOGY, 1966–1967

JULY 7, 1966—"FORMAL BRIEF FILED ASSAILING SAXON RULING TO EXPAND UNDERWRITING AUTHORITY OF BANKS"

Submitted in behalf of 114 investment and underwriting firms against Comptroller of the Currency James J. Saxon, with the Port of New York as a codefendant and intervenor. The dealers' brief reviews the record back as far as 1915, charges that "Mr. Saxon's permissive regulation" of September 1963 "will continue to create illegal competition" and that the dealers are threatened with "future injury" so long as commercial banks can underwrite and deal in the very kinds of securities that Congress, in order to protect against conflicts of interest and other results it deemed harmful to the public, deliberately forbade banks to underwrite and deal in."

SEPT. 16, 1967—"BRIEF OF JUSTICE DEPARTMENT LAWYERS BACKS SAXON ON BANK UNDERWRITING ISSUE"

The federal government today denied categorically that Comptroller of the Currency James J. Saxon had broken national banking laws with his permissive rulings to allow commercial banks to underwrite and deal in state and local government securities not secured by general taxing powers. . . .

Shortly before the Justice Department handed its answer to the district court, a brief from the Port of New York Authority in the role of an intervenor in the security dealers' lawsuit against the Comptroller, was also accepted by the Court. . . .

The intervention of the Port of New York Authority in this lawsuit is an outgrowth of the fact that the investment bankers sought and failed to find relief from Comptroller Saxon's ruling that banks could share in the underwriting of a $37.5 million port bond offering last October. The dealers declared in their complaint to the district court that the Port of New York "does not have the power to levy taxes on anyone. It builds, owns and operates bridges, tunnels, terminals and the like. It has plans for issuing $500 million of bonds in the near future. These bonds, like its bonds already outstanding, will be secured primarily by revenues paid voluntarily by customers of its facilities."

October and November, 1966. Case assigned to Federal District Court Judge Alexander Holtzoff, eighty-one, who "evidently has viewed his mission in life to make and maintain his mark as a rugged individualist."

Comptroller Saxon announced that he would step down upon expiration of his term in November; after a few weeks, President Johnson nominated as his successor William B. Camp, Saxon's First Deputy. Judge Holtzoff held stormy hearings in the middle of November, and invited the Federal Reserve to contribute an opinion.

DECEMBER 5, 1966—"INTENT OF CONGRESS HAS BEEN DISTORTED BY SAXON RULINGS, FEDERAL RESERVE HOLDS"

The Governors of the Federal Reserve System today reaffirmed their belief that rulings by the Comptroller of the Currency to permit commercial banks to deal in and underwrite tax-free revenue bonds are unlawful. . . .

In the Federal Reserve view, only those bond issues that "represent an unqualified promise by a state, or by a lesser governmental entity with general powers of taxation, to make all payments of interest and principal when due" can be considered general obligations, which are eligible for underwriting by banks. The Federal Reserve rejected as "irrelevant" the argument that, in some instances, "revenue" securities involve a lower degree of risk than certain "unconditional promise" securities.

> *DECEMBER 14, 1966—"SAXON BANK UNDERWRITING RULINGS HELD UNLAWFUL BY COURT. JUDGE HOLTZOFF SAYS GENERAL OBLIGATION MUST BE BACKED BY ISSUER'S TAX PLEDGE. DECISION HAILED AND DEPLORED BY BANKERS; APPEAL TO THE SUPREME COURT IS PLEDGED"*

As a result, the Federal Reserve definition of a general obligation bond is now the law of the land. There are singular implications. Under the Federal Reserve definition, several of the State governments are unable to issue "general obligations" underwritable by commercial banks because such states do not exercise the power of property taxation. Texas, a frequent market borrower of high credit rank, is one such state.

With the passage of time, the Holtzoff decision will probably go down in the book as a makeshift bridge between an old banking law and one that in due course will supplant it. When this occurs, it is perhaps too much to expect that the public officials will write their intentions into the law in plain language.

> *FEBRUARY 17, 1967—"JUSTICE DEPARTMENT TO APPEAL RULING ON BANK UNDERWRITING," TOGETHER WITH THE PORT OF NEW YORK AUTHORITY*

Commercial banks may continue to underwrite and deal in tax-free revenue bonds until the Appellate Court hands down its decision, but they would do so at their own risk, counsel said.

> *MARCH 17, 1967—"PROXMIRE BILL WOULD LEGALIZE SAXON BANK UNDERWRITING RULES"*

At the request of the National League of Cities, Senator William D. Proxmire, Democrat of Wisconsin and a member of the Senate Banking and Currency Committee, introduced a bill that would permit commercial banks to deal in and underwrite tax-free revenue bonds in accordance with a Federal bank investment ruling that is now the subject of a Federal court dispute. . . .

. . . . He was persuaded to introduce this bill by claims made by the cities that broader competitive bidding for revenue bonds would reduce borrowing costs. . . .

April 10, 1967. As the government filed its appeal, Senator Proxmire asked the Comptroller and the Federal Reserve Board to join in a study to resolve their differences and make a report by the time hearings on his bill began in July.

> *MAY 24, 1967—"JUSTICE DEPT. DROPS UNDERWRITING CASE—BUT PORT AUTHORITY WILL PRESS APPEAL IN DISTRICT COURT"*

The decision to drop the Government's appeal case was made by Solicitor General Thurgood Marshall, who said that the Government had, at best, "a very doubtful case". . . .

Both Justice Department lawyers and counsel for the investment bankers, the Washington law firm of Covington and Burling, admitted puzzlement over what legal line the Port Authority would follow. . . .

The Justice Department, in effect, was in a position of having to represent two clients —the Comptroller's office and the Federal Reserve Board—who were disputing with each other. The result was to burden the Justice Department with "a divided client."

Amplifying on the action taken by Solicitor General Marshall, Justice lawyers said that Mr. Marshall had informed Mr. Camp that his was "not a sound case," and that if "Mr. Camp wants to retain the permissive regulation he should take it up with Congress". . . .

Legislation is pending before the Congress under the sponsorship of Representative Fernand J. St. Germain, Democrat, of Rhode Island, and Senator William Proxmire, Democrat, of Wisconsin, that would expand the underwriting authority of commercial banks along lines favored by former Comptroller Saxon.

The Key Marks of a General Obligation

May 25, 1967. The decision of the Justice Department not to appeal to a higher court the decision of Federal Judge Alexander Holtzoff in the bank underwriting case has the effect of entrenching further the Federal Reserve Board's definition of a "general obligation" of local government so far as the national bank laws are concerned.

The heart of this definition is the pledge of the general power of taxation as bond security. The key condition is that the tax pledge, whether direct or indirect, must be "unconditional." The central bank's definition, which was adopted by Judge Holtzoff, is as follows.

LANGUAGE OF THE JUDGE

The phrase "general obligations of any state or of any political subdivision thereof" contained in R.S.5136, 12 U.S.C., section 24, paragraph seventh, is limited to obligations that are supported by an unconditional promise to pay, directly or indirectly, an aggregate amount which (together with any other funds available for the purpose) will suffice to discharge, when due, all interest on and principal of such obligations, which promise (1) is made by a governmental entity that possesses general powers of taxation, including property taxation, and (2) pledges or otherwise commits the full faith and credit of said promiser; said term does not include obligations not so supported that are to be repaid only from specified sources such as the income from designated facilities or the proceeds of designated taxes.

AUGUST 14, 1967—"BANKS' UNDERWRITING OF MUNICIPALS IS SEEN SAVING ISSUERS MONEY"

Municipalities would realize large savings if commercial banks were authorized to underwrite municipal revenue bonds, as provided for under a bill pending in the Senate, a study by the Comptroller of the Currency's office has found.

The study, requested by Sen. Proxmire (D., Wis.), concluded that bank underwriting of such bonds would "inject added competition" into the underwriting market that would "lead to a significant reduction in the interest paid by municipal authorities." The savings would exceed $27 million each year by 1975, according to the study.

D. COMMENTARY ON THE TESTIMONY

Bushels of documents are now available on the controversy, and the purpose of this section is merely to evaluate the summary statements and original analyses of data prepared in conjunction with the hearings on S.1306 before the Subcommittee on Financial Institutions of the Committee on Banking and Currency of which Senator Proxmire was a member during the summer of 1967. The testimony came from some forty organizations, banks, investment dealers, law firms, and federal agencies, including the Treasury Department and the Federal Reserve.[2]

The essential points of the debate, in this writer's opinion, involved methods of answering two questions:

1. Would more competition for revenue underwritings lower the interest cost to local governments?
2. Can the commercial banks be trusted?

The debate itself covered all aspects of the municipal field, especially the credit-worthiness of revenue bonds not secured by the full faith and credit of issuers, the nature of demand for bonds, the method by which bids are made, the techniques of marketing, and the relationship between rating and market price, plus other topics covered in this book as well. Nevertheless the essential questions seem to be the ones identified above.

The protagonists devoted major efforts to the first question. The Federal Reserve prepared a report entitled "Interest Cost Effects of Commercial Bank Underwriting of Municipal Revenue Bonds" based upon multiple-regression mathematical analysis of sixteen variables characterizing some 6000 bond issues offered during the first half of 1966.

In addition, the National League of Cities and the Committee for Broadening Commercial Bank Participation in Public Financing commissioned a professor of business economics at the University of Chicago to prepare a report titled "The Economic Consequences of the Exclusion of Bank Competition from the Underwriting of Revenue Bonds," based upon further application of multiple-regression analysis to the characteristics of 9120 relatively large bond issues reported by *The Bond Buyer* between April 1959 and March 1967.

On the other side, the Committee for Study of Revenue Bond Financing, representing the investment bankers, commissioned a professor of business administration from Harvard to write a critique of the Federal Reserve and commercial bankers' studies. What ensued in the hearings was a high-level

[2] Hearings (a).

discussion of econometric analysis of various hypotheses framed by the researchers to demonstrate that the introduction of competition by commercial banks would—or would not—reduce the cost of borrowing to local governments.

For a number of reasons, enumerated in part below, neither side can be said to have proved its case. Some of the reasons are highly technical, as illustrated by the discussion of the effects of logarithmic functions on the results of an analysis to show that an increase in the number of bids would tend to decrease the reoffering price. And that discussion led to differences of opinion regarding the significance of spread, or dealers' profit, in the several analyses and the extent to which a reduction in spread would be passed on to the issuer. Also involved was the unresolved issue as to whether any savings in cost of issuing could be found as the number of competitive bids increased over some effective number such as three, given the nature of syndicate operation.

The arguments are generally unconvincing, moreover, because of the fairly low indicia of correlation (squared correlation coefficients) which measure the percentage of variance of the dependent variable explained by the estimating equations, even though the various results were deemed "statistically significant." In addition, the samples were composed of relatively large issues, leaving out of account most of the issues that are handled on a local basis by small banks and investment bankers without reference to the "general market" served by New York and other central city underwriters.

The most unconvincing aspect of the testimony, however, is the reliance on analysis of yields for different categories of rated bonds. Yields for similarly rated bonds can vary within a wide range, assuming constant market conditions, so that bonds can be described as selling like "high" or "low" AA bonds. These ranges of yields in a rating category were obscured in the analyses but would seem significant enough to offset the extremely small variations in net interest costs upon which the conclusions rested. The disputants agreed, however, that the difference in basic characteristics between general obligation and revenue bonds affected their rating and yield structures, regardless of bank underwriting, so that one can anticipate that average ratings of general obligations would remain above average ratings for revenue bonds, and yields for revenues remain above yields for unlimited obligation bonds.

With no implication that commercial banks would suffer financially if they were not allowed to underwrite revenue bonds and much testimony by the investment bankers that they could not compete with commercial banks, and with no conclusive evidence that the local governments' position would be measurably affected, the second question assumes paramount importance. Can the commercial banks be trusted?

This question of trust is fairly embarrassing, but it strikes at the heart of the issue. The Glass-Steagall Act was passed originally because of a series of undesirable activities in banking during the Roaring 'Twenties, when speculative securities underwritten by commercial banks were lodged in the portfolios of fiduciary accounts as well as in the bank's own investment accounts. The Crash was a moment of truth, and the investment bankers suggest that conflict of interests would lead to inevitable tragedy if the commercial banks were again enabled to underwrite the possibly speculative and unguaranteed revenue bonds of the future. Moreover, many investment bankers claim that the commercial banks (and a few of the larger investment banking houses) would dominate the revenue field as they have come to dominate the general obligation field, effectively driving the smaller investment bankers out of the municipal bond field.

The issue is thus moral and political, rather than economic, and it will ultimately be resolved within the Congress as an expression of trust or a withholding of such expression. On balance, however, a decision in favor of the investment bankers would seem to be the most reasonable course, for there is a lack of convincing evidence that local governments would be significantly benefited or commercial banks significantly damaged by such a decision. Allowing commercial banks to underwrite revenue bonds, on the other hand, would appear to benefit the banks in many ways, severely handicap the investment bankers, and produce only highly problematic benefits, if at all, for the local governments in whose name the battles are being fought.

Chapter IX   Should Industrial Revenue Bonds Be Tax-Exempt?

During the writing of this chapter, Congress passed legislation revoking tax-exempt status for industrial revenue bond issues over $1 million sold after January 1, 1969, and thus partially resolved one of the most complex issues ever to confront the municipal bond field. Bills have been introduced to raise the limit to $5 million.

The controversy touches all of the fundamental principles relating to municipal bond finance and serves as a curtain-raiser in this book to the question about the desirability of retaining tax exemption itself as treated in Chapter X. It should also be clear to the reader that rating industrial revenue bonds is especially difficult and that the debates about ratings and bank underwriting covered in the two preceding chapters are often focused directly on the industrial revenue bond situation.

In this chapter we first describe the origin and growth of industrial revenue bonds, in form not much different from the railroad bonds of the 1870's. Then, the arguments for and against their use are evaluated, with respect to the nature of the remedies proposed for the control or elimination of the practice.

A. ORIGIN AND GROWTH OF INDUSTRIAL REVENUE BONDS

From small beginnings in 1936 in the South, the industrial revenue bond technique was adopted by a majority of the states and made widely available to large-scale industries in the 1960's. We begin with that story as told to the Joint Economic Committee by James Reilly, one of the market's avid promoters of this type of financing.

Industrial development bonds are issued by local government bodies, city, State, county, municipality, etc., to buy or build plants and equipment to be leased to private enterprise. The most common variety of industrial development bonds is a revenue bond, which is supported solely by rents derived from the facility. Some issues, however, have been general obligations which pledge the credit and taxing power of the issuer in addition to rents from the project.

The primary purpose of industrial development bonds is to attract new industries to areas by offering lower costs than would be incurred through traditional methods of corporate bond financing. Since the interest on municipal bonds is exempt from Federal income taxes, local governments are usually able to borrow funds in the capital markets at interest rates lower than those available to private borrowers.

Typically, a municipality will sell bonds to purchase a site and build a plant for a particular company, usually to the company's specifications. It is then leased to the company for a period of time sufficient for rental payments to cover principal and interest on the bonds. Should the tenant default, he is subject to eviction and another company is then sought to fill the premises. If the plant was financed by revenue bonds, any loss must be stood by the bond holders.

The first industrial aid bond was issued in the State of Mississippi in 1936. Authority for the issue came from Mississippi's then new "balance agriculture with industry" (BAWI) plan which was State sponsored and legislatively approved, and made industrial aid financing available to all Mississippi's communities. The first issue originated in Durant, Miss., for the construction of a factory for the Realsilk Hosiery Mills. The amount of the issue was $85,000. Between 1936 and 1950 only Mississippi and Kentucky had authorized the use of industrial development bonds, but during that period very few such bonds were issued.

In 1952 the city of Florence marketed an issue of bonds convertible into stock.

The first issue of industrial development bonds by Durant, Miss., was of the general obligation type. Today only Mississippi uses general obligation bonds extensively, though Tennessee, Arkansas, and Louisiana have made some use of this technique. Both revenue bonds and general obligation bonds are tax exempt, but they differ in the credit standing behind the issue. Since general obligation bonds pledge the full faith and credit of the municipality they have the advantage of being easily marketed. However, most States limit the amount of local bonded debt to the value of local property. Communities are often restricted to small scale financing and one issue may exhaust the possibility of further general obligation financing for many years.[1]

Relation to Other Building Authorities

Some distinctions must be made between financing of industrial plants and financing for schools and other public facilities. For this large category of nonindustrial uses, a nonprofit corporation is created; it acquires a site and erects a building using funds secured by the sale of tax-exempt bonds; the facility is then leased to the local government under terms and conditions that fit the particular jurisdiction. States in which public buildings have been constructed on the basis of such leases include, according to Reilly's count, California, Colorado, Georgia, Illinois, Indiana, Kentucky, Maine, Michigan, Missouri, Pennsylvania, West Virginia, and Wisconsin. Many bond issues of this type carry a guarantee as to principal and interest from the state or from some other governmental entity with taxing power,

[1] JEC—*Financing* (h).

but the more easily perceived nature of the public purpose and the guarantee combine to make such bonds significantly different from and less controversial than their industrial revenue cousins.

State Enabling Acts

By the end of 1967, according to the Investment Bankers Association (a vigorous critic of the practice), over forty states had passed enabling acts permitting use of such lease-rental financing, and the remaining states were at least considering its adoption. The legislative and judicial history of these enabling acts is available in the reports of the IBA's Municipal Industrial Finance Committee and in numerous briefs and court decisions, but the essential points brought out by the IBA are the following.

1. Since the 1914 Supreme Court decision in Union Lime Co. versus Chicago & Northwestern Ry. Co., the Court has refused to review decisions by the highest court in a state concerning the propriety of definitions of "public purpose" or "public use" in state enabling acts.

2. By amending their constitutions, where necessary, and by passing legislation that removes obstacles to industrial revenue bond financing, states have encouraged the practice, leaving critics with only their appeal to Congress.[2]

About the only incontrovertible aspect of the situation is that the volume of industrial revenue bonds issued has increased dramatically during the 1960's. Figure 18 shows the use of this type of financing, by state, to the end of 1966, with the major application in the southern and central states. The volume of bonds issued prior to 1956 aggregated about $5 million, but the annual volume began to grow slowly but steadily during the rest of the decade. By 1961 the market began to keep closer track of the volume, as shown in Table E for the most recent years.

Table E   Industrial Revenue Bonds Issued, 1961–1967

Year	Volume ($ millions)	Volume as Per Cent of All Tax-Exempt Issues
1961	$ 72	0.09%
1962	84	0.10
1963	119	0.12
1964	191	0.18
1965	212	0.19
1966	504	4.55
1967	1,325	9.30

Source: *The Bond Buyer Statistics*

[2] IBA (b).

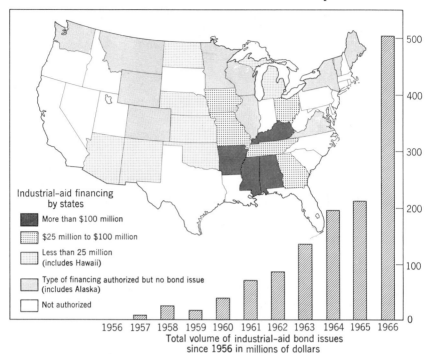

Figure 18 Map of the United States showing sales of industrial revenue bonds by state, with graph showing total sales of such issues, 1956–1966.

During the years when the volume of industrial revenue bonds repre-sented one or two tenths of one per cent of all tax-exempt bonds issued, as was the case until 1966, even the occasional incidence of major corporations in the roster of firms that took advantage of the privilege could be accepted by all but the most determined critics, but the increase in volume to the point where it represented 5 or 10 per cent of total volume, with the lurking possibility that the volume might continue to climb until every factory in every community was financed by tax-exempt bond issues, sounded a gen-eral alarm. The critics of the situation in 1966 found their fears realized as the 1967 stampede of large corporations into industrial revenue bond lease financings took place in a tight market. The final count for 1967 showed that 13 bond issues absorbed 63 per cent of a volume two and one half times as great as seen in 1966. The 13 major issues of 1967 are shown in Table F.

In the absence of controls, there is no convincing method for projecting future volume, since the only limits on the high side are the willingness of local communities with suitable enabling acts to undertake industrial building programs and, depending on the yield of such bonds, the capacity of investors to absorb the bonds offered. Some market observers, however, have assumed a constant rate of growth, thus calculating that the volume of

Table F   Major Industrial Revenue Bond Issues of 1967

Amount of Issue ($ millions)	Issuing Authority	Corporation Signing Lease	Date of Issue
$130	Mississippi Industrial Port Dev.	Litton Industries, Inc.	11/14/67
97	Scottsboro Ind. Dev. Board, Alabama	Revere Copper & Brass, Inc.	12/5/67
85	Courtland Ind. Dev. Board, Alabama	U.S. Plywood-Champion Papers, Inc.	11/28/67
82.5	Middletown, Ohio, Ind. Building	Armco Steel Corp.	2/21/67
80	Wickliffe, Ky., Ind. Building	West Virginia Pulp and Paper Co.	7/11/67
75	Crossett, Ark., Ind. Dev.	Georgia Pacific Project	9/27/67
60	Fort Madison, Iowa, Ind. Dev.	Sinclair Petrochemicals, Inc.	5/18/67
53	Albany Dougherty Payroll Dev. Auth., Georgia	Firestone Tire & Rubber	11/21/67
46	Union City Ind. Dev. Board, Tenn.	Goodyear Tire & Rubber Company	12/27/67
35	Spartenburg Co., S.C. Ind. Rev.	Hyston Fibers, Inc.	12/15/67
33	Livonia, Mich., Ind. Rev.	Allied Supermarkets Inc.	6/28/67
30	Warren Co., Ky., Ind. Building	Firestone Tire & Rubber Company	6/15/67
25	Iberville Parish, La., Ind. Rev.	Hercules, Inc.	12/15/67

$831.5 Equals 63 per cent of total $1325 tax exempt industrial revenue bonds sold in 1967.

Source: *Bond Buyer Statistics*

such bonds might be around $3 billion in 1968 and $7 billion in 1969, in order to expound on the implications of the practice, as discussed in the following section. With controls, the flow of such industrial revenue issues can be limited to insignificant amounts.

B. ARGUMENTS FOR AND AGAINST THE PRACTICE

This section evaluates the arguments in the debate concerning industrial revenue bond financing. We begin with the defense and end with the strong hypotheses advanced by the opposition.

Pro: Legality

By the time an industrial revenue bond has reached its ultimate home in an investment portfolio, it has run a gamut of legal controls:

1. The State government must have passed the enabling legislation.

2. In most instances, sometimes as the very last step, the enabling legislation will have been tested in the courts, typically on the question of whether the law itself, or a particular lease, satisfies applicable definitions of public purpose.

3. The legislative body of the community or the directors of the special district have approved the form of contract negotiated with the prospective corporate lessee.

4. Sometimes the bond issue terms have been approved by the local electorate at a special referendum.

Pro: Certified as Tax-Exempt

In addition, as a condition precedent to the offering, the Internal Revenue Service in most cases has issued a letter certifying that the proposed terms and conditions of the lease qualify the issue for tax-exempt status with respect to interest payments so that the issue can be accepted by the underwriters as technically valid as a tax-exempt security, an essential precondition to the application for credit rating and the establishment of prices and yields for the various maturities being offered in the bond issue.

In general the Internal Revenue Service has held since 1957 that interest is not taxable on obligations issued by municipally owned corporations regardless of the purpose for which the bonds were issued. More specific rulings were made in 1963: bonds issued by a nonprofit corporation formed under the general corporation laws of a state for the purpose of financing the acquisition, lease, and sale of industrial facilities would be considered as having been issued on behalf of a political subdivision within the Code if (a) the municipality issuer had a beneficial interest in the nonprofit corporation while the bonds were outstanding, (b) there was a reasonable likelihood of a vesting of full legal title in the municipality at some point, and (c) either a state or a political subdivision had approved the specific bond issue in question.[3]

Pro: Essential for Local Development

Competition among localities for new industry does not increase national productivity by itself but merely distributes growth potential among

[3] JEC—*Financing* (h), p. 166.

the various communities. We must assume that the firm involved has found an efficient solution to its locational problems by agreeing to sign the long-term lease only after it has (a) determined that it would be feasible to have a factory operation in the specified region, given the availability of labor and raw materials, the cost of transportation, and the proximity to markets, and (b) selected the particular locality served by the issuer of the bonds.

Proponents claim that industrial financing of this type is an essential weapon in the armory of economic development specialists working on behalf of cities and states throughout the country. A former president of the American Industrial Development Council wrote as follows:.

Formerly, regional differences in wage rates were a major determinant in plant location decisions. More recently, wage payments on a national basis have leveled off and this factor has been neutralized to a large degree. . . . Thus considerations given to the cost of money for capital expenditures occupy a much higher position of importance than in former years. . . . The industrial developer must have at his disposal every possible attractive financing proposal. . . . The use of tax concessions and tax exemptions at the local level has not been widely used.[4]

Pro: Right of Self-Determination

Regardless of possible conflict with the priorities that may be assigned by the federal government for the development of one or another backward region, and regardless of the availability of federal or state programs of assistance to state and local governments, many people feel that a local community has the right—or, perhaps, the duty—to define its own best interests and to take such steps as it can within the law to win the prize in the nationwide competition for local employment and income growth. The same idea is found in the statement that industrial revenue bond financing supplements other programs of economic development.

Pro: Employment Generator

Another claim relates to the multiplier effect of stabilized or increased employment in the community. The rewards of a successful local development campaign are many: local pride is boosted and new investment follows; the new corporation, like a good citizen, may pay money in lieu of taxes on the factory; new construction for additional workers' housing adds to the tax base of the municipality; larger payrolls help support local stores and services. Far from being a source of jeopardy to local finances, the new factory is seen by the proponents as a potent force for direct and indirect benefits.

[4] Lease Rentals (a).

Pro: Expanding the Tax-Exempt Market

It appears to be true that the interest costs of an industrial revenue issue are higher than for securities of equivalent quality that carry the full faith and credit pledge of the municipality (although Reilly notes that the differential has narrowed over the years), but some underwriters claim that the higher yields have successfully attracted new buyers of tax-exempt bonds, including certain institutions that had been waiting for high yields and were willing to accept the risks attendant on such financing, and certain individuals who would not have been interested in general obligations. Thus the introduction of a large volume of industrial revenue bonds is said to supplement the efforts of those who have been trying to broaden the market for all tax-exempt securities, even though the yields on all local bonds, general obligation as well as limited obligation types, are forced upwards.

The Cons

The standard term of reproach in the annals of industrial revenue bond financing is "abuse" or sometimes "misuse," a term that implies that use of the technique is a privilege rather than a right held by local government; presumably the only way to abuse a right is to fail to use and defend it. Known for their use of the word "abuse" are the Advisory Commission on Intergovernmental Relations, the Investment Bankers Association, the AFL-CIO, Congressman Henry Reuss of Wisconsin, and an assortment of Treasury and other federal officials.[5]

The comments below represent an interpretation of their statements both on "abuses" of the privilege and on the bad effects of industrial revenue bond financing. The difference between an abuse and a bad effect is the difference between a discussion of alternative methods of financing (using taxable corporates or tax-exempt bonds) and a discussion of the subsequent effect on the economy and the market once the tax-exempt route has been selected.

These opponents of industrial revenue bonds seem to have four major areas of abuse or misuse in mind: the perversion of public purpose doctrines; excessive benefits to the industrial tenant if he purchases part of the new issue of bonds (and unwarranted benefits to the issuer through arbitrage); deliberate and unnecessary avoidance of the sources of taxable loans; and interregional pirating of firms.

[5] ACIR (b).

Perversion of Public Purpose. The complaint about the perversion of public purpose, the use of public funds for the benefit of a private corporation, seems to be an extremely weak reed, under the circumstances. One is entitled to assume that the question of propriety in this regard had been fully considered at the time the state's enabling act was passed and, if not then, in the course of the litigation that so often is required to clarify the allowable scope of state statutes and local ordinances. In the opinion of a leading municipal bond attorney,

> *Public Purpose:* The issuance of bonds by a political subdivision of a State for the industrial development of its area in order to relieve unemployment is not more, per se, an abuse inconsistent with the public interest than the issuance of its bonds for any other legally authorized purpose.
>
> Indeed, in a given case the State legislature and the governing body of the political subdivision and often the State courts have determined that the public interest is served best by the proposed action. . . .[6]

The distinction between residential and nonresidential urban renewal programs that involve land takings with resale to private parties and industrial financing programs that provide facilities for industry may be fairly small in relation to public purposes, and even the Advisory Commission on Intergovernmental Relations, for all its concern about abuses, acknowledged that "governments in the United States since the beginnings of the Republic have freely intervened in and assisted the private economy to enable it better to achieve popular ends," and goes on to discuss the canals, turnpikes, railroads, drainage and irrigation projects, banks, utilities, sports arenas, tourist and recreation facilities, area redevelopment and small business development projects that have characterized local programs through the years.[7]

Double Tax Benefits and Arbitrage. A second form of abuse involves the purchase of part or all of the newly issued bonds by the industrial corporation that occupies the premises thus financed. Although it is said the practice faded out as soon as industrial revenue bonds became more widely accepted and the benefited firm was no longer expected or required to help in the underwriting, the objection to the practice stemmed from the double benefits created: (a) the firm deducted the portion of lease payments used to amortize the bond issue from its gross income as a business expense (as it could not do with mortgage amortization or corporate bond retirements), and (b) it did not include in its gross income subject to taxes the interest received on the tax-exempt bonds purchased. There is general agreement on the impropriety of this situation (but disagreement as to means of con-

[6] See JEC—*Financing* (d)—letter.
[7] ACIR (b).

trolling it since corporations would retain the right to purchase any other tax-exempt securities).

Related to this practice is the arbitraging procedure sometimes used by issuing governments and other instrumentalities, in which funds are raised through the sale of tax-exempt bonds and reinvested (pending the application of the funds toward new construction or the retirement of an outstanding issue) in higher yielding U.S. Government securities. This also is a practice that is increasingly discouraged.[8]

Unnecessary Avoidance of Private Capital Sources. The abuse is found in the unnecessary inducements given to a private corporation that is presumed to have access to internal or borrowed funds, even though the cost of such funds is greater than under the various financing plans available from local industrial building authorities. The claim is that the private capital markets are unfairly by-passed and, moreover, that inefficient production is generated since it would not have been profitable without the benefits of tax-exempt financing. The sticky problem with this reasoning, however, is the establishment of criteria for blue-ribbon firms occupying facilities erected by tax-exempt funds. The criteria would have to differentiate between the public purposes being served in various localities. For example, take three firms with triple-A credit ratings. The first corporation wants to lease space in the World Trade Center or Kennedy Airport from the Port of New York Authority. The second corporation wants to lease a facility to provide employment in Appalachia or in a ghetto area of an eastern city under a federal program. The third corporation wants to lease a special-purpose building built to its specifications in Alabama, Arkansas, or Alaska. At the present time, we have no basis for differentiating among these three situations, for each of which a local authority might issue large amounts of industrial revenue bonds.

Interregional Pirating. If the practice of pirating firms is a problem in the United States, as many observers claim, then industrial revenue financings admittedly can aid and abet it, but there may be more feasible ways of prohibiting piracy than by eliminating tax exemption on the bonds involved in the alleged transaction. Suppose that a community X makes a deal with a corporation to construct a factory with up-to-date machinery to make Product B (an improvement on Product A) that can only be manufactured with the new machines. Upon signing the lease, the corporation announces that it is going to phase out production of old Product A at its antiquated factory in another community Y. Should the firm have built its new factory for Product B in community Y? Is this piracy? What should community Y have done to obtain the new factory for itself? Was the corporation dealing in good faith with knowledge of antipirating rules?

[8] *Bond Buyer* (d).

Should the new bond holders of the issue sold by community X be deprived of the tax-exempt feature of their interest receipts? The administrative problem is to prevent piracy in the first place, and/or to be able to identify it after the fact; the elimination of industrial revenue bonds would not appear to solve the pirating problem.

The Perceived Effects of Larger Volumes

The opponents of industrial revenue bond financing have enumerated many situations in which they feel the effects are undesirable as the volume of financing rises:

Item. "These bonds conflict with federal economic programs for local development," said Representative Reuss in his speech to the Investment Bankers. (Ed. note: But not with local programs.)

Item. They are issuable even in times when the federal government may be trying to dampen the economy by restricting credit and raising taxes. (Ed. note: But so are all other securities.)

Item. "Projects far beyond the community's employment needs are undertaken. When this occurs labor is imported, the local economy is disturbed and community facilities are strained. In addition, the community may saddle itself with excessive contingent liabilities in the form of debt service bonds." [9]

Item. The consequent rise in interest costs for all tax-exempt securities would be a disaster for both the market and the local governmental issuers. This view has been best expressed by a prominent investment counselor as follows:

As long as industrial revenue bond issuance was largely confined to small issues for small or modest sized companies in States with economic resources well below average, it could be tolerated in our market because the volume was inconsequential in relation to total tax-exempt issues. . . .

The flow of investment funds available to absorb additional tax-exempt financing is far from unlimited. . . . There can be some growth in these sources, probably enough to absorb the growth in state and local financing for generally accepted public purposes. But a sudden large addition as is threatening in the industrial revenue field (and is potential in the area of arbitrage) can only be absorbed if there is a relative drop in tax-exempt prices to a level making them attractive to the major life companies with tax brackets around one-third of the 48% corporate rate. This can mean a 15% loss in the market value of long tax exempts, assuming no market change in the other departments of the bond market. Herein lies the real threat to our market, and in turn to the independent ability of states and localities to do their own financing.

When rates moved sharply higher in a disorderly market, the Federal government would no doubt feel impelled to assist state and local financing programs. This assistance could take the form of a subsidy interest payment to those issuers who sold taxable securi-

[9] ACIR (b), p. 14.

ties or, more likely, a direct loan program at nominal interest rates that could be financed with other sales of "participations in government assets." In either case the private market involvement with state and local financing would be seriously curtailed, as would the independence of that financing from federal control. It would, of course, be more desirable to end industrial revenue financing by denying tax deductability to the lease rental. (Unfortunately there is no similar workable approach to cover the pressing problem of arbitrage.) . . . If the Treasury really wanted to conspire to eliminate tax exemption they would let these abuses continue until the market value of tax exemption deteriorated. Then the rest would be easy as there would be little for anyone to defend.[10]

This letter to the Municipal Forum of New York (an association of municipal bond experts) from Mr. John F. Thompson, then with Scudder, Stevens & Clark, New York City (now with Equitable Securities), on a very real threat to the market and to local government exemplifies the thinking of those concerned with the practical implications of continuing high volumes of industrial revenue bonds in contrast to the more abstract reasoning of those who feel that industrial lease financing confers an unfair competitive advantage on certain corporations and certain communities.

However, Mr. Thompson, an investment counselor, has an eloquent opponent in Mr. Marquette de Bary, an investment banker, and with much fervor these two leaders of the municipal bond field debated the subject in the press and on the rostrum of the Municipal Forum. Mr. de Bary regards industrial revenue bond financing as a form of laudable self-help for local communities, citing, for example, data to show it was three times as effective in creating jobs in Tennessee as the federal Economic Development Administration, and asserting with considerable evidence that 85 per cent of the *number* of industrial revenue bond issuers were issues of $10 million or less, that the benefited companies were generally small and unpirated, that the bonds, their leases secured, had lower than A ratings, and that only one-quarter of their facility costs were represented by the bond issues.

Of greater relevance here, however, is de Bary's demonstrations that the Treasury is not losing revenue if recognition is given to income taxes on the firm's higher profits and dividend distributions, and that the relatively higher yields on industrial revenue bonds are a small price to pay for making them attractive to investors in order to finance individual projects that represent a minuscule portion of American enterprise. Finally, with regard to the Thompson argument concerning the threat to the market, de Bary writes:

Time has a way of dimming unpleasant memories but it wasn't very long ago—in the early to mid-fifties—that cries were heard that high yielding turnpike revenue issues were taking investors away from the then orthodox types of G.O. and Revenue municipal issues. When Ohio Turnpikes offered a juicy 3¼% the depressed municipal market caused the Bond Buyer Index to move up to 2.11%. Before that it was just revenue issues,

---

[10] *Bond Buyer*, June 16, 1967.

municipal utilities and the like, that were frowned on as diverting factors in orthodox municipal finance.[11]

The Thompson and de Bary positions in fact complement each other. Both acknowledge the boost to yields induced by the influx of industrial revenue bonds, Thompson reflecting the concern of a portfolio manager watching his valuations on older bonds fall as yields increase (which they were doing in large part as a response to the monetary and fiscal conditions of the times), and de Bary expressing his firm belief as underwriter in the capacity of the market to accommodate itself to fundamental changes in the national economy and to provide capital for the development of local public economies. Their debate has been rendered moot by the action of the Congress in removing tax exemption from the larger industrial revenue issues, as discussed in greater detail in the following section.

C. THE REMEDIES PROPOSED AND LEGISLATED

A number of suggestions have been made by Treasury officials and interested parties with respect to industrial revenue bond financing. Again they seem to fall into four categories, enumerated below and discussed in greater detail in the concluding section:

▶ Suggestions that the interest on industrial revenue bonds be declared taxable or, alternatively, that the lease payments not be allowed as deductions from the taxable income of the tenant corporation.

▶ Suggestions that control be effected and the volume of such financing be reduced by the introduction of some mandatory review procedure, perhaps conducted by the states, perhaps in conjunction with the Securities and Exchange Commission.

▶ Suggestions that the issuers and the underwriters, and even the investors, exercise a new high degree of self-restraint, abiding by a code of good conduct that would eliminate all the criticisms as to form and volume.

▶ Suggestions that somehow the privilege be rationed, perhaps restricted to certain regions, or certain classes of communities and certain types of firms, a procedure presumably to be directed by some agency of the federal government.

Hundreds of articles appeared in *The Bond Buyer* and other journals beginning early in 1966, as the federal government appeared to be making some determinate moves to control industrial revenue bond financing and to control arbitrage and/or eliminate tax exemption and/or introduce

[11] Lease Rentals (b).

new forms of subsidy or return of tax collections to state and local governments. The names in the news included the Secretary of the Treasury, the Assistant Secretary, the Commissioner of Internal Revenue, the heads of the Securities and Exchange Commission and the Federal Reserve System, the Council of Economic Advisors, and assorted senators and representatives (especially Patman and Reuss). At this writing, the matters are very much on the public agenda.

Evaluation of Proposed Remedies

Some of the criticisms are well taken but relate to situations no longer of major significance. For instance, firms no longer seem to purchase the bonds issued to finance their facilities, because the market has come to accept such bonds. Almost all situations have considerable individual merit and have run the gamut of the self-regulating constitutional and quality-control inspection, topped with letters of approval with respect to tax exemption from the Internal Revenue Service. To an increasing degree, it is said, firms make payments in lieu of real-estate taxes and otherwise assume the burdens of "good citizenship" in the new community.

Some of the proposals relate to conditions that are exceedingly difficult to measure or control: industrial piracy, the inability to obtain other financing, and the competition among localities for more employment that makes 100 per cent financing an "essential" adjunct to development programs.

Some of the proposals are hard to fathom. The Advisory Commission, for instance, apparently recommends that the size of a project be limited to the size of the existing surplus labor force, but a small town wants a big plant so that it can grow and, even in a certified area-redevelopment area, it might be unwise or impossible to restrict the size of plant for a given community.

It is probably also unlikely that the Commission could find many examples of a community willing to "saddle itself with excessive contingent liabilities in the form of debt service on the bonds" and even less likely that the underwriters and investors would be interested in a bond issue, except at prohibitive yields, that bore such a risk.

The threat of market reactions to a flood of industrial revenue bonds, along the lines spelled out by John Thompson, however, is undoubtedly real. In the next chapter we examine the problem created by yields so high that the value of tax exemption as a benefit for state and local government can be questioned. The remedies proposed relate partly to this issue, and, although it may be possible to prohibit the issuance of tax-exempt bonds either for the purpose of industrial financing or for arbitraging (investing the proceeds in higher yielding taxable securities), defining and administering a rule that limited new bond issues to "generally accepted public purposes" would be difficult because of the matter of the constitutionality of passing any statute that appears to limit the freedom of state and local governments to issue bonds for any public purpose they choose or that appears to tax the interest to be paid on these bonds. Thus the control of industrial revenue bond financing is inextricably involved with the global problem of the privilege or right of tax exemption itself.

The proposal that new issues of industrial revenue bonds be registered with the SEC does not seem to concern proponents of such financing. The following assertion by a group of underwriters who do not agree with the Investment Bankers Association's stand against the practice may well represent the feeling of all the market professionals who underwrite and deal in such issues:

Municipal bonds have always been exempt from Federal regulation and we fully believe that this independence should be continued. However, should the S.E.C. conclude that municipal industrial bonds should be subject to registration, there would be no cause for great concern. There is adequate precedent to allow the area of municipal finance to be treated according to its needs. For example, banks, in consultation with the S.E.C. prior to enactment of the Securities Amendment Acts of 1964, were recognized to perform operations and activities sufficiently unique so as to permit their filing of registration statements, not with the S.E.C., but instead, with the Comptroller of the Currency.[12]

Significance of Current Legislation

During the spring of 1968, a House-Senate conference committee approved a measure to withdraw tax exemption from local government issues over $1 million that are secured only by lease-rentals from private firms. (Subsequent legislation may raise this limit.) The measure came after the Senate had voted to prohibit execution of a comparable regulation issued unilaterally shortly beforehand by the Treasury, a vote interpreted as a rebuke to the Treasury for intervening in what Congress considered its own domain of fiscal policy. The measure also followed passage of amendments clarifying the definition of permissible revenue-secured issues to include bonds issued for airports, facilities for "public events" such as conventions and trade shows, public entertainment or recreation, activities serving two or more hospitals, and sewage disposal and other municipal services.[13]

Such legislation is designed to eliminate the larger industrial revenue bond issues, but it is presumably subject to attack by those who hold that a Constitutional amendment would be required to enable Congress to tax the interest on bonds legally issued by local governments. Consideration of that concept is reserved for the next chapter. In any event, although Con-

[12] Lease Rentals (c).
[13] Lease Rentals (d).

gress has changed the nature of the controversy, it is useful to summarize the comments made in this chapter.

Industrial revenue bond issues fit neatly into the economic development programs of local areas, and although competition in development does little more than redistribute economic activity, it is part of a process that will continue, with all the characteristics claimed by proponents: legality, essentiality, expansion of the local economic base, and expansion of the market for tax-exempt bonds (at higher yields). Moreover, many of the objections to the use of industrial revenue bonds have been removed by improved procedures or have been discounted because of the inherent difficulty of obtaining agreement on basic objectives and definitions.

On the other hand, the new restrictions on their taxable status reflect a Congressional finding that the demand for tax-exempt securities is too limited, because of the operation of the tax laws, to justify raising the cost of financing to all local governments and depreciating the value of outstanding securities, over and above the general increase in interest rates, merely to provide facilities for a handful of major corporations, much less to open up the tax-exempt market to all local governments and all manner of business firms for this type of bond issue.

Thus the recent Congressional resolve can be justified only as a temporary expedient pending more fundamental changes in fiscal and monetary policy to relieve the tenuous state of the capital markets in the mid-1960's. These basic problems, yet to be tackled by the Congress, include particularly the tax code which limits the marketability of local government securities and the unresolved issue of greater financial support for local governments to enable them to cooperate on improvement of the quality of the urban environment. In short, the controversy over industrial revenue bonds is only part of the larger debate over the allocation of national resources in behalf of local community development.

Chapter X Should Any Local
Public Securities Be Tax-Exempt?

Municipal bond finance is currently based entirely on the exemption from federal income taxation of securities issued by state and local governments. The five parts of this chapter discuss the implications of eliminating the exemption and explain our position that it ought to be retained:

A

We begin with a discussion of the Constitutional questions that have been raised in connection with the power of the federal government to tax the states, together with examples of the way the significance of the exemption is being whittled away by legislation and administrative fiat.

B

Next we consider the theories which suggest that the nation would benefit by the elimination of the exempt status of local public bonds.

C

There will be substantial real and distributive costs if exemption is removed. Some of the costs will be tangible in the form of compensation to be paid to holders of outstanding bonds. Some of the costs are anticipated as the result of adjustment by governments and investors to a new market structure. Calculating the margin of benefits over costs is, of course, a key step in making the decision about eliminating the exemption.

D

A number of proposals have been made to augment the revenues available to local governments, and these programs must be viewed as supplements rather than as alternatives to local programs to finance capital outlays.

E

This last section brings together the judgments made above for evaluation as a whole. The program that appears to promise the larger quantum of net benefits calls for retention of exemption, in addition to the structural changes in intergovernmental relationships that are essential to make the institution of local government viable and to relieve undue pressures on the limited market for tax-exempt securities.

A. CAN CONGRESS ELIMINATE TAX EXEMPTION—THE CONSTITUTIONAL QUESTION

The immunity of interest on state and local bonds from federal income taxation is a little like the weather: people like to talk about it, but no one does much about it.

Few of the cases considered by the Supreme Court in recent years have dealt with the issue directly; to date, bills introduced in Congress call for the elimination of a particular "abuse" or for the taxation of a particular transaction rather than the elimination of the exemption itself. If, indeed, the Constitution protects the exemption, then Congress cannot remove it by statute. No move appears to have been made as yet to start a proposal for amending the Constitution through Congress or the state legislatures. It is generally felt that few state legislatures, and very few Congressmen, would be willing to take the political risk of standing for the elimination of a doctrine that appears to protect local independence and initiative and to lower the cost of local government.

Reciprocal Immunity

The basic concept is that of "reciprocal immunity." If the states may not tax federal activities, then the federal government may not tax state activities nor those of the political subdivisions of the states. Not only would an amendment or legislation on the subject have to deal with the question of compensating present holders of outstanding issues and of instituting some alternative method by which local public facilities could be financed, it might also be expected to provide for the taxation by the states and their instrumentalities of federal activities and Treasury securities located within the states.

Constitutional History

The best summary of the Constitutional aspects that this writer has seen is found in the first chapter of Roland Robinson's enduring book, *Postwar Market for State and Local Government Securities*. His one-paragraph summary below is followed by a review of developments since his book was published.

> The exemption of state and local governments securities from the taxation of the federal government originated in the constitutional division of sovereignty in the United States. Some constitutional lawyers, including a number of specialized municipal bond attorneys, feel that the doctrine of reciprocal immunity between the states and the federal government first stated in *McCulloch v. Maryland* in 1819 would make a federal tax on interest income from state and local government obligations unconstitutional. Many others, apparently including a majority of academic and federal government lawyers, feel that the passage of the 16th Amendment removed this bar and that thereafter the federal government could have taxed the income from state and local government obligations. Since Congress explicitly exempted taxation of such income by statute in 1913, that is where the matter has since rested. In effect, the issue has not been adjudicated.[1]

McCulloch was the cashier for the Baltimore branch of the bank of the United States who refused to pay a tax Maryland had levied on the property of the Bank. The federal government's attorney, Mr. Daniel Webster, said to the court: "An unlimited power to tax involves neccessarily a power to destroy," and since the shoe is now on the other foot, the writers in the municipal bond market's stable are concerned with the power of the federal government to destroy the institutions of state and local government. A recent editorial in *The Bond Buyer* quoted Mr. Justice Douglas:

> If the power of the federal government to tax the states is conceded, the reserved power of the states guaranteed by the Tenth Amendment does not give them the independence which they have always been assumed to have. They are relegated to a more servile status. They become subject to interference and control both in the functions which they exercise and the method which they employ. They must pay the federal government for the privilege of exercising the powers of sovereignty guaranteed them by the Constitution.[2]

Reciprocal Taxation by the States?

The pages of *The Bond Buyer* have once again been filled with speeches and letters demonstrating that Congress does not have the power and should not be encouraged in any case, to tamper with the present system. Taxation, however, is a two-edged sword and might serve the needs of the states quite well, as a well-known municipal bond attorney pointed out.

[1] Robinson, p. 3.
[2] *Bond Buyer,* May 8, 1967.

With the states having the power to tax the income from bonds of the United States and its various agencies, etc., the present dilemma of the states as to sources of needed revenue would be substantially relieved and they would be freed from their present embarrassing position of having to go, hat in hand, to Washington for Federal subsidies and, at the same time, they would be relieved of Federal dictation which, as we all know, is a necessary corollary to Federal subsidies, for "the hand that pays the piper calls the tune." [3]

The Atlas Case

A recent chapter in tax exemption's constitutional history is the Atlas case, which tested a portion of the Life Insurance Company Income Tax Act of 1959 and was won by the government against the insurance companies. The Joint Economic Committee researchers found that life insurance companies would not be significant purchasers of municipal bonds, following the adverse decision of the court in the Atlas case, until the tax law itself was changed. The following lucid explanation of the complicated Atlas case comes from a paper read to the New York Municipal Analysts Group shortly before the Supreme Court decision.

Since reserves are established by law and held by the insurance company for the benefit of the policyholders the income going into reserves has been traditionally tax free. Although the 1959 law specifically declared it was the intent of Congress to exempt income from Municipal Bonds, the Internal Revenue Service ruled that a company must allocate to policyholders a pro-rata part of every item of income including municipal bond income. The Atlas Life Insurance Company complained that this constituted a tax on municipal bond interest and that the municipal interest should not be applied to the policyholder's share but go to the company's share. . . .

At par the municipal portfolio of the Atlas Company yielded 3.06%. When the tax return was figured according to the I.R.S. ruling the municipal yield was reduced to 2.12%. . . . If the Atlas decision is unfavorable to the industry the yield of a current coupon tax exempt bond will decrease as policyholders' surplus increases (as a percentage of assets). . . .

Our conclusion is that if the industry loses the Atlas Case with resulting loss to the insurance companies of tax exempt advantages for all intents and purposes the bulk of the industry will be out of the Municipal Bond market except in times of very tight money. . . . A municipal would have to have a 5.5% coupon to have the same effect as a bond with a 3.90% coupon (now has).[4]

The Atlas case serves as a prime example of how exemption is reduced in scope by determined opposition from the Treasury; other examples are represented currently by the joint IRS-Treasury statement concerning reinvestment of tax-exempt proceeds in higher yielding treasuries ("arbitrage") and by the recent legislation with respect to the deductability of rental payments that are the revenue sources for industrial revenue bond

[3] MFOA (b)
[4] Readings (d).

issues. Thus, until Congress provides a permanent set of definitions, the significance of tax exemption will be determined by interpretation and the market will have to adjust to such changes in the guidelines.

B. ECONOMIC BENEFITS BY ELIMINATION

The spur toward elimination of tax exemption on local public securities has come from economists interested in both the level and the distribution of national income and from the Treasury, which claims it loses more than state and local governments gain. In this section we look at both sets of arguments.

The Equity Argument

Volumes have been written about tax-exempt bonds as a tax loophole for the rich. As expressed by Ott and Meltzer, two economists whose writings have been widely quoted in relation to the tax and fiscal implications of the exemption clause, "The exemption is inequitable because it discriminates among individuals in similar economic circumstances and principally benefits taxpayers in the highest income brackets." [5]

This argument is valid of course, but one must note that high tax rates which encourage some but not all taxable institutions and individuals to avoid taxes by investing in municipal bonds have effectively limited demand for bonds to such taxpayers and thus forced the yields to rise.

The Efficiency Arguments

The other economic arguments are largely in terms of efforts to increase total national income by using resources efficiently, with any inefficient use considered suboptimal. As summarized by Ott and Meltzer,

Risk investment is reduced because potential investors are encouraged to purchase tax exempts;

A misallocation of resources in the private sector and between the public and private sector results from the encouragement given to local government projects;

The subsidy is inefficient because, first, federal revenues are reduced more than interest costs to states and municipalities; second, the borrowing which is subsidized is not directly correlated with need; third, the least benefit is obtained by communities with the lowest credit rating.[6]

These points, however, are far more debatable than the question of equity. For instance, although some investors may avoid risk investment by

[5] Ott-Meltzer, p. 3.
[6] Ott-Meltzer, p. 3.

loading a portfolio with tax-exempts, another class of investors may have increased its willingness to make real capital investments as a result of the capital outlays provided by local governments, and it remains to be demonstrated that local government projects represent a misallocation of the resources available for investment in national growth. The matter of federal revenue reduction is discussed below, and comments about the needs of local communities, especially those with the lowest credit rating, appear in Section D.

Does the Treasury Lose More Than Local Governments Gain?

Since the 1939 hearings before the Senate Special Committee on Taxation of Governmental Securities and Salaries, the economists have been hard at work in an effort to show who benefits (and how much) from tax exemption. The major studies referred to in this book are well known to such men as Representative Wright Patman, Chairman of the Joint Economic Committee and the House Committee on Banking and Currency, and to the staff of the Secretary of the Treasury; the exchange of letters below constitutes a concise summary of the politico-economic situation at this writing, but the Treasury's position is not wholly substantiable, as the comments that follow the letters indicate.

Text of Letter to Mr. Fowler

Dear Mr. Secretary:
    In our committee hearings on March 15, 1967, the chairman and other members of the Banking and Currency Committee, as well as the Federal Reserve Board, expressed concern over the inequities involved in the exemption from Federal income taxation of interest payable in certain public securities. . . .
    I would appreciate your close attention to the proposal made by the Federal Government to provide compensation for any interest differential between what a locality pays on a tax exempt security and what it would have to pay on a taxable security. I believe that the Treasury would gain more revenue in taxing these securities than it would pay out in compensating the difference.
    In closing, I would like to point out that the members of the Committee fully recognize the tremendous needs of our localities in financing schools, sewerage facilities, health facilities, and other local government projects. But we do not believe that such practices as tax exempt securities are the best procedure in aiding our local communities.
    We would appreciate your answers as soon as conveniently possible.

Sincerely,
WRIGHT PATMAN
Chairman

Text of Letter to Mr. Patman

Dear Mr. Chairman:
    Thank you for your letter of March 21 requesting information relating to tax exempt bonds. . . .

Your letter also raises a question as to the relationship between the interest savings to states and localities from tax exemption on bonds compared to the Federal revenue loss from this tax exemption. This topic was discussed in a Treasury paper for the Subcommittee on Economic Progress and printed as Chapter 20 of volume 2 of *State and Local Public Facility Needs and Financing.*

The analysis presented there indicated that, "over the life of state and local bonds issued in 1965, the excess of Federal revenue loss over interest saving to state and local governments is therefore estimated to be between $0.6 and $1.0 billion."

The estimated interest saving to the states over the life of these bonds was estimated to be $1.9 billion–$2.6 billion.

I do not believe that any further study of this differential would produce significantly different results. Thus, the belief that you express in the last sentence of the first page of your letter would seem to be a reasonable possibility, namely, that the Treasury would gain more in revenue in taxing these securities than it would pay out in compensating the difference. Tax exemption of state and local bonds is, of course, a very complex issue. You may be interested in the discussion of the pros and cons of your proposal . . . (in) . . . *Federal Tax Treatment of State and Local Securities,* by Ott and Meltzer.

Sincerely yours,
HENRY H. FOWLER [7]

In fact, economists have generally abandoned the effort to measure exactly how much local governments save in interest payments because of tax exemption and how much the federal government loses in taxing such interest. The reasons for this frustration are two-fold:

1. Every holder of an outstanding bond is in a unique tax bracket, so that any estimate of the whole population of investors in municipals must be the result of a whole series of unsatisfactory approximations.

2. The estimates of savings are based upon sales of tax-exempt bonds by multitudinous local governments at interest rates which were some unknown number of basis points below what they would have been if the issue had been of taxable bonds of the same quality; any estimate requires extensive approximations back through the life of all outstanding bonds.

Recourse is now generally made to the technique developed by Ott and Meltzer which estimates for the bonds sold in any one year all the savings and all the lost federal revenues that will accrue over the life of the bonds issues in that year.[8]

Treasury's Estimates Reviewed

Thus the Treasury declares that, in 1965, state and local governments would have had to pay between $1.9 billion and $2.6 billion more over the life of the issues of that year if they had been sold at yields that would have prevailed in the absence of exemption. And in the absence of exemption,

[7] Letters in *Bond Buyer,* April 19, 1967.
[8] JEC—*Financing,* Chapter 20.

and assuming an "aggregate average marginal tax rate" of 42 per cent, the Treasury would have collected taxes amounting to $2.9 billion on their minimum estimate (or $3.2 billion on the maximum saving). By subtraction it is found that the federal government lost more than the issuers saved in the range of $600 million to $1 billion.

Reference to the Ott-Meltzer text reveals that the federal government's tax take would be much smaller if the average marginal tax rate applied was the one calculated for holders of corporate securities generally (then 14 per cent) rather than the marginal rate for the institutions and well-to-do individuals currently holding municipal bonds (42 per cent).[9]

Thus it might be alleged that, after a period of conversion to a market without tax exemption, the government would not be losing half as much as the state and local governments were saving. If, for instance, the Treasury receives $2.9 billion at the 42 per cent marginal rate, then total taxable interest on municipals must have been $6.9 billion, which produces taxes amounting to only $970 million at the 14 per cent marginal rate, compared with local interest savings of $1.9 billion (for the maximums given in the Treasury statement, the revised tax receipts would be $1.1 billion, far less than projected local interest savings of $2.6 billion). However, Ott and Meltzer believe that it is reasonable to assume the higher marginal tax rate of 42 per cent and that the shift of lower income taxpayers out of corporate bonds and into municipal bonds would be relatively small.

C. THE ECONOMIC COSTS OF ELIMINATION

Removal of exemption, whether for presently outstanding issues or for new issues only, will affect the national economy, the local public sector, and the investment community in various ways both in the short run and over a longer period. The commentary below covers these costs and effects of conversion, first with respect to the nation, then local government, and finally the market.

Effect on the Nation

The major distributive cost for obtaining the economic benefits of the preceding sections found by Ott and Meltzer is that the tax structure of the nation would become less progressive or more regressive if state and local taxes have to rise to finance capital outlays.

In addition, the benefits to the Treasury may be reduced if the process of conversion is slowed down by retaining the exemption with respect to

[9] Ott-Meltzer, Chapter V.

bonds already issued. Their statement of the case provides a summary view of these fiscal aspects:

If the exemption is removed from outstanding state-local securities, the revenue gain to the Treasury will reflect (1) the revenues received from taxing the interest on the outstanding bonds until they mature, (2) the yield from taxing capital gains at maturity, and (3) the loss of revenue from realized capital losses sustained when the exemption is removed. The present value of the algebraic sum of these three items is about $4.5–$5 billion. The Treasury would receive a net gain of receipts, in present value terms, from taxing outstandings. However, taxing the interest on outstanding issues complicates management of the federal debt; on balance those shifting into municipals will discard more long-term federal securities than those shifting out will acquire at present yields. Yields on federal government bonds will rise. Taxing outstandings tends to cause equity yields to fall slightly and produces a sharp decline in commercial bank earnings. These estimates of the revenue gain and attendant capital market changes are discussed in Chapter VI.

If the federal tax exemption is removed, inequities arise whether the tax applies to new issues only or to new issues and outstandings. In the former case, present holders obtain windfalls as the value of their securities increases in response to the shrinking supply; in the latter case, they suffer capital losses. Methods have been devised to avoid such capital losses if outstanding issues are taxed. However, the inequities, compliance, and administrative problems are fewer if the exemption is removed from new issues only.[10]

There is, of course, no way of predicting whether Congress would choose to eliminate exemption on outstanding issues and pay compensation in order to obtain current tax receipts on interest income and capital gains receipts on what would have automatically become discount bonds. Quite possibly they would follow the precedent set in 1941 when existing Treasuries remained exempt but future issues of federal securities became taxable. One team of writers has suggested that outstanding issues be taxable but subject to a 50 per cent tax credit, with the hope (which all investors share) that compensation by the government would be "obvious and generous." [11]

Effects on State and Local Government

What happens to state and local finances if tax exemption is removed is a serious concern. It may only be an intensification of the present difficult situation or, because of the difference in degree of change in the market for different types of issues, qualitatively different. The late Cushman McGee, one of the most respected of the municipal bond empiricists, was quoted during the 1959 tax hearings as follows:

It is my opinion that the burden would vary, issue by issue, municipality by municipality, with the lower credit ratings bearing the progressively heavier burden, and the unrated issuers critically affected. The burdens would be so substantial that thousands of

[10] Ott-Meltzer, p. 7.
[11] Readings (e).

municipalities would not be able to borrow within the maximum interest rates permitted by the state and local laws. To measure the harm of such a proposal is beyond arithmetical calculation alone.[12]

Ott and Meltzer adopt more measured tones in coming to a somewhat similar conclusion, the burden of which is thrown upon the devices considered in Section D to augment local revenues. In addition, they are small comfort to those who hope that reciprocal taxation by state and local governments would help cure the added fiscal imbalance created by higher interest costs on local government for a number of reasons: (a) only states and localities with income taxes would benefit, (b) areas with holders of large amounts of federal bonds would benefit disproportionately, and (c) few states have given localities the right to tax income, in addition to the question whether localities most affected by loss of exemption would be the ones to which the increments of state revenue would be redistributed. Ott and Meltzer's summary of conclusions include these anticipated results:

> Interest costs of states and municipalities will rise "sharply" if the exemption is removed—more than the usual comparisons of yields of outstanding corporates and municipals would suggest. This argument is based on the view that municipals are not as attractive as corporates (and other securities) in terms of "marketability."
> The understated rise in interest costs will prevent some local government units from borrowing. This will curtail necessary state-local outlays.
> Alternative subsidies will reduce the fiscal independence of the state and local governments and produce further centralization in government.[13]

These dollar costs and effects on local governments are as difficult to measure as are the changes in the cash receipts of the Treasury and the changes in market responses, discussed next. Of even greater importance, however, are the noneconomic values that figure so prominently in the conclusions reached in the last section of this chapter.

Effect on the Market

One's perspective in judging the national, local, and market effects depends upon whether one is making an estimate for the period immediately following the removal of tax exemption before the characteristics of the holders of municipal bonds have changed substantially, or for the long-run period when municipal securities would be just like corporate securities in terms of taxability. Taking the long view concerning the amount by which average municipal interest would rise, Ott and Meltzer reported as follows, as part of their very careful investigation into yield differentials.

> A number of capital market experts were asked for their opinion on the yields of municipals if the exemption feature is removed. In general, these experts believe (1) that

[12] Quoted in Readings (e).
[13] Ott-Meltzer, p. 3.

yields on municipals would rise by more than the current differential between new issue yields on municipals and public corporate bonds. This view is based on the assumption that private placement yields are the relevant ones at which the large institutional buyers would become active in the market for municipals if they were taxable. (2) They suggest that the municipal yield curve—that is, the curve relating yield to maturity and time to maturity—would have a much lower slope after removal of the exemption feature. This conclusion is based on the assumption that there would be increased institutional buying at the short end. (3) The market experts generally agree that municipals would not sell at a discount because of the serial forms of such issues.[14]

The Treasury's opinion on the impact that taxable municipals at higher yields would have on the amounts held by different classes of investors was based in part on the Ott-Meltzer study. The Treasury anticipated that life insurance companies might reenter the market (since they already seek municipal issues if the yields are sufficiently attractive) but that the casualty insurance companies would switch into preferred stocks over time. Individual investors would include fewer persons of high income and a greater number in lower tax brackets. In addition, nonprofit corporations, pension funds, and state and local trust funds might also come into the market for high-yield municipals. The prognosticators have not attempted to calculate the extent of such shifts, even assuming a constant volume of new bonds issued each year.

The interrelated effects on national, local, and market operations are also related to the patterns of yields and the general structure of interest rates and tax rates at the time exemption is removed. These patterns are the subject of Chapter XV, to which the reader is referred. In the next section, we return to the larger arena of state and local revenues to consider the possibility that greater federal assistance might obviate part of the need for bond issues.

D. FEDERAL PLANS FOR AUGMENTING LOCAL REVENUES

What happens to state and local finances even if tax exemption is retained is also of great concern, and a plan of assistance to ameliorate the effect of having removed the exemption feature would also be useful if the exemption feature were retained. Absent exemption and the need for federal assistance might be greater, but the same techniques can be used.

Certain criteria are universally applicable in judging the merit of a proposal for federal augmentation of local revenues. Will it have greater benefits than costs? Will it help one area without penalizing another? Will it advance the general welfare, adding to the national wealth? Will it advance the general welfare by effecting a better distribution of wealth, narrowing the gap between rich and poor areas? Is it easily administrable? Is it

[14] Ott-Meltzer, p. 5.

politically feasible? Would it be better to change the system in some way other than instituting a program that really only treats a symptom; for example, would consolidation of local governments be a better solution than an assortment of subsidies to shore up the individually weak units?

Three broad areas of federal assistance can be defined for discussion below. The first is the grant-in-aid or categorical assistance type; the second has to do with loans and borrowing; the third is the notion of tax sharing, or redistributing the revenues available to the federal government.

1. Categorical Federal Aid

Federal aid has been expanding for a number of years, and it may be expected to continue to do so whether or not exemption is retained. A short quotation from the Council of Economic Advisors says much:

> The grant-in-aid approach is flexible. It enables the Federal Government to single out the most urgent needs and to apply suitable remedies directly . . . to pay for a greater share of costs in States and areas where needs are greatest relative to available resources . . . (to) encourage innovation . . . (and) better planning.
>
> At the same time, the categorical grant mechanism is open to some criticisms. State and local officials are sometimes bewildered by the number, variety, and complexity of eligibility and matching provisions. A special effort is necessary to keep them informed of latest developments, so that all eligible units of government may share equitably. And some localities resent Federal standards and "supervision" in grant programs.[15]

2. Subsidies for Borrowing Costs

Ott and Meltzer consider a number of proposals for assistance in the event exemption is removed and the costs of borrowing increased; all of them to one degree or another could be helpful in the current era while exemption is still with us: [16]

1. The Selzer plan (1941) called for the federal government to pay some fixed proportion of local government's annual interest payments. Ott and Meltzer thought highly of this proposal, and it is basically the solution advanced by Eiteman-Coleman (1967).

2. The Lyle Fitch tax credit proposal (1950) involved "a tax credit that in principle equalizes the after tax yield on corporate and taxable municipal bonds . . . (and) would allow municipals to sell at lower before tax yields than corporates without inequity among taxpayers." Essentially the same plan was suggested in a recent policy statement issued by the Committee for Economic Development: *Growth and Taxes* (1961).

3. The Treasury Department Committee on Intergovernmental Fiscal

[15] Federal (a), 1967, p. 164.
[16] Ott-Meltzer, Chapter VII.

Relations suggested in 1943 that the Treasury redistribute to the states the revenue from taxing new issues of state and local government securities.

4. Hanson and Perloff (1944) suggested that an Intergovernmental Loan Corporation be established with a revolving fund to lend money to local governments at the federal borrowing rate plus a service charge.

Federal Guarantee of Bond Interest and Principal. The Joint Economic Committee staff inquired as to the effect of a federal guarantee which would be either (a) added to the tax-exemption feature or (b) in lieu of tax exemption. All the investor groups expressed a preference for the status quo, to which they had adjusted. If the guarantee were added, the credit quality would generally rise, yields would generally fall, and municipal bonds would become less attractive investments, the guarantee doing "more harm than good":

> . . . If municipal securities were to be guaranteed by the Federal Government, and the interest income were to be taxable, the resultant yield on municipal securities would be around the yield of Federal agency securities or perhaps somewhat higher. Investor groups such as fire and casualty insurance companies would find yields at these levels unattractive, causing them to turn to alternative investments. . . .[17]

3. Tax Sharing in Review

With or without tax exemption, the very idea that the state and local governments could look forward to a day when the federal government, which seems to have such a vast capacity for raising money through income taxes, would share some of the proceeds with its poor relations, has caused excitement. The idea was suggested back in 1913 when the income tax came in; its current versions are creatures of the 1960's. (There are still those, of course, who would prefer to have the federal government either reduce or eliminate the income tax.)

The debate about tax sharing, which is looked upon as a device to help cushion the shock of conversion to a peacetime economy as well as a device for helping local governments, has produced a substantial literature which cannot be discussed in detail here, although it is useful to view the proceedings with regard to the municipal bond field.

A survey of this literature indicates that far more attention is devoted to the size of the gap between municipal revenues and municipal expenditures (a gap that may even be closing on its own, as discussed in Chapter XIV) than to the distinctions between current expenditures and capital outlays that are vital to municipal bond finance. The debate appears to transcend the problem of bond finance (with or without exemption) and to

[17] JEC—*Financing*, p. 23.

concentrate on the relative merits of tax credits and direct block grants (with and without strings).

The debate has become deeply enmeshed in another level of problems involving formulas for determining relative tax efforts by states and for distributing the benefits among the states, with a great deal of attention paid to the suspicion that apportionment of federal funds to localities within a state and to priority projects that are in line with national goals may be too important to be left to local politicians. Although it is somewhat surprising nevertheless to find no mention of municipal bonds in a book of essays entitled *Revenue Sharing and the City* with contributions from five leading economists, it implies that more thought must yet be given to the relationship between federal assistance programs and the institution of tax exemption.[18] We attempt to evaluate the connection in the section that follows.

E. A REASONABLE FUTURE FOR TAX EXEMPTION

In the four preceding sections of this chapter, the reader has been exposed to the arguments in support of the drive to eliminate tax exemption for state and local securities. In essence the case suggests the following:

1. The Constitution does not mandate the exemption.

2. The exemption is unfair and inefficient with respect to the allocation of resources.

3. The Treasury loses more revenue than local governments save.

4. The benefits exceed the costs imposed on nation, community, and portfolio manager.

5. The federal government has many ways of compensating local governments for any loss in revenues sustained by a conversion to taxable status for municipal bonds.

In this writer's opinion those arguments are unconvincing for a number of reasons. On technical grounds alone, the Treasury's findings concerning its revenue loss vis-à-vis local savings are reversible if an equally possible assumption is made concerning the marginal tax rates for new classes of individual and institutional holders.

The ultimate questions, however, involve more than technical considerations. They require evaluation of basic attitudes concerning the institutions of local government in the United States. Our reasoning proceeds along the following lines.

To begin the rebuttal, we can observe that, although the Constitution is a flexible document, the Supreme Court is not likely to reverse its traditional sidestepping of the issue of reciprocal immunity unless it is pre-

[18] Readings (f).

sented with arguments that indicate that doctrine has outlined its usefulness.

If scholars had come to understand the dynamics of local communities (as Chapter XII indicates has not yet happened) *and* if the voters had been consistently frustrated in their attempts to improve local governmental functions (as the dismal record of voting on metropolitan-wide issues demonstrates has not happened either), then the justices might find reasons for countenancing the drastic interventions by federal and state governments in the functioning of local governments that would be required in the absence of the exemption. Instead the Court has not pressed for direct federal involvement in local administration, except with respect to reapportionment of election districts and civil rights. The implications of both these topics for the structure of urban areas are only beginning to be felt.

The Court and the Congress are therefore understandably reluctant to remove exemption, for the alternative is not only increased federal assistance but an inevitably increased measure of federal control. But federal control implies agreement with respect to national goals and national standards that can properly be imposed in the form of criteria for federal assistance, and the plain fact is that such agreement on principles is still pending and that effective means for administering federal programs involving intangible standards, such as in education, have not yet been found. Compensating local governments for higher interest costs in the absence of exemption involves the same considerations as apply to revenue sharing, especially if the amount of federal funds for compensation or block grants is relatively small so that choices must be made regarding the capital projects to be certified for compensatory subsidy.

Additional thoughts could be penned about the intangible effects on local government if exemption is removed, and about the inherent problems of revenue sharing and federal assistance, but the point has been made sufficiently on the basis of the limitations of our knowledge about urban dynamics to enable us to reject some of the arguments in favor of elimination, without resorting to flag-waving about the virtues of independent local government. There are too many insidious deficiencies in local government for such an accolade.

The deciding element, however, is in the matter of choice, where individual choice does not significantly restrict opportunity for another. The degree of inefficiency and inequality introduced into the national economy because of tax exemption is relatively slight with the exemption, but the loss to local government if exemption is eliminated would be incalculable but very large. On balance, exemption is not hurting the economy or interfering with other programs very much. Meanwhile, every effort must still be made to improve the kinds of choices being made by voters and their representatives in connection with the urban environment, but there are enough strings attached to present modes of federal assistance through grants, subsidies, and loans to obtain improvement. Thus elimination of exemption is neither necessary in itself nor sufficient to effect change noticeably. Elimination would remove some significant measure of choice from local government generally and from smaller units most in need of municipal facilities other than those for which federal grants are available.

One could recommend the elimination of exemption, however, if that act would increase the demand for municipal bonds, for tax-exempt securities, even at fairly high yields, are now attractive to only a few types of investing institutions and individuals. Moreover, although the Joint Economic Committee feels that current sources of investment demand for tax-exempt bonds will probably be sufficient during the next decade, excessive reliance has been placed upon the investment demand of commercial banks for tax-exempt bonds. Unfortunately, elimination of tax-exemption appears to limit still further the demand for state-local securities.

One hope is that the supply of bonds offered may slacken enough to lighten the pressure, especially if federal and state grants-in-aid continue to increase. *The Bond Buyer* reports that both the Tax Foundation and the National Industrial Conference Board optimistically predict a lighter demand for current and capital funds in relative terms (that is, compared to the demand in recent years) up to 1975; George Break of the Brookings Institution is considerably gloomier about the size of the revenue gap, however. The selective elimination of exemption for industrial revenue and arbitrage bonds will have a beneficial effect.[19]

When demand and supply are in balance without excessive yields required, exemption still permits taxable institutions and individuals to purchase bonds, whereas nontaxable institutions avoid municipal bonds. Basically, removing the exemption merely transfers bonds from taxable to nontaxable hands without benefiting local governments or significantly helping the federal Treasury.

To summarize this argument is to say that the case for elimination of tax exemption has not been made strong enough to justify an end to the doctrine of reciprocal immunity and the imposition of another fiscal burden on local government. It follows then that exemption deserves a reasonable life expectancy so long as the demand for tax-exempt securities is supported by high tax rates and so long as the supply of bonds does not overwhelm the industry.

[19] Readings (g).

3

Problems for the Bond Analyst

Chapter XI   The Scope of Municipal Bond Evaluations

A. INTRODUCTION

The chapters of Part 3 are devoted to the work of the municipal bond analyst and thus constitute an exploration of the politico-economic environment in which the municipal bond market operates. For our purposes here, the bond analyst is a person who is responsible for interpreting trends in public administration and local public finance in order to establish probabilities concerning local governments generally and a given issuer in particular.

Our hypothesized analyst knows how the market functions and how resolution of the critical issues discussed in Part 2 would affect the market. His problem is to understand existing policies and practices affecting the creditworthiness of bond issuers and to consider how proposals for the introduction of modern methods of decision-making into local government might change the nature of new issues of local public securities. In addition, he is vitally concerned with his ability to forecast market reactions to changing supply and demand factors.

Although every trader, underwriter, and investor is a part-time bond analyst, relatively few of the large institutions have established fully staffed research activities. Major reliance is placed upon the materials published by the several rating agencies, which, as noted in Chapter 7, are themselves underendowed and understaffed. Thus the balance of this chapter is profitably devoted to an evaluation of credit analysis in its present limited form.

In Chapter XII we consider four important trends in public administration in terms of their probable effect on municipal finance:

1. The analysis of local government expenditures, exemplified in the work of urban economists.

2. The restructuring of local government, as exemplified in the work of the Advisory Commission on Intergovernmental Relations.

3. The Establishment of planning, programming, and budgeting systems at the local level.

4. The revision of state constitutional and legislative restrictions on the issuance of local debt.

Chapter XIII then takes up the possibility of applying systems analysis to the municipal bond field as a whole, with an evaluation of attempts to forecast economic variables.

B. CREDIT ANALYSIS

The purpose of credit analysis is to provide investors with a means of minimizing risk and of maximizing profits. As the risk of actual default has diminished over the years [see Hearings (a)], the attention of the municipal bond community has been directed to the far more subtle matter of quality differentiation among bonds and issuers. A poor quality rating, or lack of a rating, tends to raise the interest cost demanded by investors.

Quality ratings, whether made by the rating agencies or by officers of the underwriting and investing institutions, have so far been based on crude rules of thumb. However inadequate these rules of thumb have become, they are the only guidelines made available to a local finance officer who wants his own community's bonds to be acceptable to the market.

The conservative investor's rules of thumb are primarily concerned with (a) the relationship between outstanding debt and the legal limitation on debt issuance, (b) the ratio of debt to property valuation, (c) the amount of debt in per-capita terms, and (d) a number of other ratios and criteria mentioned in the paragraphs below.

The combination of lack of data, lack of theory, and incredible variation among local governments has limited professional writings on the subject. One of the best known expressions of the attitude of the conservative investor is found in "A Checklist for Determining Debt Policy," compiled for the Municipal Finance Officers' Association.[1]

The checklist, however, is of little use in a changing urban environment. For instance, when it reports a rule that direct and overlapping debt should not exceed 10 per cent of assessed valuation, it cannot show what the rule should be when properties are reassessed so that they narrow the difference between "true" and assessed valuations or when numerous special districts contribute to the debt burden that "overlaps" that of the issuer. Moreover, the general increase in the level of municipal salaries and in the scope of local government operations means that a ratio of debt service to

[1] MFOA (c).

total budget is of little significance. So too are the ratios of direct debt as a maximum multiple of total municipal expenditures.

Lack of data and a shortage of research-minded institutions, both public and private, are only partial explanations of the absence of theoretical underpinnings for the rules of thumb. It has been sufficient in the past for a community to show that its bonds meet all the legal tests and that the issue has a reasonable set of purposes and a reasonable schedule of repayments, given a depression-prone economy. As the complexity of the urban environment in the United States has increased, and with less likelihood of prolonged economic distress for the nation as a whole, the emphasis on the quality of a bond, over and above its risk of default, has brought about a coordinate expansion in the number of relevant political, social, and economic factors that the community must take into account in developing suitable internal policies; thus the need for a more rational series of tests has grown, especially with respect to revenue bond issues.

Information Required for Analysis

Credit analysis to establish a municipality's credit in general and the relative standing of its specific bond issues in particular stands out as one of the major links between a local government and the investment community. A thorough job of credit analysis will cover the same topics that should be considered by local officials in determining debt policy for their governmental unit. It is to the Investment Bankers Association of America (IBA) that most analysts have turned for a detailed exposition of the material to be considered in establishing credit. The IBA's list of "information suggested for inclusion in a bond prospectus" is the standard takeoff point for credit analysts, bank examiners, local finance officers, and public administration specialists.[2]

IBA Forms

The information required with respect to any general obligation issue, according to the IBA forms, includes: a general report on finance, detailed descriptive material about the locality, a detailing of property valuation by type and of all types of bonded debt, an abstract of the legal provisions and the untapped debt capacity, debt service requirements for the next five years, information about past operating revenues and expenditures, past tax collection data, and a variety of other information. With respect to municipal revenue bonds, the information is similar except that much greater stress is put upon the technical provisions and bond-retirement priorities of the debt structure.

[2] See also ACIR (c), pp. 64–70.

The IBA also suggests that the credit analyst should consider the character of the community as well as the financial data. Character includes

its moral responsibility, the historical background of the community, and its attitude toward debt in the past. The principal criterion is whether the municipality has defaulted at any time in the past. If it has defaulted, the first thing that should be looked into is the cause of the default, because there might or might not have been mitigating circumstances. The worst possible cause of default would be bad faith, where a municipality is simply trying to take advantage of some loophole to escape paying bonds it is perfectly capable of paying.[3]

It was also recommended that the character of municipal officials be investigated, together with the ability of local banks to weather economic adversity, a caution born during the depression, when some banks closed, preventing access to municipal funds.

C. STATE OF THE ART

The municipal credit analysts who work for the major underwriters and investing institutions, however, look askance at these formidable lists of important factors, for they are faced with a number of operational problems for which there seem to be no solutions at the present time, given the lack of substantive research about the nature of local development. They find that most of the prospectuses published by the issuing bodies or their representatives fail to include many of the material facts called for in the IBA formats. Where such material is furnished, the analyst is still lacking the means of evaluating it, for he has no reliable source of comparative data for other communities and no store of accumulated research to suggest whether a given ratio is high or low, whether a given rate of change is fast or slow, or whether events in the past are suitable indicators of future conditions. In some cases the sheer mass of relevant data available, especially for major states and cities and their related governmental entities, requires a greater expenditure of research talent than the analyst's employer has made available to him. The effect of some of these problems can be seen in the chapters on the mechanics of bond sales and on ratings.

The Advisory Commission on Intergovernmental Relations has also become aware of the present impasse that maintains the unverified status of rules of thumb and impedes the implementation of worthwhile research projects. One of the Commission's strongest recommendations in its study of means by which states could provide technical assistance to local debt managers is for the states to undertake the systematization of data collection and dissemination on the basis of IBA formats.

[3] IBA (a), p. 103.

Validating Rules of Thumb

The major problem in the eyes of the Advisory Commission is to find some way of measuring an issuer's economic ability or capacity to carry debt or other forms of fiscal loads. Their report on technical assistance considers each of the suggested ratios in turn. Per-capita debt is found to be a useful means of comparison, provided that the comparisons are supported by accurate population figures and related to the "economic base" of the community, two conditions that are extremely difficult to satisfy, especially in an era and in a region characterized by rapid changes in economic activity.

When debt is to be related to property valuations, the essential question is the comparability of the assessment bases among the communities being analyzed, although the Commission found that the number and sophistication of studies providing data on estimated full valuations was on the increase.

Interrelations

When debt service is compared to revenue on an annual basis, or when debt obligations are related to tax levies, or when an analysis is made of the distribution of revenues and expenditures by purpose in an effort to gain insights into the fiscal structure of the community and its ability to retire the new debt in proper style, the need for interrelated tests and for reliable comparative data becomes overwhelming. There is even the risk that extensive detail, such as the requirement that each bond issue be shown with all its sinking fund and other transactions (where some cities may have over a hundred such issues outstanding), may obscure the overall picture the analyst is attempting to draw. The Advisory Commission, in showing how officials, taxpayers, and bond investors share a concern for the extent to which localities have encumbered their legal borrowing capacities, gives a cogent example, however, of the necessity for incorporating all the borrower's operations into the analysis, even those that appear to be self-sustaining and hence not affecting the general credit:

Dedication of revenue from self-financing projects or from non-property taxes to pay revenue bond or limited tax liability bonds may so reduce general revenue as to require replacement revenue that increases fiscal loads. The extent of utility transfers to general funds or from general to enterprise funds may be crucial in reviewing a bond issue. Therefore, utility statements are germane to the appraisal of general obligations, and selective general obligation tests are relevant to the appraisal of revenue bonds.[4]

[4] ACIR (c) p. 52.

Municipal finance in all its dimensions is far from being an exact science. An investor has no sure guidelines to follow in selecting a credit-worthy bond, nor can a municipal finance officer be sure that he has matched sources of repayment with outstanding bond issues in the most efficient manner. There is certainly an interplay between the basic economy of an area and the fiscal capacity of the communities in it. There is some relation between the ratings given to specific issues and the rating given to a municipality's general obligations after it has entailed revenues for those special purposes. There is a kind of restraint on local borrowing imposed by state statutory and constitutional restrictions. There is a more subtle form of restraint in the interplay between the investment community's credit analysts and the local finance officers, but one cannot ordinarily measure the impact of the general market on the specific issuer.

Prospects

Over the coming years the art of credit analysis is surely going to be improved by the application of a more scientific approach to the subject, most likely within the university research community using data collected by the states. There seems to be less likelihood that sustained research can be expected within the investment community with its divisions among types of competing institutions or within any of the levels of government (partly because of the concept of federalism that gives fiscal independence to local government) or among the many professional and industry-wide associations that serve these various interests. As the need for better legislation and information is explored by such agencies as the Advisory Commission and many other distinguished organizations, and as the budgeting process at the local level begins to reflect the advances in methodology being instituted within the federal establishment and within industry, we may expect the conservative investor to put aside some of the rules of thumb and to grapple with the more sophisticated intuitions that his credit analysts will provide. Finally, we can expect local governments to improve their bond prospectuses in the struggle to improve their ratings. Some suggestions have been made for revenue bond prospectuses comparable to those filed with the Securities and Exchange Commission covering corporate securities.

In Chapter XII we consider the implications for credit analysis, and for the market generally, of attempts to understand the local economy, to rationalize the structure of state and local government, to control the budgetary process, and to revise the existing pattern of restrictions on the issuance of debt.

Chapter XII Impact of Trends in Public Administration

A. INTRODUCTION

State and local government was given slight attention in the early post–World War II years as economists, political scientists, and public administrators devoted their time to more pressing matters of economic growth, business cycles, depressed areas, and national goals. Now the revived interest in the local political economy will bring changes that the bond analyst cannot afford to ignore.

Scope

This introductory section covers some of the general patterns that have generated this revival of concern. The emerging developments in the field will be covered in four succeeding sections: (B) the attempt by urban economists to understand the operations of local government; (C) the attempt to restructure state and local government and to improve intergovernmental relations; (D) the attempt to control expenditures through capital budgeting and PPBS (planning, programming, and budget systems), and (E) the attempt to revise state restrictions on issuance of debt by local government.

In recent years a substantial amount of progress has been made in understanding the nature and the developmental problems of the nation's urban areas. An excellent analysis of the situation as of the beginning of World War II is found in *State and Local Finance in the National Economy* by two economists, Alvin H. Hanson and Harvey S. Perloff. The question was how to manage the local economy after the war, since "a nation so large in geographic extent and so varied in industrial and social development demands a large reliance upon local responsibility and local government." [1]

Their writing came during wartime, when the Council of State Govern-

[1] Hanson-Perloff, p. v.

ments was urging state and local governments to restrict operations, pay off debts, and prepare for large expenditures after the war; the timing of these postwar expenditures could be used to counteract another depression. The authors were concerned about the then-current trend to locate industry in rural areas outside the tax jurisdictions of urban communities, a trend that might create "extremely embarrassing" fiscal situations, as indeed has been the case. They were also concerned about the accumulated distortions of depression and war, the threat of inflation, and the urgent demand to reduce the amplitude of economic cycles. Even more important, perhaps, were underlying maladjustments and deficiencies they perceived in the fiscal, economic, and governmental structures of states and localities.

Postwar Urban Problems

Some of the conditions and problems they described are still with us, but their prescriptions appear rather pallid for the 1960's. We can no longer rely on "overall planning" at the local level to correct "the decline in the property-tax base and the high cost of supplying municipal services," and we no longer seriously suggest that state and local governments can manage their local economics and provide an acceptable level of services without financial assistance and intervention by the federal government. Since the Hanson-Perloff book, moreover, we have added almost 60 million persons to the population but have halved the number of governments in being.

As of 1966, about two-thirds of the population lived in metropolitan areas, and the political significance of the fact that a majority of the metropolitanites are living in the suburbs is just beginning to be appreciated. These suburbanites generally have higher incomes, more of the children, and fewer of the aged, the nonwhites, and the poor. The tabulation reproduced below from the *Economic Report of the President, January 1967,* as Table G tells that familiar story.

For those who see "the city" as the repository of our most visible social problems, the economy is heavily penalized by the present rather unsatisfactory distribution of resources among cities of varying sizes and their suburbs. In the words of the Council of Economic Advisors,

> In short, too many cities realize the worst of all possible worlds, with strained budgets, inadequate expenditures for public services ranging from education to law enforcement, burdensome property taxes which spur the exodus of wealthier taxpayers and discourage job-creating business, and partial, excessively costly solutions to problems that extend far beyond the city's jurisdiction and control.[2]

Although the municipal bond analysts are generally concerned with the aggregate local public economy or "the problem of the cities," they are much more concerned with the qualitative measurement of individual

[2] Federal (a), 1967, p. 157.

Table G   Characteristics of Population or Area, 1966

| Characteristic | All Areas | Metropolitan | | Non-metro-politan Nonfarm | Farm |
		Central Cities	Outside Central Cities		
Population (millions)[a]	101.5	58.3	64.3	57.1	11.8
Percent of population:					
Children under 18 years of age[b]	36.4	33.6	37.6	37.6	38.7
Aged (65 years and over)	9.4	10.4	7.3	10.6	9.9
Nonwhite	11.8	21.6	4.4	9.4	12.4
Poor[c]	17.1	18.2	9.6	23.4	26.5
Median family income (dollars)	6,569	6,697	7,772	5,542	3,558

[a] Excludes inmates of institutions and all members of the armed forces except those living off post or with their families on post. Metropolitan data exclude and farm data include the relatively few farms within Standard Metropolitan Statistical Areas.
[b] Never married children living in families.
[c] Poverty is defined by the Social Security Administration poverty-income standard; it takes into account family size, composition, and place of residence.

Note.—All data from Current Population Survey, March 1966, except median income from March 1965 Survey.

Source: *Economic Report of the President, 1967*, Table 25, p. 155.

governmental units, with the precepts under which they are governed, with their interactions, and with the response of the capital markets to their invitations for bids on issues of long-term bonds.

Every Issue Is Unique

The local public economy includes a formidable number (81,303 in 1967) of discrete governmental units. Some are large, some small, some general in powers and functions, some severely limited in their resourses. The economists and political scientists, of necessity, must reach for generalizations about these various units, but it must be remembered that the bond market has no alternative but to consider each applicant for credit as a distinct entity and as a proper subject for individualized scrutiny when it brings its new issue of bonds to market.

The latest full Census of Governments in 1967 revealed that the number of governments in the United States continued to decrease sharply, a consequence primarily of the consolidation of school districts. Special districts (autonomous units of government organized to accomplish functions that general governments could not or would not handle) have continued to grow in number. Table H is the 1967 enumeration of the complex governmental environment with which we must deal.

Table H   Distribution of Local Governments, 1957, 1962, 1967

Type of government	1967	1962	1957 [a]
U.S. Government	1	1	1
State governments	50	50	50
Local governments	81,253	91,186	102,341
Counties	3,049	3,043	3,050
Municipalities	18,051	18,000	17,215
Townships	17,107	17,142	17,198
School districts	21,782	34,678	50,454
Special districts	21,264	18,323	14,424
Total	81,304	91,237	102,392

[a] Adjusted to include units in Alaska and Hawaii, which were reported separately prior to adoption of statehood in 1959.

Source: *Nation's Cities*, November 1967, p. 29.

A local government in one state can be compared to a local government in another state, however, only if account is taken of the differences in those laws which provide powers to the local government and various kinds of taxable resources, grants-in-aid, and other means of financing the expenditure authorized by the voters. Each community is unique in terms of its location, which is a strong determinant of its ability to provide employment opportunities in agriculture, natural resource development, manufacturing, services, and recreation. Each community is uniquely situated in a region or a metropolitan area, serving as a new or old central city, or perhaps a high- or low-income suburb. It may be a community self-conscious about its environment, using city planning, zoning, urban renewal and beautification, and other techniques to the hilt. Its citizens may have more or less interest in education, cultural opportunities, and social welfare programs. In short, there are as many subtle variations among communities issuing bonds as there are between people in a cross-section of the population. The multifaceted attempts to understand, restructure, control, and modernize local finance patterns, as discussed in the sections below, promise to demand an increasing share of the bond analyst's time in the years ahead.

B. UNDERSTANDING THE URBAN ECONOMY

To understand the complex urban environment, the bond analyst, in company with a wide range of public administrators, sociologists, economists, city planners, and other professionals, needs to have some theories of urban economic development, some methods of explaining diverse local expenditure patterns, some techniques for measuring the effects and effectiveness of alternative forms of public investment, and a feel for the social and political forces at work. In this section we evaluate the economists' work to date in explaining municipal expenditure patterns and discuss briefly some of the techniques and concepts that will be of significance to the bond analyst.[3]

We have not tried to cover theories of urban development which are concerned (a) with economic job-creating relationships among regions and metropolitan areas, (b) with the distribution within metropolises of employment locations, residential areas, and other activities, and (c) with critical problems of transportation and land use. To investigate these problems of economic growth and urban development, some economists have used mathematical models of various kinds: input-output models of the local economy; interindustry, interregional linear programming models; intrametropolitan allocative models; and, to a limited extent, dynamic programming models.

A smaller number of economists have concerned themselves with theoretical problems of local public finance, the relationship between a decentralized and very heterogeneous system of local governmental decision-makers and the type and cost of public services offered, the cost-benefit calculations that are increasingly called upon to establish the suitability of alternative public projects for services that have no market price, and the implications of different types of federal and local programs of assistance. Although detailed consideration of this growing body of useful approaches is also beyond the scope of this book, we can predict that the bond analyst of the future will find himself immersed in the writings of these urban economists and regional scientists, for they are building new foundations for municipal fiscal policy. The next section is a birds-eye view of their activities.

An Interpretation of Research Findings to Date in the Field of Municipal Finance

Understanding why and how local governments spend money is a basic, fascinating, and statistically messy process. In the following few paragraphs we attempt to give the reader an impression of the results of the work to date as it relates to the changing nature of the municipal finance function.

1. Economists have found the different socioeconomic characteristics of the community to be more helpful than size or location of the community in explaining expenditure patterns for particular municipal services or

[3] Readings (h).

functions. The level of income of families within a given jurisdiction, for instance, is a much more reliable guide to the level of educational expenditure than is the size of the population in the community. Total population, in contrast, tends to be correlated with expenditures on functions such as police or transportation.

2. Data expressed in per-capita terms tend to produce more meaningful analyses than data expressed as totals.

3. For many categories of expenditure, the levels and, even more importantly, changes in the levels tend to be dependent upon intergovernmental flows of funds. For example, a local welfare program, which is reported as a municipal expenditure, is typically a stepchild of federal and state programs and may be financed more by transfer payments than by local tax receipts.

4. In general, long lists of factors considered as partial determinants of the level of expenditure in a community can be boiled down to a manageable number by formal mathematical analysis (usually a multiple-regression program). However, leading economists such as Werner Hirsch and Harvey Brazer have been critical of studies that fail to differentiate between current operating expenditures and capital outlays, pointing out that the forces that influence investment outlays are qualitatively different from those affecting current expenditures.[4] In addition, the findings of such studies are hard to apply, as Seymour Sacks has noted:

> . . . Analyses of intra-jurisdictional variations in local government expenditure such as those carried on by William L.C. Wheaton and Morton J. Schussheim, *The Cost of Municipal Services in Residential Areas* and Walter Isard and Robert E. Coughlin, *Municipal Costs and Revenues Resulting from Community Growth* are not phrased in terms suitable to local government fiscal problems. Moreover, they emphasize capital considerations which are entirely different in order of magnitude for any given period of time than are . . . operating expenditures.[5]

5. Moreover, much of the research has been in the form of scholarly projects that are difficult to compare among themselves, since one may cover 122 central cities in 1962, another 14 metropolitan areas in 1957, still another all cities and towns in a New England state in 1960, each with different groups of variables, different categorizations of functions, different perceptions of intergovernmental relations and flows over time. Since the national economy and the activities within metropolitan areas have also changed impressively in recent years, an analysis performed on comprehensive data first available from the Census of Governments of 1957 has probably not been repeated using comparable data from the 1962 Census and may not be relevant to the local problem which the 1967 Census measures. In short, we need better data (to be analyzed on computers) and a well-

---

[4] Readings (i).
[5] Readings (j).

financed continuing central research effort comparable to those set up to explore problems at the national level before significant new perceptions will be available for the bond analyst.

6. In any case, a full explanation of how a community made its expenditure decisions in the past can never be a reliable guide to its future decisions, because of the element of choice in planning.

Choices, Given Perfect Knowledge of the Future

Let us assume for a moment that a municipal government has the ability to predict its future in terms of income potential for its residents, the amount of economic activity of various sorts that will be going on at some future date, and the nature of influences that will affect it beyond its control by virtue of national programs (such as the building of the Interstate Highway System).

Even with full knowledge of future magnitudes to eliminate the factor of uncertainty in estimating future revenue flows, the municipal officials will still have wide choices regarding the kind of community they will build. However important personal income may be, the link between local economic growth and physical planning is not determined by it.

From the economist's point of view, one of the critical questions is the distribution of income or available resources; we have a choice between letting the rich get richer and the poor poorer, taxing the rich to build facilities for the disadvantaged, or providing public benefits in equal amounts per capita, the latter step maintaining the status quo to the extent this can be managed within the microeconomy of the city.

In addition, the city government can encourage either high- or low-density development; it can use its resources either to provide facilities of interest to those living outside the community at greater or less cost to those in other jurisdictions. It can choose to adapt to the future as it is known or to make the future adaptable to the community's desires. The choice will remain for a time with the voters in each community. The problem is to make urbanization not only palatable but desirable in human terms. Economic analysis of regional problems and potentialities can only be the servant of planning for people. The regional scientists, the economic geographers, the social scientists, and the urban designers are all contributing to our ability to define and implement choices for the urban environment at different scales. Mathematical models are increasingly important as a means of investigating alternative choices; data are improving, and since fundamental economic change takes place relatively slowly, the impact of structural economic change in the United States on the capacity for comparable change in any given locality can be measured more accurately and, if we will, differences compensated for more efficiently than before.

New Ways of Studying Public Finance

A prime example of the kind of economic research directed toward the explanation of local financial structures which will eventually help bond analysis is a recent study of public finance in Pittsburgh and Allegheny County.

The patterns of fiscal trends that the study uncovered for its metropolitan area can probably be found in many of the older metropolises in the country. The project was made possible through a demonstration grant administered by the Urban Renewal Administration, Housing and Home Finance Agency (now the Department of Housing and Urban Development), supplemented by funds from the A. W. Mellon Educational and Charitable Trust to represent the one-third local share. The work was performed by the staff of the two urban redevelopment agencies serving Pittsburgh and the surrounding county. The Pennsylvania Economy League, Inc., Western Division, a well-known nonprofit governmental research organization, and Dr. Robert C. Wood of M.I.T. (and, under Johnson, Secretary of the Department of Housing and Urban Development), served as consultants. The authors stated:

> The overriding question warranting attention is not whether community improvements and services can be financed. Rather, the key word is "how"—how can the urban area make more efficient use of all its financial resources to meet present and future demands upon it? . . . .
> (Our) examination leads one to suspect that the single greatest fiscal deficiency in any large urban community is a shortage of knowledge about the true nature of its debits and credits—its abilities to raise and spend money. As far as can be determined, no major urban area in the country today can forecast with clarity and accuracy the extent of financial support that will be needed from citizens in the near future for community improvements and services. . . .[6]

They began by distinguishing municipal functions financed by tax revenues (such as law enforcement, construction and maintenance of streets and highways, refuse collection and disposal, tax collection) from "public" functions financed by taxes as well as by private contributions (such as education, health, social welfare, utilities, housing, recreation, culture).

In order to comprehend the "fiscal habits" of Allegheny County's 129 municipal governments, 109 school districts, 131 public authorities, and 210 major private community agencies, data were obtained for each of these decision-making units and analyzed with regard to the effect that

[6] Federal (b), p. 5.

population, size, wealth, density, age, education, and other factors play in the shaping of public budgets.

On the basis of a factor analysis of 40 socio-economic variables, supplemented by informed opinions, a *"community typology"* was developed. This indicated that Allegheny County is comprised of seven distinct types of communities reflecting various stages of urban development. The statistical classifications are: (1) affluent; (2) industrial; (3) declining; (4) rapidly growing; (5) slowly emerging; (6) rapidly maturing; (7) central city. The researchers found that:

   . . . Differences in population size, occupational distinction, land use, wealth and youth are closely associated with differences in spending, taxing, contributing and debt management. However separated physically within the area, communities showing similarities in these respects show also similarities in the management of their fiscal affairs. Certain of them "cluster together" in discernible types and share common problems and prospects. So the lesson many officials have learned by experience—that their control over tax rates and debts is sharply limited—is demonstrated mathematically. And the conclusion many students of urban life have arrived at—that physical planning and fiscal planning must go hand in hand—is affirmed once again.[7]

Fiscal Factors by Type of Community

   The kind of factor analysis that was applied to classify the various jurisdictions in Allegheny County makes possible systematic comparative interpretations of fiscal data ordinarily handled by a bond analyst on a city-by-city basis.

   For example, the study showed per-capita assessments of real property for the affluent and industrial areas (the latter so classified because a substantial share of their revenues come from taxes on industrial property) rising appreciably faster than for other types of communities, with the City of Pittsburgh about average for the county as a whole. However, the city had the highest per-capita amount of revenues and expenditures in the county, a telling comment on the problem of the central city.

   Revenues are rising faster than expenditures in affluent communities because of the rapid buildup in assessable property, the reverse being seen for the declining communities. The slowly emerging communities show up in the bottom ranges, and the rapid-growth type is characterized by slightly accelerating assessments and slightly lagging revenues and expenditures on a per-capita basis in comparison to the rapidly maturing type.

   When per-capita expenditures are analyzed by function, as shown in Figure 19, some other significant relationships appear. Public safety and utility operations constitute relatively large percentage shares of central city and declining areas budgets, whereas streets and highways absorb relatively high percentages in budgets for other types of communities. Education expenditures, in amounts per capita, are visibly lower in the central

[7] Federal (b), p. 29.

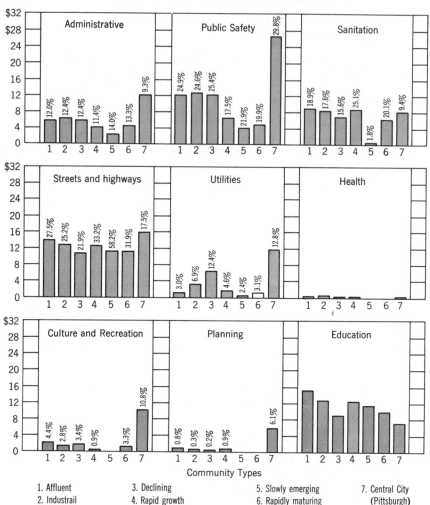

Figure 19 Per-capita expenditures by function and percentage of total budget by type of community, 1961 (Pittsburgh study).

city and declining areas, and not unexpectedly highest in the affluent areas.

The point to be made here is that few such studies are available to bond analysts, even though the general drift of the conclusions of such studies is well known. The Pittsburgh study demonstrates the value of categories that are more subtle than the usual central city-suburban or large-small breakdowns found in the few studies that are available. The Pittsburgh type of study, moreover, may establish reasonable expectations for capital investments required in given communities to accommodate emerging needs and to rehabilitate obsolete facilities, but explicit justifications for new projects and programs require a great deal more than analysis of past trends. Such justifications are discussed in Section D, on budgeting policy.

C. RESTRUCTURING LOCAL GOVERNMENT

The structure of local government in an area determines the kind of bond issues sold, and as the reader has seen in Figure 1 and in Chapter III, a bond issue is a financial consequence of a complex political process.

This section outlines some of the reasons why the local finance problem is endemic, and then considers the proposals that have been advanced to reassign the obligations of states and their local governments and to reapportion revenue sources among them.

Endemic Problems of Local Public Finance

Since the Republic was founded, Americans have wanted their local communities to be financially independent and locally controlled. The demand for municipal services, especially in metropolitan areas, however, has increased faster than the financial resources available to local governments, primarily taxes on immovable real property. Income and other taxes are generally available only to the federal and state governments. The problem is how to match these financial resources with the responsibility for providing public services.

Voters have consistently turned down proposals for metropolitan government and other "rational" plans in favor of a continuance of local government as it is, a political haven for both suburbanites and residents of the ghetto.[8]

Moreover, our political economy is constantly in motion. The population is growing. The product mix offered by American industry is constantly changing; so are the locations selected by producers. The center of population has been moving west ever since the start of the Republic. The Census of 1860 showed that European immigrants were taking the places in the eastern areas vacated by the settlers heading west. The Census of 1860 also revealed that many eastern cities had suffered a loss of population between 1850 and 1860.

One hundred years later we still have a continuing western migration, together with migration of southern nonwhite families into the central cities of the north and north central states, and migration out of central

8 ACIR (d).

cities as families moved to the suburbs. Inevitably, the local political economy is in a state of disequilibrium with respect to the supply and demand for governmental services. The demand for services is virtually unlimited and is ordinarily quite inelastic; that is, the demand does not get smaller as the price increases.[9]

For some municipal services there can be supply prices set by market forces, such as electric power, but for other services to be supplied the question is whether cost by itself is the proper price. For example, central cities supply streets and policemen in large quantities for the benefit of suburban commuters who have elected to live in a different tax jurisdiction, but the suburbanites naturally resist extra charges for such services in addition to the package of services they have bought and paid for in their own communities. As Vernon [10] has pointed out, the majority of Americans now live in suburbs, quite content with their grass, good schools, and like-minded neighbors, and quite unwilling to shoulder financial burdens that they have so far been legally able to avoid.

Defining National Goals

The metropolitan finance problem has many other dimensions, over and above the disparities in services and resources among communities of different types. Three important factors subject to change are the lack of a national urban policy, economic competition among local communities, and the lack of standards for services provided by individual communities. Some measure of local financial independence will be properly given up in the process of improving both the efficiency and the distribution of municipal services.

Our national goals have rarely, until recently, been designed to foster the growth of cities, much less to improve their livability or to assure their financial viability as independent units, nor have state governments focused their attentions on the cities. Embedded in our intellectual heritage is a well-documented antiurban agrarian bias.[11]

Nevertheless, every implementation of a national goal has an ultimate effect, large or small, upon urban areas, and taxes levied by the federal government have a different effect in each jurisdiction. Given the diversity and relative independence of local government, we cannot make detailed plans for the development of the country as a whole, nor determinations of which regions and which cities should be allowed to grow.

Moreover, our national interest in the urban problem is only of recent date. The urban economy was "discovered" in the days of the National Re-

[9] Readings (k).
[10] Vernon, Raymond.
[11] Readings (l).

sources Planning Board, shortly after "housing" as an industry came to national attention in 1931 with the President's Conference on Home Building and Home Ownership. The national interest in transportation as a system, rather than a set of railroads, highways, and other modes, was only generated after automobiles had altered local circulation patterns and airplanes and trucks had changed the basis for the local economy.[12]

Defining Local Goals

Our theory of government allows local communities to develop as they wish, subject only to restrictions imposed by their state charters and by competition from other communities. The idea is that each community shall determine the scope of its own general government and be prepared to pay for the activities it undertakes. Each community can decide how much education, how much police protection, how much street cleaning and garbage removal, and how much of any other public service its citizens require.

However, federal and state programs of assistance to local governments have the effect of introducing new standards into municipal administration and of diverting local funds from other uses. Formerly having made its own decisions on the scope and level of service, a local government could draw up a budget to balance revenues with the indicated expenditures. Where it was desired to spread expenditures for a capital investment over a number of years, the money could be borrowed through the sale of municipal bonds, as approved by the voters.

Local financial independence was a more meaningful concept before the American family acquired the degree of residential mobility that now characterizes the nation. In days gone by, one lived and worked, almost by necessity, in the same community and the same political jurisdiction over a substantial period of time, and the chances were good that a voter approving a bond issue would be around during the years that it would take to pay off the debt. The chances were also good that he would be benefiting fairly directly from the improvements made, for the scope of public improvements was narrow and their visibility high. But now the typical voter will change his jurisdiction in the course of the next decade. The purposes for which municipal funds are expended have become much less visible as a greater proportion of the budget is directed to intangible social benefits, and the average voter's mobility implies that he will not have been in the community long enough to have had much say in the adoption of the municipal budget itself.

[12] Federal (c).

Proposals to Improve Local Government

It became settled doctrine with the reports of the Kestnbaum Commission in the early 1950's that the structure of state and local governments had to be improved, given "the erosion of the competence of local government" and the way the states were by-passed as local units began to deal directly with the federal government.

On the basis of those findings, Congress in 1959 established the Advisory Commission on Intergovernmental Relations, composed of representatives from all levels of government and charged with the continuing task of recommending changes to strengthen the system of federalism. Since then the Advisory Commission has called for a number of pieces of federal legislation, has bombarded the state governments with urgent appeals for reform at the state level, and has necessarily had its attention riveted on the problem of the metropolitan areas that contain most of the operative problems of an intergovernmental nature.

In *Metropolitan America: Challenge to Federalism,* an official summary of the Advisory Commission's work through 1966, Profesor Frieden justified this concentration of effort on metropolises:

> Local governments within metropolitan areas receive more revenue per capita than those in the rest of the country, but they depend more heavily on property taxes and other local sources and less on State aid. They also spend more per capita overall, mainly because of a greater need for services that are basically urban, such as police and fire protection and urban renewal and housing. Within metropolitan areas, total central city expenditures per capita are greater than those in the suburbs. Expenditures for education and highways tend to be higher than in the suburbs, but most other outlays, particularly for police and welfare, are higher in the core cities. . . . The facts of population disparities, government structure, and expenditure patterns . . . go a long way toward explaining the conflicts of interest between local governments with different needs and varying resources.[13]

The Advisory Commission has tried to determine what should be done. The Commission has suggested programs to ameliorate the social and economic disparities in metropolitan areas which involve promoting wider opportunities for individual choice with respect to employment and urban housing, in addition to increasing state contributions to public welfare programs, and housing relocation in urban development programs. The Advisory Commission has also recommended large increases in federal and state support of water, sewer, and pollution-control projects.

Responsibility of the States

Implementing such recommendations is, of course, beyond the power of the Commission, but gradually Congress and the states have begun to take

[13] ACIR (e), p. 28.

small steps in the general direction of greater control, coordinative planning, and realignment of powers and responsibilities. To improve state-local relations within each of the several states, the Advisory Commission, according to Frieden, recommended that the states: (a) grant to local governments functional powers not reserved or restricted by general legislation; (b) liberalize municipal annexation of unincorporated areas; (c) control new municipal incorporations; (d) authorize creation of functional area-wide authorities; (e) authorize voluntary transfer of functions from municipalities to counties and vice versa; (f) authorize interlocal contracting and joint enterprises; (g) grant selected extraterritorial powers; (h) authorize formation of councils of public officials; (i) authorize creation of metropolitan area study commissions; (j) authorize creation of metropolitan area planning bodies; (k) establish a unit of state government for metropolitan area affairs; (l) establish a state program of financial and technical assistance to metropolitan areas; (m) extend control over special districts; and (n) be able to resolve disputes among local units of government in metropolitan areas.

Such measures are a combination of giving local governments greater flexibility and of tightening state control over the system. In many of its reports the Commission has voted in favor of techniques to force local communities to meet minimum standards, especially in the context of planning for education, welfare, urban development, and transportation. Grants-in-aid thereby would become subject to review and control at both the metropolitan and the state levels, a procedure that is unwieldy but promises a variety of benefits in the name of both efficiency and equity.

Reforming the Property Tax

An effort possibly of greater significance to the bond analyst is the Commission's desire to have the states "smooth out the fiscal contours of a metropolitan landscape broken up by local government boundaries." In putting primary responsibility on the states to deal effectively with this problem by providing more assistance in financing local government services, the Commission recognized that

The property tax is the major, and in many cases the sole, source of tax revenue of local governments. In 1962 it accounted for over 87 per cent of local tax revenue. The extent to which local units use the property tax is, therefore, probably a good general index of the pressure of local public service needs and the degree to which the locality based on property tax effort will direct funds to those communities having the most acute public service needs and showing maximum local tax effort.[14]

A number of states employ some method of equalizing property tax information by converting undervaluations to some measure of true value,

[14] ACIR (e), p. 165.

and, as municipal bond experts are well aware, there are innumerable techniques by which states contribute directly to the construction of educational facilities and other projects by reference to a formula based on local tax and socioeconomic characteristics. Along these lines, Professor Frieden reports that the Commission recommended that each state

examine its present system of grants, shared taxes, and authorization for local nonproperty taxes, and remove all features that aggravate differences in local fiscal capacity to deal with service requirements in metropolitan areas and that encourage or support the proliferation of local governments within these areas.

Formulas for distributing State grants and sharing State taxes can have a significant effect on the relative ability of localities to deal with their public service problems. State grants and shared taxes may also aggravate disparities by acting to proliferate local governments within metropolitan areas, whether or not these effects are intended. In some cases, a State shares income tax revenue with local governments, or authorizes local governments to impose an income tax, solely on the basis of place of residence. Wealthy citizens, in particular, are thereby given a tax incentive for leaving the central city and incorporating suburban communities in order to get a share of the State income tax and thereby lessen their property tax load. In other cases, where State grants are made to all incorporated units, there is a tendency to stimulate new incorporations without regard to whether they are in the interest of the best long-range pattern of governmental development in the area. Annexation by an existing municipality or incorporation with adjoining territory to form a much larger unit might be more desirable alternatives from the standpoint of removing or forestalling disparities in services and finances.[15]

The Advisory Commission's job is to make recommendations for legislation to the several states and to the Congress. Their packages of proposed laws and their suggestions for built-in controls in grant-in-aid programs can only be evaluated on an individual basis, but even though the local voters and their state legislators are often reluctant to change ancient ways, some of the changes are clearly necessary and constructive. The challenge is to give the residents of a local community more effective control over their own institutions as part of a more satisfactory system for planning metropolitan-wide facilities and services. As we shall see in the next section, capital budgeting systems promise to be important innovations in the process of improving local government and represent one of the important links between the municipal bond market and the intergovernmental reformers.

D. CONTROLLING INVESTMENT

Role of Capital Budgets

Few areas of importance to the municipal bond system are changing faster than the field of budgeting. It is still uncertain to what extent local

---

[15] ACIR (e), p. 166.

officials will be required to recast their accounts to accord with modern concepts of program budgeting of planning, programming, and budget systems (PPBS), but the opportunities to do so will increase over the coming years; some municipalities have already had notable success in adapting the program budgeting approach for parts of the public business they administer. It is an even greater question to what extent the principle of local fiscal independence will confound attempts to apply program budgeting to federally supported activities of certain types that require the co-operation of a multitude of individual governments in a given metropolitan area and that imply a rationing of assistance among these governments.

The Advisory Commission on Intergovernmental Relations, in its study of methods by which states could help local govenments, made a strong and useful statement about budgeting in general, with examples of standard forms of budgets that can serve to introduce the subject:

> The usefulness, indeed the necessity, of long-term capital planning cannot be over-emphasized. While most States have statutory requirements as to annual budgeting by local governments and some require the filing of local operating budgets with State agencies, the need for a capital budget is only beginning to be recognized. The States should foster the development of local capital budgets and, in conjunction with their programs of technical assistance to local debt management, should require that such budgets be filed with the State agency administering such assistance.
>
> *Capital budgets and long-term programs.* No aspect of budgeting is of more importance to debt technical assistance than the planning of a long-term capital program. Indispensable as are data of the past and current condition of local governments, debts are paid in the future; and a knowledge of future financing, even on an estimated basis, is a tool of the first importance in both the local and State evaluation of proposed bond issues.
>
> This study is concerned with four elements of planning:
>
> 1. *The capital improvement program* is stated in terms of the physical improvements required for a specified period of years in the future. Such a program is the creation of a community, normally through a local planning agency, that should start with a physical inventory of capital improvements and be extended into the future by an appraisal of replacements of existing assets and the addition of future improvements.
>
> 2. *The capital budget* should correlate capital improvement receipts, comprising long-term bonds, short-term notes, and various revenue sources, with capital expenditures arranged by priorities for a specified number of years.
>
> 3. *The long-term program* should incorporate the capital budget and should include debt service on outstanding and proposed obligations as well as the current operation cost that is importantly affected by the nature of future capital improvements.
>
> 4. *The annual budget,* to which the community is legally committed, would set forth one year of the long-term program, the later years of which are subject to annual revision.[16]

---

[16] ACIR (c), p. 29; see also ICMA (c).

Philadelphia's Method

In an earlier compilation of materials, the International City Managers' Association published a description of development programming in Philadelphia by Robert B. Shawn.[17]

Philadelphia has achieved a certain renown for leadership in this field, and Shawn describes its comprehensive approach for reviewing, analyzing, and scheduling development activities. He defines programming as a mechanism for taking stock of what existing programs exist and how they can be applied, identifying inadequacies and designing new programs to meet needs, and "scheduling existing and new programs over an extended time period within the limitations imposed by the resources made available during any given year." The programming system, serving both planning and management purposes, has value because "it provides a framework for making rational decisions."

Internal Systems

With considerable experience in long-term forecasting and planning of its operations, the City of Philadelphia found itself with a number of budgeting systems already in operation. These systems included: (a) planning operations orientated toward producing a comprehensive plan for guiding the physical development of the city; (b) capital programming procedures that provided "a method for scheduling capital projects according to their physical relationships within the guidelines of established fiscal policy"; (c) urban renewal and redevelopment procedures; (d) operating budget analyses that were being used to examine the efficiency of various city operations; and (e) budget forecasting methods that were used to examine the implications of future city operations, given the continuance of existing policies.

The Philadelphia planners then split municipal activities into six major categories for development programming. These categories were composed of programs and activities concerned with the following: (a) housing and the physical environment related to housing, including construction of public and private housing, residential conservation and renewal, and maintenance of minimum housing and environmental standards; (b) maintenance of a prosperous economic climate, including such programs as industrial financial assistance, economic promotion, employment training and retraining, special facilities, in providing locations for commercial and industrial facilities; (c) individual and family services covering health,

[17] ICMA (d).

Table I   Illustrative PPBS Program Structure

I. Personal Safety
   A. Law enforcement
   B. Traffic safety
   C. Fire prevention and control
   D. Safety from animals
   E. Protection and control of disasters natural and man-made
   F. Prevention of other accidents

II. Health
   A. Physical health
   B. Mental health
   C. Drug and alcohol addiction, prevention and control

III. Intellectual Development and Personal Enrichment
   A. Preschool education
   B. Primary education
   C. Secondary education
   D. Higher education
   E. Adult education

IV. Satisfactory Home/Community Environment
   A. Comprehansive community planning
   B. Homes for the dependent
   C. Housing (other than that in A and B)
   D. Water supply
   E. Solid waste disposal
   F. Air pollution control
   G. Pest control
   H. Noise abatement
   I. Local beautification
   J. Intra-community relations
   K. Homemaking aid/information

V. Economic Satisfaction & Satisfactory Work Opportunities for the Individual
   A. Financial assistance to the needy
   B. Increased job opportunity
   C. Protection of an individual as an employee
   D. Aid to the individual as a businessman
   E. Protection of the individual as a consumer of goods and services
   F. Judicial activities for protection of consumers and businessmen alike

VI. Leisure-Time Opportunities
   A. Outdoor
   B. Indoor
   C. Recreational activities for senior citizens
   D. Cultural activities

VII. Transportation-Communication-Location
   A. Motor vehicle
   B. Urban transit systems
   C. Pedestrian
   D. Water transport
   E. Air transport
   F. Location programs
   G. Communications substitutes for transportation

VIII. General Support
   A. General government management
   B. Financial
   C. Purchasing and property management
   D. Personnel services
   E. Unassignable EDP
   F. Legislative
   G. Legal
   H. Elections

Source: Federal (d), Hatry-Cotton.

welfare, and assistance programs; (d) services to property, such as refuse disposal and street maintenance; (e) transportation services providing means for moving people and goods and including rail transit operations, arterial construction and maintenance, port facilities; and (f) support and general administrative activities, planning operations, courts, and other similar types of programs.

Since programs that fit into these categories may be governmental or private, may have specific geographic applications or be citywide in effect, and may play different roles in the process of development, the Philadelphia planners attempt to specify the role to be played by a program, to compare its effectiveness to other programs with a claim on the city's resources, and finally to project a sequence of events related to the program over an appropriate time period.

Planning, Programming, Budgeting Systems

Efforts are now being made to get other cities to follow Philadelphia's lead, and wide publicity has been given to an important study by Hatry and Cotton recently released as one of the first publications of the State-Local Finances Project, directed by Dr. Selma J. Mushkin, under a grant from the Ford Foundation to George Washington University, in cooperation with the Council of State Governments, the International City Managers' Association, the National Association of Counties, the National League of Cities, and U.S. Conference of Mayors.[18] In addition to an excellent review of the doctrine of planning, programming, and budgeting systems for local government generally, this study provides an illustrative program structure, focused on "the individual citizen—his needs and wants," the short form of which is reproduced as Table I.

The Hatry-Cotton program structure (a) incorporates more categories of "general government" such as law enforcement and traffic safety than seemed to be represented in the Philadelphia approach, and (b) appears to be more in line with the program approach taken by the federal government in its programs for the assistance of state and local governments.

Metropolitan Area-Wide Budgets

The real test for program budgeting will come as the federal government attempts to provide for review of federal program grants to local governments at the metropolitan level. According to the eighth annual report of the Advisory Commission on Intergovernmental Relations:

Beginning in July 1967, all applications for grants or loans for certain physical development projects within Standard Metropolitan Statistical Areas must be accompanied by

[18] Federal (d).

the review and comment of an area-wide body authorized to carry on comprehensive planning for the metropolitan community.

The possible scope of such review proceedings, and indeed the implications of the relationship between a metropolitan planning agency and a metropolitan program review agency, have been explored most extensively in a study prepared for a Senate government operations subcommittee under the direction of Professor Charles M. Haar, later Assistant Secretary of the Department of Housing and Urban Development.[19]

This study's list of major federal programs affecting urban and metropolitan development does not include major federal programs relating to health and personal safety, but it does enumerate those programs the authors felt required metropolitan coordination prior to a federal grant and those that should be reviewed at the metropolitan level.

The federal programs then requiring metropolitan coordination included: Urban Planning Assistance, Waste Treatment Works, Area Redevelopment, Open Space Land Acquisition, and Highways. Among those suggested as candidates for review at the metropolitan level were: Hospital and Medical Facilities Construction, Community Renewal Programs, Urban Renewal Projects and Urban Renewal Demonstrations, Public Facility Loans, Advances for Public Works Planning, Public Works Acceleration, Civil Works Projects, Surplus Land Disposal, Land for Recreational and Public Purposes, Public Housing, Low-Income Housing Demonstrations, Senior Citizens Housing Loans, F.H.A. Mortgage Insurance, Mass Transit Loans, Mass Transit Demonstration, and Airports. Programs for College and Medical Facilities Construction and School Construction in federally impacted areas were in a less urgent review category. The report also calls for "referral of municipal and operating agency data" from all local governments to the metropolitan review agency.

Problems of Implementation

At this writing, the federal criteria for the functions of a metropolitan review agency do not employ the programmatic terms of the Hatry-Cotton study, which in turn conceives of programs in somewhat different ways from most of the local communities that would make up any given metropolitan area. Moreover, whole new sets of federal programs, such as the attack on poverty and the improvement of educational systems, are being incorporated into local and metropolitan thinking, but it is unclear what level of local government will have cognizance of them or what budgetary pigeonholes can accommodate them. Other examples of programs hard to fit into old accounting categories are mental health facilities, pollution

[19] Federal (e).

controls, reorganization of local governments themselves, and bloc grants to the states for use by local government.

Haar's report, *The Effectiveness of Metropolitan Planning,* suggests that the metropolitan review agency should review municipal and operating budget data on a continuing basis. Sooner or later we may have to come to grips with the problem of trying to understand relative tax efforts and expenditure levels within a metropolis, and some current use may be made of periodic local fiscal data, but it will be some time before any metropolitan review agency will be in a position to examine suitable economic and political data, in conjunction with the fiscal data, in order to weigh alternative courses of action in a truly comprehensive and programmatic style.

Haar's study suggested that there were three methods by which metropolitan planning might ultimately be implemented: (a) requiring conformance by the localities with a metropolitan master plan; (b) requiring conformance by the localities with the recommendations of the metropolitan planning agency on local development proposals; and (c) permitting appeal to a higher authority by the agency or the local government units upon nonconformance.

Independence Versus Agreement on Objectives

Among the very real problems that now make the review process less than ideal, of most significance is the lack of substantial agreement among citizens of any metropolis about the objectives of a metropolitan plan—for example, should the area have a form that is dominated by a strong central business district? Even with agreement, it is difficult to encompass all functions now performed by local government, both general and special, in a unified analytic system, but many functions are related logically to programmatic categories such as "individual development" or transportation, and some of the partial analyses may help provide a framework for considering related programs and a wider set of values and policies than might have been considered before introduction of review proceedings and adoption of the concept of programming. It will be a substantial improvement over the present state of affairs if any review agency (operating without significant funds, staff, or powers at its disposal and trying to influence events by persuasion rather than by coercion) is able to help applicants for federal grants take steps to improve the stock, flow, and quality of data which are required for comprehensive program analyses at any level of government.[20]

[20] Readings (m).

E. REVISING RESTRICTIONS IMPOSED BY THE STATES

History

As the indebtedness of local governments has grown from a relatively small figure to become an important factor in the capital markets, the fundamental laws under which local governments operate have been changing in the direction of more and more control by the states. In recent years the Advisory Commission on Intergovernmental Relations (ACIR), established by the Congress in 1959 to provide means of improving the effectiveness of federal, state, and local government, has taken the lead in studying and recommending remedial legislation on such matters as state laws pertaining to local indebtedness. The following quotation is from ACIR's historical summary of such restrictions.

There have been several periods during the past century when many local governments found it difficult or impossible to keep up payments on their indebtedness. By far the most serious of these, in terms of the proportion of all outstanding bonds involved, was the crisis of the 1870's.

The serious depression of the 1870's came after many localities had floated bonds for aid to railroads, commonly to assure or encourage the location of routes through particular areas. Some State governments had been seriously embarrassed by over-issuance of "internal improvement" debt for similar purposes in the 1830's. One by-product of that experience was the widespread adoption, during the 1840's and 1850's, of constitutional restrictions on State borrowing powers. Accordingly, the pressure for public efforts to expand transportation facilities was shifted to the local government level. Many of the local railroad-aid bonds were to purchase stock of which the dividend earnings, it was fondly hoped, would provide for debt service plus some surplus for general government financing.

With onset of a sharp depression, many debt-loaded governments found themselves in difficulty, and numerous bond issues went into default. Firm figures are not available, but it has been estimated that in the course of this crisis there was at least some delay in servicing for about one-fifth of all local government debt outstanding. Because of the optimism, haste, and carelessness which marked many of the railroad-aid transactions, local officials and taxpayers often felt they had received little or nothing for their money, so they sought means to avoid honoring such debt. A period of costly and bitter litigation ensued.

Two important developments can be traced to this yearly crisis. There was, in the first place, a sharp contraction in the availability of long-term credit for local governments. Through the 1880's they were forced to finance their essential capital outlays largely on a pay-as-you-go basis, rather than by borrowing. Secondly, restrictions on local government debt and borrowing were written into many State constitutions, as more fully described below.

Another period of debt difficulty for local governments occurred in the 1890's, again involving railroad-aid bonds in many instances. However, this crisis was less severe and widespread than that of the 1870's.

An easier period followed, but during the 1920's difficulties again began to develop, particularly where considerable amounts of "special assessment" debt had been issued to finance improvements for actual and prospective subdivisions. With the onset of the Great Depression of the 1930's, trouble spread. In many communities, the property tax base diminished as assessed valuations were cut back, though rarely at the pace of the decline in market values. Nationwide, assessed values dropped 18 per cent, but in some States there was a considerably greater decline. Delay in property tax collections spread, and delinquency mounted from 10 percent in 1930 to 26 percent in 1933. Meantime, local governments were carrying the brunt of expansion in public welfare needs, multiplying their expenditure for aid to the needy. Some local governments were also embarrassed, along with other depositors, in having their current resources lost or at least temporarily tied up in closed banks.[21]

The crisis of the nineteenth century had led to restrictions written into constitutions and statutes in a majority of the states. The Depression experience precipitated more legislation but, more importantly, it focused attention on the functioning of the local economy over business cycles. Accordingly bond analysis began to take on new significance; the rating services found new customers, and the banking institutions set to work designing credit analysis forms.

The bulk of the revenue issues offered in the post–World War II period has not yet been tested by a serious recession or suffered from more localized economic troubles, but cautious institutional investors quite properly assume that a rash of defaults or financial embarrassments in connection with new forms of revenue bonds for which credit data are untested, such as for new communities, would have the undesirable effect of leading both to greater federal intervention in local affairs and to additional state restrictions.

The Effort to Revise the Network of Restrictions

In its summary of findings the Advisory Commission found that borrowing by local governments is now subject to an extensive and complicated body of law, expressed in the provisions of state constitutions, statutes, and individual government charters, and interpreted by official rulings and accordant decisions. These legal provisions deal with many aspects of local government debt—not only with the amounts that may be borrowed, but also commonly with permissible methods, purposes, time periods, and other conditions of borrowing and taxing.

The Advisory Commission's report discusses three main types of restrictions involving (a) a limit on indebtedness, expressed as a percentage of the local government's property tax base (its assessed valuation); (b) a limit on tax rates that can be imposed specifically for debt service or for various

[21] ACIR (a), p. 19.

purposes including debt service; and (c) the requirement of a local referendum to authorize the issuance of bonds.

The Advisory Commission recognized the legitimate and strong concern of the states with the borrowing power and practices of local governments subject to their jurisdiction, but it pointed out that existing legal provisions are in most states critically in need of intensive review and major change. It stated its belief that the present maze of constitutional and statutory restrictions on local government borrowing constitutes a serious impediment to effective local self-government in the United States.

Furthermore, it noted that state-imposed restrictions do not encompass all types of local bond issues, but commonly apply only to local governments' issuance of full faith and credit debt. Various legal doctrines and devices by which local governments can issue nonguaranteed or "revenue" debt, usually exempt from such state restrictions, have developed, and in recent years there has naturally been an extremely rapid growth of "unrestricted" local debt as local officials found opportunities to create special authorities to handle new projects. Thus the use of revenue bonds has in some states spread far beyond its initial limited application to the financing of utility type facilities of local government.

Debt Ceilings

The most common type of restriction—a ceiling limit related to the local property tax base—the Advisory Commission found was subject to numerous technical deficiencies, for it pertains only to the past trend in a small area without reference to economic growth for its surrounding area. Moreover, even though property tax receipts have grown impressively (see Figure 26), the Commission stated,

It purports to measure economic capacity by reference to only one revenue source, the property tax, which provides less than half of the revenue of most local governments in most states.

This type of limit is, in most states, imprecise and potentially discriminatory because of the nature of the property tax base to which it refers. The real level of limitation is determined by local assessment practices rather than being closely governed by the legal provisions.

Being commonly applicable to only full faith and credit debt, this type of limitation offers no assurance that aggregate local debt will be kept within prudent bonds.[22]

Effect of Restrictions

In a parallel study the Commission considered the effect of restrictions on the ability of local governments to raise revenues.[23] Restrictions on

[22] ACIR (a), p. 2.
[23] ACIR (f).

property taxes arose in the same historical periods that produced restrictions on issuance of debt, when such limitations had become the means by which citizens could effectively reduce or contain local government expenditures under the stress of depressed economic conditions and by which they could also express their dissatisfaction with the conduct of public business by local officials.

The general effect, heightened during the 1930's, was to curtail property tax revenues for local governments and, to the extent that assessments were also kept at low levels, to restrict the ability to issue debt. This procedure, according to the Commission, often crippled government services severely; in some cases total collapse of local government was averted only by increased state fiscal aid financed for the most part by new consumer taxes, many of which were enacted as "crash programs" during the early 1930's. The problem remains even with the postwar growth in property tax revenue as the result of new construction, higher property values, improved administration, increased assessment ratios, and higher tax rates; however:

> There is no recent, reliable, and comprehensive source of nation-wide information regarding percentage limitations on local debt expressed by *statutory as well as constitutional* provisions of the various States. Until about 1939, a presentation on this subject for each state appeared annually in the authoritative reference source, Moody's Municipal and Government Manual, but the proliferation of enactments then led to abandonment of the effort, and it has never been revived. Recent limited-focus presentations on this subject suggest why any attempt to "summarize" all existing provisions comprehensively in an intelligible form would be doomed to failure. . . .[24]

A similar statement may be made about any other aspect of local government in the United States for which comprehensive, comparative, and up-to-date data are desired. The lack of data, however, has not impeded the widening perception of the need to reappraise the structure of laws applicable to municipal corporation. In the view of David M. Ellinwood, the present handicaps under which local governments labor as they attempt to use their credit economically, effectively, and responsibly include: (a) legal limitations in maximum rates of interest that public bodies may pay; (b) the vagaries of the bond market itself; (c) ill-advised state regulations on maximum maturities, amortization schedules, and call provisions; (d) the occasional requirement that a local government be required to obtain large down payments on bond issues; (e) ill-advised specificity in laws relating to the purposes for which local governments may borrow; (f) ill-conceived referendum requirements typically higher than a majority; (g) lack of freedom of action and choice in areas involving selection of security recitals, types, and forms of debt; and (h) restrictions on the amounts that can be borrowed.

Ellinwood goes on to express a widely held sentiment:

[24] ACIR (f), p. 28; see also JEC—*Financing* (c), p. 153.

There are some students who argue that the power to incur debt should not be limited by law at all, that the only limitation should be the practical inability to borrow when credit becomes so tenuous investors will refuse to lend. . . . Because debt limits have been a part of our governmental provision for approximately a hundred years, it may be that we must accept, as a matter of practical politics, the continuance of some type of limit. Hopefully, new revised limits will be more realistic than those now most prevalent.[25]

A Prediction

We can evaluate Ellinwood's statement by taking a backward glance over this chapter. It is more than practical politics that makes continuance of stated debt limits likely. A more potent factor is the rudimentary state of the art of credit analysis in technical terms and in terms of financial support with the municipal bond institutions. As we saw in Sections B, C, and D, economic analysis is in its infancy, only a few steps have been taken to make local governments more viable, and adequate techniques of programming and budgeting are found in few municipalities.

Until such time, therefore, as the combined forces of federal, state, and local governments and investing institutions provide effective understandable guidelines for local fiscal policies, and until such time as there is evidence of greater agreement as to the objectives and standards of local activities on the part of suburbanites and central city residents, it is difficult to imagine a lifting of restrictions. Instead, we can assume that voters will continue to employ these arbitrary but familiar forms of control over local officials and their propensity to tax and to spend.

[25] MFOA (e).

Chapter XIII   On the Possibility
of Systematic Forecasting

The bond analyst has, in general, two goals: (a) to make reliable judgments about credit with respect to the bond issue itself, as we discussed in Chapter XII, and (b) to make predictions regarding the volume of bonds to be offered and the general price level for them.

The studies reported below indicate that the supply of bonds offered or remaining in dealer inventories affect the price level, which in turn has a reciprocal effect on the willingness of issuers to come to the market at any given time.

A. TYPES OF INTEREST-RATE CYCLES

In a study published for the Investment Bankers Association, for instance, three types of interest-rate cycles in the municipal bond market were described: (a) the long cycle over one or more full business cycles; (b) an intermediate cycle whose length and intensity appear to depend upon changes in investment demand and monetary policy; and (c) very short cycles of three to four months' duration produced by supply and demand factors in the money market.[1]

Short Cycles

The study considered eleven short cycles in the municipal bond market during the 1955–1960 period. A short cycle is defined as a period from a peak yield to a low yield and back to the former peak level; if the yield average continued to climb to another peak thereafter, a new short cycle would begin when the average began to decline.

[1] IBA (c).

The findings of that IBA study were that (a) fluctuations in yields or interest rates and sizes of inventories were substantially greater in the municipal market than in the market for government or corporate securities; and (b) changes in municipal dealer inventories came before changes in municipal yields. For the study, yields were measured by *The Bond Buyer*'s 20-Bond Index, and inventories were measured by an observation on the number of "bonds in major accounts" and in the *Blue List,* all sources that were familiar to the dealers. The IBA reported rather unhelpfully that, on the average, an inventory peak preceded a yield peak by 7 to 8 weeks, with a range from 2 to 19 weeks.

The IBA felt, nevertheless, that there was value in forecasting the relationship between inventories and yields, even though the lead times were variable and subject to being overridden in significance by changes in monetary policy, such as changes in the Federal Reserve discount rate. The importance of their study, in their eyes, was the discovery that "much of the instability in the municipal market is the product of the large swings in dealer inventories." The peculiar nature of dealer inventories, however, makes it difficult to control them and makes it a fairly slow process to reduce them, given "the great multitude of coupon and maturity combinations" represented in the inventories.

B. PRIVATE FORECASTS

Except for that IBA study, very little has been published on the analysis of short-term bond price cycles, perhaps because the industry is constantly in the process of making its own private predictions. Every dealer every day has to make a series of decisions concerning the bidding on new issues for the day and week and concerning the inventory of bonds he holds as the week begins. He is hardly in a position to specify what his inventory position will be thereafter, for a favorable market with a rise in price level and a dip in yield will, as the IBA noted above, immediately convert a liability into an asset. The necessity for these daily and weekly exercises in market forecasting was described in detail in Chapter I.

The investment community is keenly aware of the movement of basic factors that influence the level of interest rates. The major banks and underwriting houses publish at least annually an analysis of the flow of funds into savings institutions, commercial banks, and business and governmental activities and the outflow of funds into mortgages, bonds, and other forms of investment. The work of individuals like Sidney Homer and of institutions such as the Bankers Trust Company has been cited at various points in this book, but the absence of writing on short cycles in the bond market is noteworthy.

Experience has demonstrated effectively, however, that the success of a municipal bond dealer in the market must be a combination of (a) "good market judgment" concerning the daily, weekly, and longer cycles of the multitudinous supply and demand factors, and (b) close attention to the needs of specific investors for certain bonds with rather clearly defined characteristics of quality, type, maturity, couponing, nature, and region of the issuer, and all the other features that distinguish one bond from another. For the time being, given the present scope of econometric research, the power to predict small changes in the price level in the market may be limited.

C. IMPACT OF PRICE CYCLES ON CONSTRUCTION OUTLAYS

Public Facilities Financing includes a long chapter that attempts to measure the impact of interest-rate cycles on the volume of new tax-exempt issues and the volume of state and local capital outlays since the end of World War II. The first section reviews the contributions of a number of economists who have published articles on the subject in recent years; the second part is the presentation of the results of a regression analysis to interpret the record of bond sales in six-month periods. The author-researcher, Paul McGouldrick, added a technical appendix describing his model.[2]

Review of the Literature

McGouldrick's essay covered previous research on the subject. Morris (probably the author of the IBA study of cycles above) had found that rising interest rates tended to dampen the amount of construction for highways, bridges, and institutions such as hospitals and jails but did not seem to influence construction rates for educational and water and sewer projects. Upon updating Morris's construction data and substituting Sidney Homer's new-issue yield index for Moody's index of AAA bonds, McGouldrick came to feel that the linkages between yield and construction were rather tenuous in the bond markets of the 1960's. He reported that Pickering for the Federal Reserve had suggested that interest-rate fluctuations affected the time of bond sales more than capital outlays themselves and that the Ando-Brown-Adams team considered bond-market information irrelevant to local decisions concerning capital outlays (except in the field of education).

[2] JEC—*Financing* (j).

McGouldrick's Model of the Bond Market

McGouldrick's own model has two parts: the first reflects the viewpoint of public borrowers (who have to decide whether to sell bonds in order to finance construction), the second that of investors. Both groups are subject to many of the same influences, and both borrowers and lenders are always considered to be reacting to past as well as current changes in desired levels of debt and bond holdings, in a pattern similar to inventory adjustment models of the economy. The following material gives the empirical flavor but not the theoretical substance of his findings as partially reported in his article and as summarized for the Committee.

Investors' Influence is Dominant

McGouldrick interprets the combination of rising municipal bond yields and a rising volume of bond sales during the 1952–1965 period to mean that the stimulating effect of rising yields on the willingness of investors to buy bonds more than offsets the depressive effect of higher interest rates on the willingness of state and local governmental units to go into debt.

On further reflection he suggests that "borrowers are more influenced by expectations of future bond yields, while lenders are more influenced by current spreads between yields on tax-exempt municipals and yields on taxable bonds and mortgages." Although this writer believes that expectation of yield is even more important in practice for lenders than for borrowers, McGouldrick's reasons are worth noting:

> This hypothesis appears plausible on several counts. Within broad limits, both institutional and individual investors can rearrange their portfolios at their own discretion, enabling them to react quickly to new situations. On the other hand, State and local borrowers are inhibited against one form of arbitrage—selling tax-exempts and investing the proceeds in higher yielding U.S. Government securities—by the fact that they will be charged with abusing the tax exemption privilege. And while some State and local units have issued callable bonds, decisions to call or not require the formation of expectations on future interest rates just as much as do decisions on whether to postpone (or to accelerate) a bond issue for financing construction of facilities. . . .[3]

The interest rate coefficients are interpreted to the effect that State and local borrowers do form and act upon expectations of future interest rates, while buyers of new issues are more influenced by current changes in the spread between yields on municipal bonds and yields on taxable securities.

Also influencing municipal borrowing are Federal grants-in-aid, which have a positive effect, and an index of needs for new construction. The regression study found that the

[3] JEC—*Financing* (j), pp. 313–315.

supply of credit funds is positively affected by deviations in the wealth of individuals in the high brackets (measured by the ratio of the Standard & Poor's stock prices index to total wealth) and increases in the share of total wealth held in the form of time deposits at commercial banks.[4]

D. SOME MARKET ADAPTATIONS TO THE PRICE SYSTEM

Large fluctuations in price are inevitable aspects of the municipal bond system as it is now constituted. We have seen that its fluctuations in price are greater, that its investor market is highly segmented because of the special impact of the income tax system, that therefore the number and type of bonds sold are infinitely varied to attract certain classes of buyers, and that state and local governments are affected by price fluctuations as much as the dealers and investors. Now we can observe how a process of adaptation and intervention operates at many points as many different actors seek to improve their relative position. Some of the points at which these actors come into conflict are discussed in the four chapters of Part 6, which follows.

Survival under the Price System

McGouldrick shows one way the price system works: high interest rates tended to dampen the enthusiasm on the part of state and local governments to sell issues of long-term bonds in the 1952–1965 period, although the continuance of high yields since then does not seem to have limited the amount of offerings. In any case the viability of the price system is based on its ability to ration credit to borrowers or issuers and to attract buyers and dealers willing to take the risks of price changes.

On the whole, the market system seems to be viable along the lines that Sidney Homer describes in Chapter XV: (a) at a given tax level, the yield of tax-exempt bonds is almost wholly determined by the yield on taxable bonds; (b) yields on tax-exempts will always rise to reach that predetermined level; (c) fluctuations in the rate are largely explainable and increasingly predictable in terms of the flow of funds and other factors that determine the general yield structure in the market; and (d) unless an issuer is willing to pay such predetermined rates, he may as well abandon the idea of marketing a new issue of bonds to pay for construction.

The bond analyst thus confronts a market that has a sensitive mechanism for setting prices but that has proved relatively untractable with respect to predictions, as is true for the securities markets generally. He is impelled, however, to continue attempts to apply modern analytic techniques for the benefit of the underwriters and investors who employ him,

[4] JEC—*Financing*, p. 13.

and, over the years to come, as the theory and data pertaining to local government credit improve; and, as new program budgeting techniques within a system of metropolitan level reviews make forecasting of local capital outlays more reliable, his ability to forecast the supply of new issues may improve. His ability to predict demand, however, will depend upon analysis of fundamental monetary and fiscal conditions as they affect the operations of commercial banks, taxable investors, and the security markets.

4

The Next Decade

Chapter XIV   Doubling Municipal Debt

The central fact in the next decade from the viewpoint of municipal bond specialists is the Joint Economic Committee's projection that, between 1965 and 1975, the dollar amount of tax-exempt bonds outstanding will increase from $94 to $199 billion. This chapter sets such a projection into the general framework of public finance, reserving for the next chapters the discussion of the implications of the projection, especially with respect to municipal bond prices. Here we observe the relationship between bond sales and the capital outlays made by local governments, total expenditures and total revenues of local governments including amounts received from the federal government, and federal finances as a whole. The emphasis is the reverse of the usual treatment of local public finance, which often exhausts the subject before mention can be made of long-term debt issued.

A. LOCAL PUBLIC DEBT AND THE FINANCING OF CAPITAL OUTLAYS

Since the Civil War, total debt outstanding against the credit of state and local governments has risen in every decade.[1] The rate of increase was slowed down during World War I and was virtually eliminated during the 1930's, and the total amount outstanding dropped to a pre-Depression level as bonds were retired during World War II. The postwar construction boom in local public facilities, however, quickly used up the surpluses gathered during wartime and generated unprecedented quantities of new bonds, including those for projects undreamed of in earlier periods.

[1] ACIR (a), pp. 16–18.

During the postwar period (1946–1966), the Joint Economic Committee concluded that long-term borrowing financed about half of the $220 billion capital outlays by state and local governments. With historical data lacking in usable detail before the early 1950's, the Committee staff observed further that

Those who have had occasion to analyze the municipal securities market and those who have endeavored to compare statistics on municipal bond sales with State and local government debt outstanding or with capital outlays will appreciate that, while all sorts of data are available on these subjects, very little has been done to link the statistics together.[2]

Bond Sales as a Means of Financing Capital Outlays

The researchers linked municipal bond sales and capital outlays by making extensive adjustments to bond sale data collected by *The Bond Buyer* and the Investment Bankers Association, correcting for time lags, underreporting, and other peculiarities, and subtracting amounts for bond sales unrelated to capital outlays. They came up with an original series of data to represent "long-term debt issued for capital outlays." Comparison of this series with estimated capital outlays for each of the years 1958–1964 resulted in an average ratio of 50.1 per cent, that is, half of capital outlays were probably financed by borrowings.[3]

At about the same time, a study by the Construction Statistics Division of the Department of Commerce reported that about 60 per cent of public construction for state and local governments had been financed by the sale of municipal bonds; and the Investment Bankers Association suggested that future new-issue volume in the municipal bond market, other than refundings and other special types, could be estimated by applying a ratio of 50.4 per cent to the forecasts of construction volume.[4] Of course, the construction and bond sales data for these two studies are different in every year from the data in the Joint Economic Committee reports, but the differences are relatively minor and the computed results fairly good.

With regard to the construction data, the reader can observe in Figure 20 that the annual amounts of state and local construction put in place, currently in excess of $15 billion, have consistently exceeded federal construction except in wartime, but are dwarfed by the combination of residential and nonresidential construction. The Joint Economic Committee found that state and local government construction expenditures, or alternatively the amounts of construction put in place, on either a fiscal- or a calendar-year basis during the 1955–1965 decade, consistently amounted to about

[2] JEC—*Needs*, p. 5.
[3] JEC—*Needs*, p. 30 and Table B-2.
[4] Federal (f), and IBA (c).

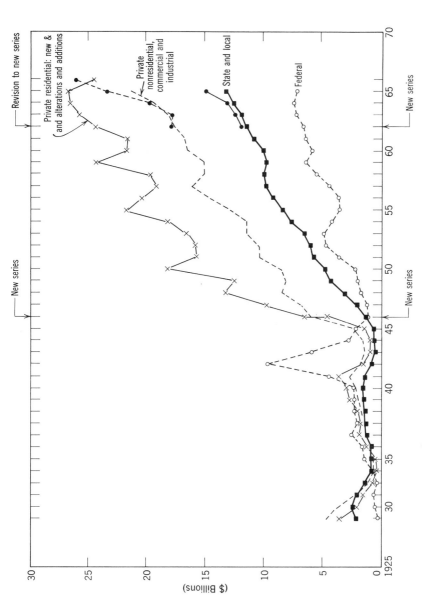

Figure 20 Value of new construction put in place, public and private, 1929–1965.

179

80 per cent of the related figures for capital outlays, with the remaining 20 per cent of "capital outlays" attributed to "equipment" and other defined items.[5] Moreover, another researcher in the same study (using slightly different figures, of course) estimated that about three-quarters of the bond sales for capital outlays during the period were initiated by local governments and one-quarter by state governments.[6] The interrelation between bond prices and the amount of construction authorized was considered in Chapter XIII above.

Projections of Capital Outlays and Debt Issued

The Joint Economic Committee's study, *State and Local Public Facility Needs and Financing,* is the most recent full-scale attempt to comprehend the trends of governmental expenditures in relation to resources, construction, and local indebtedness. It provides the kind of projections called for by the Investment Bankers Association and stands as the best set of expectations available to the bond analyst at this writing.

Annual capital outlays for structures and equipment as defined for the Joint Economic Committee study include state and local new construction plus purchases of existing structures plus net purchases of equipment less compensation for construction in process. The method of projection required a series of assumptions concerning Gross National Product, personal income, and the sources of state and local receipts (which were assumed to equal expenditures); then the outlays for structures and equipment were related to expenditures by means of linear-regression calculations.[7] In the projections:

1. Total state and local expenditures which were 7.7 per cent of GNP in 1947 and 9.6 per cent in 1962 are found to be 10.6 per cent for 1975.

2. Annual capital outlays for structures and equipment as a per cent of total expenditures for all purposes by state and local governments were found to be 16 per cent in 1947 and 29 per cent in 1962 and were held to the 29 per cent level in 1975.

The projections of capital outlays were also based on the results of an extensive survey of capital requirements over the 1965–1975 decade for all spending units—state and local agencies, private nonprofit organizations, private investor-owned companies, and, where appropriate, the federal government. Each of these groups has its own characteristic means of financing, but, as shown in Table J, state and local governments are expected to provide two-thirds (or $327.8 billion) of the $499.1 billion total.

[5] JEC—*Needs,* p. 29 and Table B-1.
[6] JEC—*Financing* (k), Table 6, p. 59.
[7] JEC—*Needs* (a)

The state and local share ranged from 15 per cent for electric and gas utilities and 30 per cent for facilities related to health to relatively higher percentages in other functional areas.

The survey covered 42 categories of facility needs clustered into the six major areas shown in Table J and identified further in Table K.

Table J   Total Capital Outlays for Public Facilities Estimated for the 1966–1975 Decade by Type of Facility, All Spending Units, and State and Local Governments

($ billions)

| | | Estimated 1966–1975 | |
| | | State and Local Governments | |
Group of Facilities	All Spending Units Total	Subtotal	Subtotal as Per Cent of Total
Water and sewer	$ 76.2	$ 56.5	74%
Electric and gas	84.9	12.8	15
Transportation	151.7	141.1	93
Education	82.2	62.0	75
Health	43.5	13.1	30
Recreational and cultural	53.1	35.0	66
Other public buildings	7.5	7.3	97
Total	$499.1	$327.8	66%

Source: JEC—*Needs*, Tables, pp. 13 and 14.

Each category constitutes a chapter in the Joint Economic Committee study. The governmental agency or private association that supplied the textual material for the specific chapter is noted in Table K, together with the dollar amount that was set down as the proportion of the total estimate for capital outlay in that category to be expended by units in the state and local government sector.

The data on capital outlays for the 1965–1975 decade were then allocated to each of the years as a basis for the calculations regarding debt to be issued by state and local governments. As noted above, bond sales were estimated to represent 50 per cent of capital outlays. The various data are shown in Table L, a summary, in effect, of the analysis which suggests a doubling of municipal debt outstanding in the decade.

Table K Type, Source, and Amount of Total Outlay, by 42 Categories, 1966–1975, for the State and Local Government Sector as Estimated by the Joint Economic Committee

Chapter in *Public Facility Needs*	Public Facility Category	Source and Author	State and Local Government Share of Estimated Capital Requirements 1966–1975 ($ millions)
BASIC COMMUNITY FACILITIES			
1.	Regional and river basin water supply systems	Corps of Engineers; Interior; Agriculture	$ 170
2.	Public water supply systems	American Waterworks Association	19,440
3.	Rural-agricultural water supply systems	Agriculture	1,100
4.	Sanitary sewer collection systems	HUD	7,750
5.	Storm sewer systems	American Public Works Association	16,000
6.	Water waste treatment plants	Interior	9,830
7.	Solid wastes collection and disposal facilities	American Public Works Association	2,170
	Subtotal, water and sewer facilities		$ 56,460
8.	Electric power	Federal Power Commission	$ 12,250
9.	Gas distribution systems	Federal Power Commission	550
	Subtotal, other utilities		$ 12,800
TRANSPORTATION FACILITIES			
10.	Highways, roads, and streets	Bureau of Public Roads	$125,650
11.	(Toll bridges, tunnels, and turnpikes) (cf. Chapter 10)	International Bridge, Tunnel and Turnpike Association	(4,000)
12.	Offstreet parking facilities	Wash., D.C. M.V. Parking Agency	2,400
13.	Urban mass transit facilities	HUD	7.600
14.	Airport facilities	Federal Aviation Agency	4,980
15.	Marine port facilities	Maritime Administration	430
	Subtotal, transportation		$141,060
EDUCATION FACILITIES			
16.	Public elementary and secondary schools	Office of Education	$ 41,800

Chapter in *Public Facility Needs*	Public Facility Category	Source and Author	State and Local Government Share of Estimated Capital Requirements 1966–1975 ($ millions)
17.	Nonpublic elementary and secondary schools	Office of Education	...
18.	(Area vocational school facilities) (cf. Chapter 16)	Office of Education	(6.300)
19.	Academic facilities for higher education	Office of Education	13,870
20.	College housing and related service facilities	HUD	6,080
21.	Educational television	Office of Education	230
	Subtotal, educational facilities		$ 61,980
HEALTH FACILITIES			
22.	Hospitals	Public Health Service	$ 3,930
23.	Clinics and other outpatient facilities	Public Health Service	810
24.	Long-term care facilities	Public Health Service	1,060
25.	Community mental health centers	Public Health Service	1,470
26.	Facilities for the mentally retarded	Public Health Service	1,070
27.	Health research facilities	Public Health Service	1,920
28.	Medical and other health schools	Public Health Service	2,880
	Subtotal, health facilities		$ 13,140
RECREATIONAL AND CULTURAL FACILITIES			
29.	State and federal outdoor recreation facilities	Interior	$ 4,400
30. s	Urban local outdoor recreation facilities	HUD	17,600
31.	Rural outdoor recreational facilities	Agriculture	. . .
32.	Neighborhood centers for recreation, etc.	National Social Welfare Assembly	. . .
33.	Arenas, auditoriums, exhibition halls	Int'l. Assoc. of Auditorium Managers	7,200
34.	Theaters and community art centers	Nat'l Council on the Arts	3,620
35.	Museums	Am. Assoc. of Museums	270
36.	Public libraries	Office of Education	1,910
	Subtotal, recreation and cultural		$ 35,000

183

Table K (continued)

Chapter in *Public Facility Needs*	Public Facility Category	Source and Author	State and Local Government Share of Estimated Capital Requirements 1966–1975 ($ millions)
OTHER PUBLIC BUILDINGS			
37.	Residential group care facilities for children	Children's Bureau, HEW	$ 560
38.	Armories	Dept. of Defense	150
39.	Jails and prisons	FBI	920
40.	Fire stations	Int'l. Assoc. of Fire Chiefs	1,370
41.	Public office and court buildings	American Public Works Association	3,250
42.	Publicly owned industrial plants	Investment Bankers Assoc.	. . .
	Subtotal, other public buildings		$ 6,250
GRAND TOTAL			$326,690

Source: JEC—*Needs,* derived from Table 2. Total varies from $327.8 billion total because of rounding and because of elimination of approximately $1 billion for police stations.

More on Financing by Type of Project

The bond analyst is necessarily curious as to the role tax-exempt bonds play in the financing of any given category of public capital investment and the extent to which federal subsidies stimulate such construction and such bond sales. The data are difficult to correlate because of the differences in definitions and the lack of certain data in earlier years, but we have matched four of the Joint Economic Committee's estimates of construction (which go back to 1952) with *The Bond Buyer's* estimates of bond financings by purpose, a series they have maintained since 1959. Inspection of Figure 21 suggests that bonds in recent years have financed a large proportion of capital outlays for schools, water supply and sewer improvements, and housing and urban renewal programs. Bonds for highways, bridge, and tunnel projects, however, have represented only a minor portion of outlays for highways.

In contrast, federal assistance as detailed in Table M has been inconsequential to date in financing education and sewerage facilities, more significant in financing health and airport facilities, and very important in

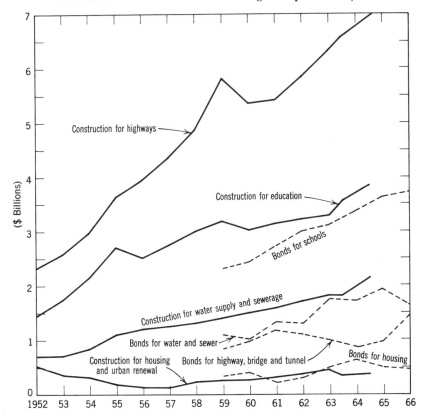

Figure 21 Construction expenditures of state and local governments, 1952 to 1964–1965, and new bond issues by function, 1959–1966.

financing highways and urban renewal projects. Thus only highway construction appears to have high levels of both bond financing and federal assistance; a more typical situation is to find the burden placed upon either local government or the federal government, although the long-term trend may well be in the direction of greater federal support.

Bond sales and amounts provided by the federal government have both been rising faster in recent years than have the capital outlays of state and local governments. In general, total expenditures and capital outlays by state and local governments have risen at the same rate, except in the 1958 recession when expenditures continued to rise but capital outlays were cut. Federal contributions to state and local outlays, however, were increasing rapidly during the recession but were cut back in 1961; since then they have continued to increase faster than outlays.

As for bonds, new issues related to outlays fell off between 1958 and 1960, and thereafter increased more rapidly than outlays until 1963, when they

Table L   Debt Issued and Outstanding, and Total Capital Outlays, for All State and Local Governments, Estimated 1956–1965, Projected 1966–1975

	Long-Term Debt Outstanding: Year-End Balance	Net Long-Term Debt Issued	Total New Debt Issued	Estimated Capital Outlays	Housing and Urban Renewal
	(data in millions)				
	(A)	(B)	(C)	(D)	(E)
1956	$44,800	$ 6,811	$ 7,340	$12,173	$260
1957	49,400	7,321	7,021	13,357	330
1958	53,900	8,006	7,195	14,489	380
1959	58,800	8,051	7,840	14,983	470
1960	63,700	8,018	8,085	14,928	580
1961	68,700	8,738	8,366	16,261	700
1962	75,700	9,680	10,651	17,251	810
1963	82,500	10,604	11,373	19,029	780
1964	88,000	11,246	10,252	20,658	760
1965	93,900	12,376	11,158	22,843	780 est.
	(data in billions)				
	(F)	(G)	(H)	(I)	(J)
1966	$108.5	$14.4	$14.2	$25.5	$0.8
1967	117.2	15.1	14.9	26.9	0.9
1968	126.2	15.9	15.7	28.3	0.9
1969	135.5	16.7	16.6	29.8	1.0
1970	145.2	17.7	17.6	31.6	1.0
1971	155.2	18.8	18.6	33.5	1.1
1972	165.5	19.7	19.5	35.1	1.1
1973	176.4	22.0	20.8	37.4	1.2
1974	187.5	22.0	21.8	39.0	1.3
1975	198.8	22.8	22.7	40.7	1.3

Source: *Public Facility Financing:* pp. 33–35: Column entries above are from Tables B–1, B–3, and B–4 in the Summary, as follows: (A) B–3/5; (B) B–3/9; (C) B–3/8; (D) B–1/6; (E) B–1/7; (F) B–4/11; (G) B–4/5; (H) B–4/6; (I) B–4/1; (J) B–4/2.

dipped before resuming a rate more in line with the growth in outlays; approximately the same relationship holds for the total new issue market.

These relationships are revealed by Figure 22, in which, for the 1956–1965 period, state and local capital outlays have been compared to (a) total expenditures by state and local governments, (b) total federal intergovernmental expenditures related to capital outlays, (c) total new bonds issued, and total bonds related to capital outlays, all of the data in 1958 constant

Table M   Federal Intergovernmental Expenditure in Relation to State and Local Expenditure, by Function, 1952–1965

| | Per Cent of State and Local Capital Outlays Financed by Federal Government | | |
	1952–1957 (6 Years)	1958–1963/1964 (7 Years)	1964/1964 (1 Year)
	(%)	(%)	(%)
Total	8.5	19.6	24.2
Highways	16.0	39.5	47.8
Housing and urban renewal	16.3	47.5	85.0
Health and hospitals	11.7	15.6	32.6
Sewerage	na	5.0	6.8
Airports	22.6	22.2	27.2
Education	3.4	1.4	0.6
All other	na	a	0.9

a: very small amounts; na: data not available.

Source: JEC—*Financing*, "State and Local Government Financing of Capital Outlays: 1946–65" (Manvel), from Table 7, p. 61.

dollars. Since the graph is on "log-log" paper, the graphs would be straight lines at a 45 degree angle if these various series were changing at the same rate; a line moving more sharply than 45 degrees from lower left to upper right is increasing faster than the capital outlay series; a line moving from upper left to lower right indicates a decrease relative to an increase in capital outlays.

Projections of bond sales, capital expenditures, and federal programs, in summary, are based upon a variety of assumptions and upon data that are suggestive but not often accurate. Nevertheless, the Joint Economic Committee study and other research materials are valuable and acceptable to the extent that the system continues relatively unchanged in terms of tax exemption, economic progress, rate of urbanization, pattern of municipal finance, and price structure in the market, to name a few of the assumed conditions. There can be little doubt that the "needs" study reflects a solid demand for capital facilities. There can be more doubt about the willingness and ability of local governments to undertake the projects forecast, and even greater doubt about the methods by which the federal government will attempt to lighten the burden. The next section, however, provides an opportunity to consider the role of the federal government in greater detail and to view the relationship between the local public economy and the national economy.

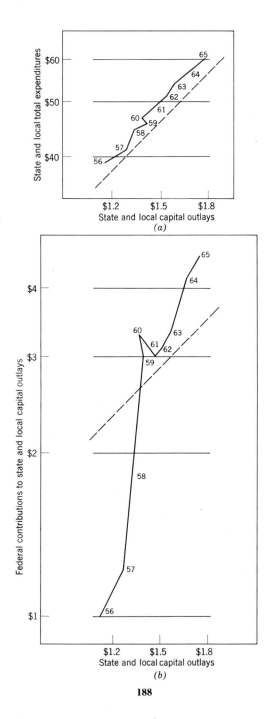

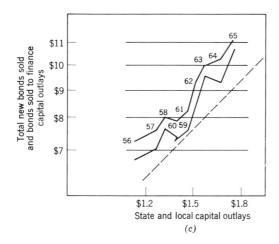

(c)

	State and Local		Federal Contributions	New Bond Issues	
	Total Expenditures	Capital Outlays		Total	For Capital Outlays
	(In Billions of 1958 Dollars)				
	(1)	(2)	(3)	(4)	(5)
1956	$38.4	$11.5	$1.0	$ 7.2	$ 6.7
1957	40.6	12.2	1.2	7.5	7.0
1958	44.0	13.2	1.8	8.0	7.7
1959	45.6	13.7	3.0	7.9	7.3
1960	46.9	13.6	3.2	7.7	7.2
1961	49.5	14.5	3.0	8.3	7.6
1962	50.9	14.9	3.1	9.2	8.4
1963	53.4	15.6	3.3	9.9	9.5
1964	56.4	16.6	4.1	10.2	9.3
1965	59.1	17.6	4.5	11.2	10.4

Source: JEC—*Financing:* Columns (1) and (2) from Table 1, p. 54; Column (3) from Table 7, p. 61; Columns (4) and (5) from Tables B2(8) and B3(9), p. 34.

Figure 22 Relative rate of growth of federal contribution to state and local programs, compared to state and local government total expenditures and capital outlays and sales of new bond issues, 1956–1965. (Data in 1958 constant dollars.)

B. ECONOMIC GROWTH AND THE REVENUE GAP

Because municipal debt in the next decade or so will increase tremendously (even if it does not exactly double), we need to explore the implications for the market of expanded federal assistance and of the role that state and local finance plays in a national economy still subject to fluctuations. These comments serve as a partial critique of the Joint Economic Committee approach and as an introduction to the topics of price, yield and interest rate in Chapter XV.

Local Public Needs and the Urban Crisis

The staff of the Subcommittee on Economic Progress of the Joint Economic Committee that prepared the report concluded that the state and local government portion of estimated public facility needs would not require any major alterations of state and local fiscal resources in the 1965–1975 period, and it also found its estimates in line with two other authoritative studies along similar lines; [8] their readers were urged, however, to consider the possibility that

(a) Our estimates of public facility requirements are too conservative or (b) that the availability of future fiscal resources of State and local governments may be underestimated by those who suggest reallocation of resources, or (c) that public facility capital expenditures is only one element in a growing pattern of required public services, and that services, rather than facilities, will make the biggest demands in the future.[9]

It is worth mentioning that the *State and Local Public Facility Needs* report projects but does not investigate national needs for housing and urban renewal, and barely refers to the physical and social needs of the denizens of the core cities in the major metropolitan areas. These problem areas were not then seen as special situations that might require dramatic activity leading to more facilities and acceleration of the expected rate of investment, nor does there appear to have been communication with the Advisory Commission on Intergovernmental Relations and its associated ranks of urban and metropolitan economists and planners. The *Needs* text, however, does include the following understatement:

No definitive projections of Federal grants-in-aid to State and local governments can be made at this time because the Federal programs are in a state of flux. The expanded operations in Vietnam are now a factor in limiting the Federal funds allocated to State

[8] Readings (n).
[9] JEC—*Needs*, p. 18.

and local bodies. When the activity there quiesces or stops entirely, the Government will proceed to implement fully its domestic programs.[10]

From the point of view of the municipal bond market, the omission of the housing and urban renewal category from the consideration of public facility needs and financing is serious, for as Figure 21 suggests, bonds sold for that purpose have become a most important component of the business. From the point of view of metropolitan planners, moreover, the coming years must see the merger of housing policies with programs for new and improved transportation systems, educational networks, and employment centers if the nation is going to implement either its social goals, primarily with respect to the Negroes and the disadvantaged segments of the population, or its efficiency goals concerning the operation of the metropolis as a desirable, well-functioning environment for the majority of people who live in the United States.[11]

Municipal Finance in the Prewar Years

Although the problems of the 1960's and the 1970's are qualitatively different from those encountered in the middle of the Depression, the following quotation from a chapter entitled "Fiscal Perversity in Boom and Depression" in the Hanson-Perloff book provides a perspective that should not be lost, since (as conservatives enjoy pointing out to their juniors) economic conditions may not always be favorable and municipal bond issuers may once again face financial embarrassment:

The taxing, borrowing, and spending activities of the state and local governments collectively have typically run counter to an economically sound fiscal policy. These governmental units have usually followed the swings of the business cycle, from crest to trough, spending and building in prosperity periods and contracting their activities during depression. In the boom of the late twenties, they added to the disposable income of the community, and bid up prices and building costs in large-scale construction activities. In the depressed thirties, the fiscal policies of the governments exerted a deflationary rather than an expansionary effect on the economy: expenditures, and especially construction outlays, were severely reduced, borrowing was restricted, and taxes weighing on consumption were substantially increased. . . .

The devasting effects of business depression on state and local finances can readily be seen from the following: tax collections of all state and local units fell from $6,798 million in 1930 to $5,715 million in 1933; tax delinquency for 150 of the largest cities rose from 10.1 per cent in 1930 to 26.3 per cent in 1933; and the proportion of state and local bond sales bearing a rate of interest in excess of 5 per cent rose from 6.5 per cent of total sales in 1930 to 37.9 per cent of sales in 1932. . . .

It is evident that the poorer areas of the country cannot finance an adequate level of services from their own resources, nor can they maintain their expenditures in depression. It is in the areas where purchasing power is characteristically at the lowest level

[10] JEC—*Needs*, p. 47.

[11] Federal (g).

that the non-federal units can contribute least to the income flow of the community when such contribution is most needed, namely, in periods of depression.

Property values dropped considerably during the depression. . . . This meant a contraction in the base of the most important local revenue producer, the property tax. Tax delinquencies rose precipitously and further restricted the tax base. The decline in property values forced a contraction in debt margins (almost all localities are limited legally in their borrowing to a fixed percentage of assessed valuation of the property within their jurisdiction), and undermined the credit standing of localities, so that many of them could not borrow even within their restricted debt margins.

Even the largest cities had serious difficulties in obtaining funds. In New York City, for example, property valuations declined from $19.6 billion in 1932 to $16.6 billion in 1935. Tax collections declined from 88 per cent of levies in 1924 to 22 per cent in 1933. Coupled with this unsound financial background was an increasing relief load. Moreover, the city had a vast amount of short-term paper which it found impossible to meet or fund. The administration was confronted with periodic crises whenever a new series fell due.

The solution of their difficulties lay in the Bankers Agreement, which involved budget-balancing provisions, tax-delinquency policy, tax-collection procedure, and further economies. The state legislature reduced the mandatory scale of wages for the teachers so that the city could more successfully complete the deflationary policy imposed upon it.

This was the price many cities had to pay in order to fund their short-term obligations or receive temporary credit. In Detroit relief was slashed in half, since loans could not be placed unless the city finances were improved. The experience of Chicago was similar. Thus, in many instances, credit could be obtained only upon a deflationary reduction in local expenditures.[12]

The Postwar Economy

The experts who have observed the post-war interaction between the national and the local economy agree with Hanson and Perloff that the operations of local governments still tend to magnify booms and to suffer in depressions (when the need for funds is greatest), but they appear to feel that the aggregated local economy (the accumulated totals of revenues, expenditures, and debt transactions from thousands of individual governmental units, each making its own budgetary decisions) appears to operate more satisfactorily and that the capital requirements for local public facilities can be furnished without undue strain, however complicated may be the process of distributing the necessary resources to specific localities. The Council of Economic Advisors holds that increased governmental expenditures—both purchases of goods and services and transfer payments—currently contribute to economic stability. The Council notes further that government outlays do not participate in the downward spiral of recession because the borrowing capacity of the federal government allows it to maintain its spending in the face of declining income receipts, while state and local governments have been able to maintain their growing

[12] Hanson-Perloff, pp. 49, 51, 57.

spending programs relatively unaffected during the mild postwar recessions. Social insurance and national defense have added especially to the postwar totals of federal outlays, and state and local outlays have been rising rapidly "in an effort to catch up with neglected needs and to keep up with the desires of a wealthier society for improved public services." [13]

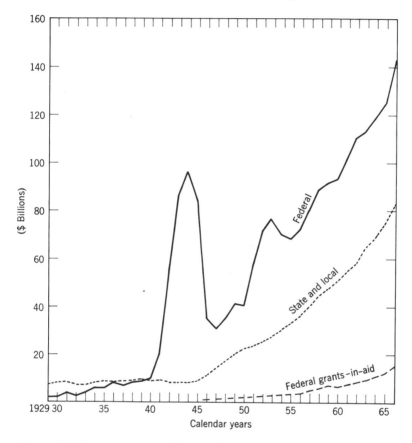

Figure 23 Government expenditures, federal and state/local, for calendar years 1929–1966, and federal grants-in-aid, 1946–1966.

Figure 23 shows total federal expenditures (still including the transfer payments that consist of Social Security benefits, interest paid, and various net subsidy payments), and the subtotal for federal grants-in-aid to state and local governments since 1929. The steady growth of these total amounts is a well-known phenomenon.

[13] Federal (a), 1966, pp. 174–175.

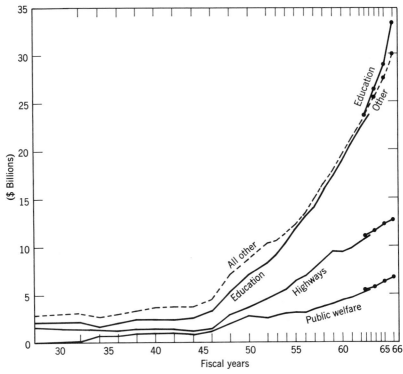

Figure 24 General expenditures by function, state and local governments, fiscal years (Census data), 1927 to 1965–1966.

State and Local Expenditure Patterns

With the strengthening of the national economy and the enlargement of the role of government generally, state and local expenditures rose impressively, especially with respect to education and highways, as shown on Figure 24. Unfortunately the data are unavailable in finer detail. The source of the data for Figure 24 is Table N, which reports that state and local governments in 1962 expended $60.2 billion for a mixture of current and capital items.

Taking total direct expenditures for 1962 (which consist of the $60.2 billion general expenditures mentioned above plus $10.3 billion for utilities and all other categories) as 100 per cent, the Census reported in another study covering all state and local governments that current operation constituted 60.6 per cent of total expenditures in 1962, capital outlay constituted another 23.8 per cent, interest on debt was 3.4 per cent, and 12.2 per cent was for other expenditures.[14]

[14] Federal (h).

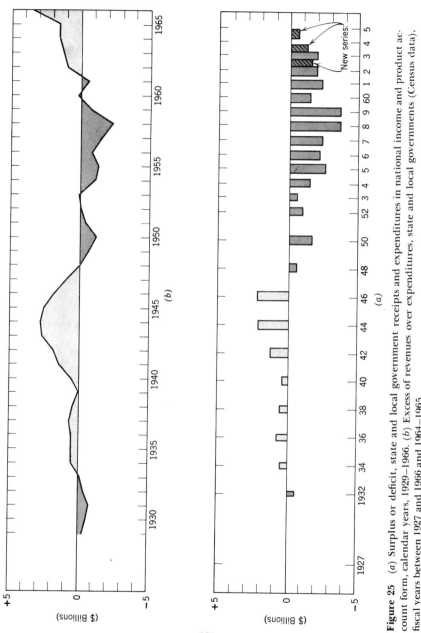

Figure 25 (*a*) Surplus or deficit, state and local government receipts and expenditures in national income and product account form, calendar years, 1929–1966. (*b*) Excess of revenues over expenditures, state and local governments (Census data), fiscal years between 1927 and 1966 and 1964–1965.

195

Table N State and Local Government Revenues and Expenditures, Selected Fiscal Years, 1927–1966
($ Millions)

	General Revenues by Source [b]							General Expenditures by Function [b]				
Fiscal Year [a]	Total	Property Taxes	Sales and Gross Receipts Taxes	Individual Income Taxes	Corporation Net Income Taxes	Revenue from Federal Government	All Other Revenue [c]	Total	Education	Highways	Public Welfare	All other [d]
1927	7,271	4,730	470	70	92	116	1,793	7,210	2,235	1,809	151	3,015
1932	7,267	4,487	752	74	79	232	1,643	7,765	2,311	1,741	444	3,269
1934	7,678	4,076	1,008	80	49	1,016	1,449	7,181	1,831	1,509	889	2,952
1936	8,395	4,093	1,484	153	113	948	1,604	7,644	2,177	1,425	827	3,215
1938	9,228	4,440	1,794	218	165	800	1,811	8,757	2,491	1,650	1,069	3,547
1940	9,609	4,430	1,982	224	156	945	1,872	9,229	2,638	1,573	1,156	3,862
1942	10,418	4,537	2,351	276	272	858	2,123	9,190	2,586	1,490	1,225	3,889
1944	10,908	4,604	2,289	342	451	954	2,269	8,863	2,793	1,200	1,133	3,737
1946	12,356	4,986	2,986	422	447	855	2,661	11,028	3,356	1,672	1,409	4,591
1948	17,250	6,126	4,442	543	592	1,861	3,685	17,684	5,379	3,036	2,099	7,170
1950	20,911	7,349	5,154	788	593	2,486	4,541	22,787	7,177	3,803	2,940	8,867
1952	25,181	8,652	6,357	998	846	2,566	5,763	26,098	8,318	4,650	2,788	10,342
1953	27,307	9,375	6,927	1,065	817	2,870	6,252	27,910	9,390	4,987	2,914	10,619
1954	29,012	9,967	7,276	1,127	778	2,966	6,897	30,701	10,557	5,527	3,060	11,557
1955	31,073	10,735	7,643	1,237	744	3,131	7,584	33,724	11,907	6,452	3,168	12,197
1956	34,667	11,749	8,691	1,538	890	3,335	8,465	36,711	13,220	6,953	3,139	13,399
1957	38,164	12,864	9,467	1,754	984	3,843	9,252	40,375	14,134	7,816	3,485	14,940

1958	41,219	14,047	9,829	1,759	1,018	4,865	9,699	44,851	15,919	8,567	3,818	16,547
1959	45,306	14,983	10,437	1,994	1,001	6,377	10,516	48,887	17,283	9,592	4,136	17,876
1960	50,505	16,405	11,849	2,463	1,180	6,954	11,634	51,876	18,719	9,428	4,404	19,324
1961	54,037	18,002	12,463	2,613	1,266	7,131	12,563	56,201	20,574	9,844	4,720	21,063
1962	58,252	19,054	13,494	3,037	1,308	7,871	13,489	60,206	22,216	10,357	5,084	22,549
1963	62,890	20,089	14,456	3,269	1,505	8,722	14,850	64,816	23,776	11,136	5,481	24,423
1962–63 [e]	62,269	19,833	14,446	3,267	1,505	8,663	14,555	63,977	23,729	11,150	5,420	23,678
1963–64 [e]	68,443	21,241	15,762	3,791	1,695	10,002	15,952	69,302	26,286	11,664	5,766	25,586
1964–65 [e]	74,000	22,583	17,118	4,090	1,929	11,029	17,251	74,546	28,563	12,221	6,315	27,447
1965–66 [e]	83,036	24,670	19,085	4,760	2,038	13,120	19,363	82,843	33,287	12,770	6,757	30,029

[a] Fiscal years not the same for all governments. See footnote e.

[b] Excludes revenues or expenditures of publicly owned utilities and liquor stores, and of insurance-trust activities. Intergovernmental receipts and payments between State and local governments are also excluded.

[c] Includes licenses and other taxes and charges and miscellaneous revenues.

[d] Includes expenditures for health, hospitals, police, local fire protection, natural resources, sanitation, housing and urban renewal, local parks and recreation, general control, financial administration, interest on general debt, and other unallocable expenditures.

[e] Data for fiscal year ending in the 12-month period through June 30. Data for 1963 and earlier years include local government amounts grouped in terms of fiscal years ended during the particular calendar year.

Note.—Data are not available for intervening years.

Source: Economic Report of the President, 1968, Table B-68

Revenue Gap Cycles

State and local governments operated with a surplus in some years and deficits in others, as shown by data from the national income accounts, which cover governmental purchases of goods and services and payment of interest but which exclude transfer payments. For each calendar year between 1929 and 1966, this comparison between total receipts and total expenditures in the national income and product accounts is charted in Figure 25a, and it is easy to observe that early in the Depression, state and local governments turned conservative, kept within their budgets, and either paid off debt or accumulated surplus funds (as they were additionally encouraged and even required to do during World War II). By the early 1960's they were in a surplus position again.

Whereas the national income series in the *Economic Report of the President* is a set of compatible estimates and derived data for every calendar year, the Census Bureau sets out annually to enumerate and add up the separate local government accounts; its results are on a fiscal-year basis, although there is little uniformity among local governments as to the fiscal-year basis used. The data were collected in 1902, 1913, 1922, and 1927 and then every second year beginning in 1932 until 1952, after which (in recognition of the increased importance of the local government sector for national economic reports) the series was put on an annual basis. Beginning in 1962, the "year" into which the Census put all local reports ending within a given year was shifted from a calendar year to a fiscal year ending on June 30; thus the reports used to be dated 1961, 1962, 1963; they now read Fiscal 1962–1963, 1963–1964, as yet another hurdle for the systems analyst. Table N shows the Census data for general (that is, excluding utilities, and so forth) revenue by source and expenditures by function.

The Census excludes from its annual tabulations for revenues and expenditures all data pertaining to publicly owned utilities (electric power, gas, water supply), to pension and insurance-trust activities, and to intergovernmental receipts and payments among state and local governments. Its totals are thus somewhat smaller than those in the national income accounts. As charted in Figure 25b, the gaps between revenues and expenditures as reported by Census indicate that since the end of World War II, state and local governments have been paying out more than they have been receiving, the deficits showing dramatically the effect of borrowing for capital investment.

State and Local Revenues

Prosperity and economic growth have given an upward tendency for all sources of revenue for state and local governments, plainly seen in Figure

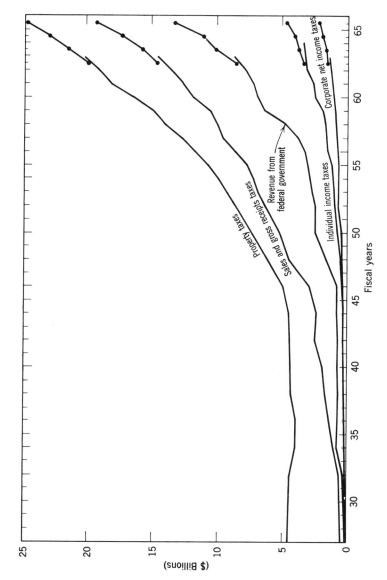

Figure 26 General revenues by source, state and local governments, fiscal years (Census data), 1927 to 1965–1966.

199

26, but a great deal has had to be written about the limits of revenue sources available to them. In the past half-century the reliance of local governments upon the property tax has diminished significantly, although between 1952 and 1962 the rate of change was trifling; during those latter years property taxes as a per cent of total general revenue for state and local governments dropped from 34.4 to 32.7 per cent, a minor change largely accounted for by the relative increase in revenue from the federal government.[15] The Advisory Commission on Intergovernmental Relations has thoroughly explored the ways the states can improve the operation of the property tax function in terms of collection and assessment and has investigated the bases upon which determinations of local fiscal capacity (ability to raise revenue) and tax effort (willingness to do so) can be made, so that distributions of federal grants-in-aid can be equitable among the several states.[16]

Revenues by Type of Government

General revenues ($50.4 billion) and federal grants ($7.9 billion) by type of government added together in Table O equal the total given in Table N for total general revenues for state and local governments. Total revenues of $69.4 billion in Table O includes all the other sources of revenue omitted in Table N. The breakdown of this total by type of government indicates that the state governments by themselves receive $37.6 billion or almost 55 per cent of all state and local revenues. The states also account for the lion's share of insurance trust revenue, almost half of the general revenue derived from taxes and charges, and none of the utility revenue.

Within the local government group, school districts, counties, and municipalities, in that order, are the major recipients of intergovernmental grants, which come overwhelmingly from the federal government via the states (with municipalities getting a slight edge on the federal grants that bypass the states). Utilities are primarily affairs of the municipalities directly, rather than operations of special districts.

Revenue by Region

The distribution of general revenue by region is shown in the chart prepared for the *Compendium of Government Finances 1962* and reproduced as Figure 27. By relating general revenue to personal income, the analyst can gain some insights regarding tax effort and fiscal capacity that have been developed by the Advisory Commission. Taxes per $1000 of personal income are relatively high in the West, and, in addition, the West obtains

[15] Federal (h).
[16] ACIR (g).

Table O   Revenues by Type of Local Government, 1962

($Billions)

	Total Revenues	Intergovern-mental Revenues			Revenues from Own Sources			
		Federal	State	Local	Total	General Revenues	Utilities	Insurance Trusts, etc.
State and local								
governments	$69.4	$7.9	$ ...	$ ...	$61.6	$50.4	$4.0	$5.9
States	37.6	7.1	...	0.3	30.1	23.7	...	5.3
Local govern-								
ments—total	43.1	0.8	10.9	...	30.5	26.7	4.0	0.6
Counties	8.7	0.1	3.1	0.1	5.4	5.2	a	0.1
Municipalities	16.8	0.3	2.1	0.2	14.1	10.4	3.1	0.5
Townships	1.7	a	0.3	a	1.3	1.3	a	a
School districts	14.2	0.2	5.3	0.3	8.4	8.4	...	a
Special districts	2.6	0.2	a	0.2	2.2	1.4	0.8	a

a: Very small amount
Source: Federal (h): *Compendium of Governments*, p. 27, Table 1.

relatively large amounts of federal grants and other types of revenue. There are substantial intraregional differences, some states showing much greater tax efforts than others. The rankings, of course, would change if personal income and revenue sources were translated into per-capita amounts or were subjected to the complex formulas proposed as the basis for revenue sharing with the federal government or for grants-in-aid under various federal programs of assistance to state and local governments.

C. SUMMARY

In the first section of this chapter the projections of capital outlays by state and local governments in response to calculated needs were reviewed, and it was noted that both bond sales and federal contributions were increasing at somewhat faster rates than capital outlays. Bond financing and federal support play a vital role in almost every category of local construction; such outlays are closely correlated with total local expenditures, and bonds finance on the average one-half of the capital costs. The projections, of course, are subject to upward revision as the nation faces its urban problems.

In the second part we considered state and local finance as a whole and in terms of the national economy. Facing the urban crisis and ending the Vietnam war will increase state and local opportunities and encourage greater federal participation, whereas economic depression (deemed unlikely by the prognosticators) would again deflate the local public econ-

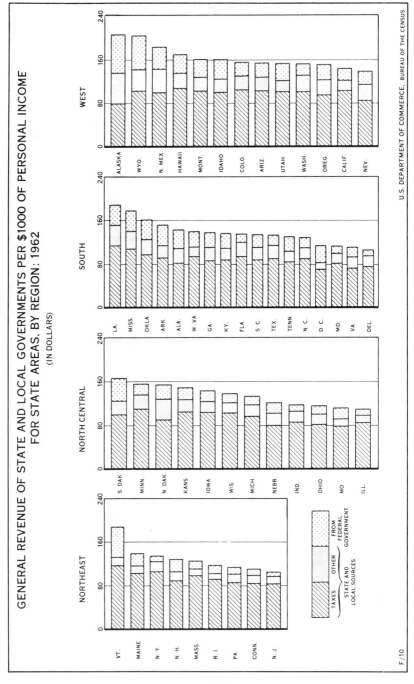

Figure 27 General revenue of state and local governments per $1000 of personal income, for state areas, by region, 1962.

omy. The assumption is widely made that the federal government would take quick action to prevent the deflationary impact of reduced state and local expenditures and to support the credit of municipal borrowers.

Both the revenues and the expenditures of state and local governments have increased regularly during the postwar period. A significant gap appeared during recent years when local governments were catching up with expenditures postponed during the Depression and World War II, were building modern metropolises, and expanding services, but there is some evidence that the size of the gap is diminishing as property tax revenues continue to grow and new sources of revenue are exploited. However comforting the overall picture is, always assuming a strong economy, there remain the serious problems beyond the scope of this book concerning the distribution of revenues to those local governments (largely in central cities) incurring exceptionally heavy social responsibilities while their fiscal capacities diminish relative to their needs.

Future Possibilities

Thus two great issues remain essentially unsolved as the municipal bond market moves into the 1970's: (a) how should capital outlays be financed, especially by municipal governments with an uncertain fiscal capacity in the event of unfavorable economic conditions but with heavy demand for capital investment as a result of suburban growth and the expectation of greater amounts and higher quality of public services; and (b) what would be the effect on particular communities if the bonds that might have to be sold to finance capital improvements were no longer tax-exempt.

If the total amount of municipal debt doubles as projected, the analysis of bond quality will become increasingly complex. The market values of the bonds issued will, of course, reflect the relative interest rates which state and local governments will have to pay on borrowed funds, but such rates will become increasingly sensitive to federal policies concerning state and local finance generally and communities with low fiscal capacity in particular. Finally, although the Joint Economic Committee was forced to assume that the market would accept a doubling of the amount of municipal debt at prevailing prices and yields, the subject of interest rates and yields as treated in the next chapter is an essential but occasionally neglected component of an overall survey of state and local finance. Although current interest is an insignificant portion of local expenditures, bond issues cannot be sold at all unless state and local governments agree to pay the interest cost determined by the market. The doubling of municipal debt projected is therefore more dependent on acceptance by the bond market than on recognition of the needs of state and local governments.

Chapter XV The Decline and Fall of Municipal Bond Prices

Practically every observer of the municipal bond market, including this writer, expects the relative price level for tax-exempt bonds to continue to fall during the next decade. The reader should recall that municipal securities will become less attractive to investors, and thus lower in price, if ratings become standardized, if tax exemption is eliminated, and if the expected doubling of outstanding municipal debt exceeds the willingness of commercial banks to absorb the volume allocated to that sector of demand.

This chapter therefore begins with an examination of past, present, and future relationships between the yields or interest rates for tax-exempt and fully taxable securities. The discussion of these relative price levels is to be sharply distinguished from a discussion of the rise and fall of the general interest rate applicable to all financial markets and considered to be a function of general economic, monetary, and fiscal expectations.

Two other aspects of the relative price level are also of special interest and are taken up in the latter sections of this chapter: the relatively large short-term fluctuations in price that are characteristic of the tax-exempt market, and the differentials in price for different quality grades of tax-exempt bonds at various points in time.

A. TAX-EXEMPT BOND YIELDS—PAST, PRESENT, FUTURE

The great question for the industry is to ascertain how far the municipal bond price level must fall, or alternatively how high yields must rise, to attract the group of upper-middle-income investors who are seen as the last best hope for increasing the volume of demand for bonds as a countervailing force to the overwhelming dominance of the commercial banks on the demand side.

In fact, municipal bond prices have typically appeared to be too high in recent years to attract a sufficient number of nonbank buyers. Frequently new bond issues have been overpriced in competitive bidding, and, to make sales, the underwriters have had to drop the price in order to raise the yield. Since in every securities market there is always a buyer if the price is right, the dealers talk about the "yield buyers" who wait in the wings for such buying opportunities. The fire and casualty companies, trust officers, and wealthy individual investors are in the general category of "yield buyers."

Lower price levels and higher yields, of course, in addition to generating additional demand, have at least two major side effects: (a) holders of outstanding bonds are displeased because the values of their portfolios are thereupon diminished; and (b) some communities may defer issuing new bonds because of the relatively higher cost being incurred, a response, however, that helps stabilize the price level by reducing the pressure caused by an oversupply of new bonds coming to market.

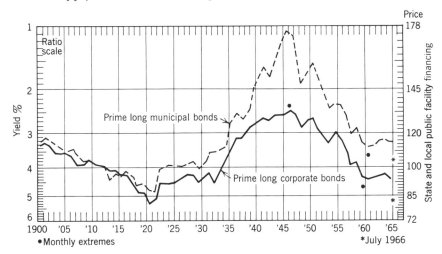

Figure 28 Prime long municipal and corporate bonds; inverted yields and index prices for fixed maturity noncallable 30-year 4 per cent bonds, 1900–1965.

A crucial factor is the relationship of municipal bond prices to prices of fully taxable bonds of comparable quality under the prevailing tax level. Figure 28 compares annual average yields (or prices) for prime 30-year municipal and 30-year corporate bonds from 1900 to mid-1966. The widening spread between the two indices after 1913 as the income tax took effect, and the narrowing spread as the volume of bonds issued grew in the postwar years are two effects that can be seen.

The Joint Economic Committee staff, having set forth capital requirements for state and local governments that would double municipal debt during the 1965–1975 decade (as described in Chapter XIV), concluded that long-term borrowing for those purposes could be

successfully financed by capital market resources, if commercial banks continue to acquire most of the municipal securities generated. However, if for any reason there is a slowdown in commercial bank asset expansion or if commercial banks find alternative investments more attractive, then a shortage of credit resources for State and local government debt financing seems likely to develop. . . . Such a shortage could be alleviated by increasing the yield on tax-exempt municipal securities to a ratio higher than the current 75 per cent of the yield on taxable securities, say to 80–90 per cent.[1]

Let it be said that commercial banks are going to be hard put to absorb their allotted two-thirds share of all new tax-exempt issues in the 1965–1975 decade. It is therefore important to review in detail the Joint Economic Committee's thinking, which was strongly influenced by an essay entitled "Factors Determining Municipal Bond Yields" submitted by Sidney Homer, an historian of interest rates and a partner in a leading bond firm, Salomon Brothers & Hutzler. His discussion of the ratio between corporate and tax-exempt yields is considered in the sections below.[2]

Ratio of Corporate and Tax-Exempt Yields

Homer conceives of yield on new issues of municipal bonds at any given time as being largely the result of (a) prevailing yields of taxable corporate bonds, *plus* (b) the demand for such bonds by investor groups. Such demand is determined, in his mind, by (a) investors' income tax rates, and (b) the flow of investible funds into their hands. Moreover, as he says, "municipal yields adjust to taxable yields."

The changing relationship between tax-exempt and taxable yields can be seen in the diagram we prepared from Homer's data (Figure 29). The nontaxable/taxable ratio is shown for every year during the 1900–1965 period. The explanation of the graph is the story told below of the municipal bond market in the twentieth century, a story that interweaves the two major themes: income tax policy and the availability of investor funds. The taxable yield referred to is for "long-term prime corporate" bonds on a pretax basis.

History of Yields in the Twentieth Century

In the pre–World War I years the municipal bond yields were about the same as corporate bond yields, with the ratio being over 100 per cent as the income tax amendment was in the process of adoption. After 1913 the effect of income taxes can be seen as the ratio begins a decline through the years to 1945.

[1] JEC—*Financing*, p. 22.
[2] JEC—*Financing* (1).

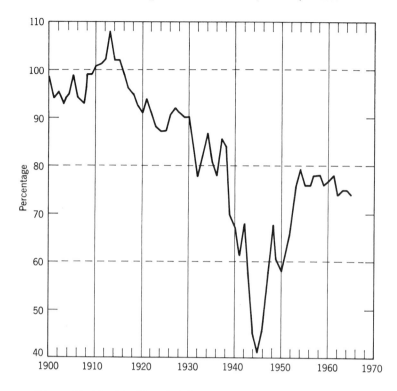

Figure 29 Municipal bond yields as a percentage of corporate (pretax) yields, 1900–1965.

As a tax rate increases, the *after-tax* return or yield of a taxable bond is lowered, and the ratio between the *pretax* corporate yield and the tax-exempt yield necessarily falls. Yields move to the point at which, with all other factors held constant, an investor would receive the same after-tax yield whether he held taxable or tax-exempt bonds. When the ratio between the two yields falls below this point of indifference, municipal yields are effectively lower than corporate yields, indicating a strong investor preference for municipals that sustains a high price level for the tax-exempt markets.

During World War I the increase in the rate of taxation was responsible for most of the fall in the ratio, as the corporate tax rate went to 12 per cent and the top-bracket individual rate climbed to 75 per cent.

During the 1920's the individual top-bracket tax rate dropped back to a low of 24 per cent in 1929, and Figure 29 shows that the ratio hovered around the 90 per cent range during that decade. The decline in the ratio began again as tax rates climbed during the 1930's; the top individual rate jumped to 63 per cent in 1932 and reached a high of 94 per cent during World War II.

The decline in the municipal-corporate ratio to 41 per cent in 1945 is explained by Homer in terms of the scarcity value of municipals at that time. New municipal financing was almost nonexistent, maturing bonds were being paid off, and even though the yields were so low that many corporations, insurance companies, and savings banks sold their holdings of municipals to obtain funds for other purposes, there were enough trust officers and wealthy individuals continuing to invest to keep the price of a municipal bond relatively high. The volume of municipal bonds, of course, was relatively small.

Yields in the Postwar Era

Tax rates continued high in the postwar years, with the corporate rate going up and the top individual rates easing a bit, but the ratio began a climb from its low of 41 per cent to the 75–85 per cent range. To make this reversal of the ratio trend understandable, it is necessary to analyze the flow of funds into the hands of investors who might be interested in acquiring tax-exempt bonds.

Beginning in 1946 the flood of new municipal issues swamped the new funds available to the high-bracket private investors, and the yield on municipals began increasing notch by notch as dealers sought new customers among institutions and individuals. Homer found that, with postwar tax rates, a ratio of about 80 per cent has appeared to attract a sufficient number of medium-bracket individuals and that municipals became "a bonanza" for corporations at those tax rates, especially for the commercial banks which are taxed at corporate levels. As Figure 29 shows, after the banks began purchasing bonds in quantity, the ratio stayed within a narrow range, with yields reasonably stable until 1966.

Relative Yields in the Future

No one can predict what the general level of long-term interest rates will be in the future, but it is reasonable to assume that the ratio of tax-exempt to taxable yields will remain high and go even higher if the expected volume of new issues offered materializes and if it becomes necessary to attract the medium-income investor into the tax-exempt market. The amount of money available for profitable investment in tax-exempts is painfully small, however, as pointed out by those who have opposed the recent unwieldy volumes of industrial revenue bonds and as analyzed by Sidney Homer for the 1960–1964 period.

He calculated that the average annual investment in bonds and mortgages by all investor groups in the 1960–1964 period amounted to $35.9

billion. This annual average was distributed among: (a) individuals and miscellaneous other types who invested an average of $5 billion a year in bonds and mortgages; (b) commercial banks (taxable at full corporate rates) that invested $7.4 billion, and (c) all the nonbank institutions put together (including foundations, pension funds, savings institutions of many kinds, life insurance companies, and fire and casualty companies), who invested $23.5 billion. Only the less than $1 billion invested by fire and casualty companies among the last category was taxable at the corporate rate; the bulk of this nonbank investment was taxable at a 20 per cent rate or less. Thus some part of the $8.3 billion investible by the commercial banks and the casualty companies and some small part of the $5 billion investible by all individuals in bonds *and* mortgages was all that was available for the purchase of an annual volume of net new municipal financing averaging almost $6 billion a year during the 1960–1965 period. Homer goes on to say:

> The table reveals the extraordinary consequences of our complicated tax laws. We start with a high graduated income tax and then enact a series of reductions or exemptions in order to avoid or soften double taxation on the individual saver who saves through pension funds, insurance companies, or savings banks. These complex laws, and the tendency of Americans to save through institutions, have resulted in an extraordinary concentration of savings in institutions which are subject to no tax or to a bracket less than half of the corporate bracket.[3]

Thus the basic problem in generating demand for tax-exempt securities at reasonable interest rates is that only an extremely small share of investible funds is held by taxable institutions or individuals. A projection of yields to be required in the future to absorb the supply of bond offerings by state and local governments must be based in part upon a projection of funds available to such taxable investors and upon predictions regarding the level of taxes and the continuance of tax exemption for local public securities. A reliable projection of funds held by taxable investors is not available because it is dependent upon guesses about how individuals will allocate their savings between taxable and nontaxable institutions, but a trend toward a higher ratio between tax-exempt and taxable bonds (or equivalently toward higher relative yields) seems inescapable in the coming decade.

B. SPECIAL CHARACTERISTICS OF TAX-EXEMPT YIELDS

Wide Fluctuations In Yield

Tax-exempt yields are also affected by the peculiarities of the municipal bond market, and it is highly likely that the markets of the future will continue to be characterized as unusually subject to wide short-term price fluc-

[3] JEC—*Financing* (1), p. 272.

tuations as they have been in the past. Roland Robinson's description of
the market in the early postwar period provides some basic insights about
the complex causes of this phenomenon.

> The yields of long-term state and local government securities fluctuate through a wider
> range than any other important long-term interest rate. . . . The average variation of
> price for the municipal series was more than twice that of the corporate series for the
> entire 1937–1955 period (Ed. note: for Robinson's data on securities having a rating
> of Aa). In the period since March 1951 (the Federal Reserve–Treasury "accord") both
> fluctuated a bit more than before and the difference in range is not quite as large, with
> the municipal average range a little less than twice that of corporate bonds.
>
> The wider range of yield fluctuation for state and local government obligations than
> for corporate or U.S. Treasury bond yields appears to be due to a combination of circum-
> stances. In addition to the general economic influences that apply to all capital markets
> equally, the valuation of state and local government securities involves pricing the privi-
> lege of tax exemption. This makes it a narrower market.
>
> A further circumstance influencing state and local government security yields is that
> this market is more subject to inventory adjustments. The supply of corporate obliga-
> tions in the secondary market is seldom very large; the supply of new and unsold cor-
> porate issues is more often zero than any other amount. The supply of Treasury obliga-
> tions in the market is concentrated in the shorter maturities; supplies of the longer
> maturities are seldom truly large. . . .
>
> But the market for state and local government securities apparently cannot operate
> satisfactorily without an inventory of significant size; sometimes it seems to need quite a
> large amount. Even though dealers may see the signs of marked adversity, they find it
> hard to reduce inventories quickly. Since many state and local government finance au-
> thorities in offering their securities for competitive bidding do not respond quickly to
> adverse market developments, inventory may pile up from new-issue marketing much
> more than is true of the corporate field, where the units are larger, financing plans can be
> changed more quickly, and the proportion of negotiated deals is larger. The influence of
> unsold inventory on this market is material.[4]

Robinson, in addition to these comments, was interested in tying his
findings into the work of the American interest-rate economists: Macauley,
Hickman, Durand, Winn, and unnamed analysts at the U.S. Treasury. He
found that there are a number of differences between municipal yield
curves and the curves for Treasury and corporate securities, partly because
of the specialized use of Treasury securities by certain kinds of institutions
that come in and out of the market, and partly because of an upward slope
of the interest-rate curve in the intermediate ranges caused by the preference of commercial banks and fire and casualty companies at that time for
the intermediate-term municipal bonds. In short, he considered the municipal market highly segmented, a fact that is well known in the industry,
since certain maturities are, indeed, priced at levels that will appeal to the
several different kinds of investors. This process of segmenting a new issue
for marketing purposes applies as well to other characteristics of the issue:
coupons, discounts, call provisions, revenue coverage required in the in-

[4] Robinson, p. 169.

denture, and even the name given to the issue. The yield curves on any given date for different grades and types of bonds reflect the underwriters' perceptions of the current preferences of these investor groups.

No recent study quite comparable to Robinson's has been made to compare price fluctuations of tax-exempt and other long-term obligations, but Sidney Homer, in observing the market in the 1955–1965 decade and projecting it forward to the 1970's, predicted that "price-wise municipals will decline more or advance less than taxable bonds" in the 1965–1975 decade. This condition obtained, in fact, during the 1966 credit crunch, about which more will be said below.

Reaction to Monetary Policy

The effects of credit tightenings that involve higher interest rates can be seen by comparing yield curves in terms of the number of basis points difference between an X-year maturity and a 1-year maturity for a series of points in time. Figure 30 is derived from data prepared by Homer for the Joint Economic Committee study; we have plotted basis-point differences for the years 1950–1965 for five maturities (2, 5, 10, 20, and 30 years) from annual averages of municipal yield scales for his "good-grade" bonds. The municipal bond yield curve tends to flatten, that is, the differential between short- and long-term yields narrows, whenever the yields on corporate and government bonds increase significantly (along with similar flattened curves), as happened in 1951–1952, 1956–1957, 1959, and generally since the early 1960's. The events of 1966 provided exceptionally interesting insights into the process. During the credit crunch of 1966, short-term yields had risen with the money market, and individual investors had buoyed the long end. Consideration of Figure 31, prepared by Sidney Homer's firm, and published in *The Bond Buyer,* demonstrates again that price levels are dependent upon a wide variety of factors applicable to limited parts of the full spectrum. The sum of these factors determines the state of the market and the direction of its many shifts, as can be seen in the following quotation from *The Bond Buyer.*

One of the few bright spots in the gloom of last summer (1966) in tax-exempts was that individual investors would bestir themselves when yields crashed through the 4 per cent barrier—sometimes regarded as the "magic number" for attracting non-institutional money. . . .

Last Summer the big commercial banks were net sellers of municipals under the pressure of business borrowing and their inability to sustain liquidity through their certificates of deposit. . . .

The pattern now has been reversed. The commercial banks have come back strongly into the market, acquiring $3.2 billion of municipals on balance in the first quarter of 1967, according to Federal Reserve figures, compared with acquisitions of only $500 million in the first quarter of 1966.

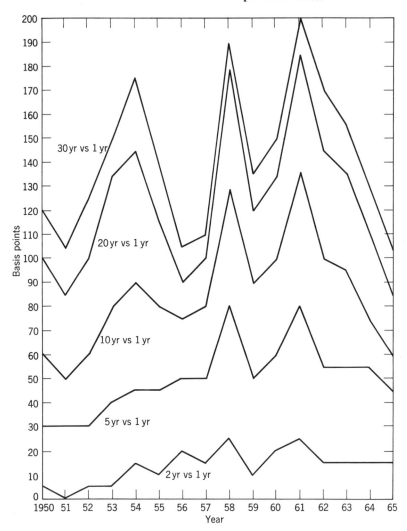

Figure 30 Difference in basis points between *Bond Buyer* average yield on a one-year tax-exempt bond and on various other maturities, by year, 1950–1965.

But the individual buyers have looked elsewhere. As a result the interest structure of the tax-exempt market has been sharply realigned.

Last Summer and Fall, the yields from short, medium and long-term maturities were nearly all the same, producing yield curves that were picturesquely compared to saucers and pancakes (see accompanying chart [Figure 31] by Salomon Brothers & Hutzler).

In the past five months there has been a major correction—some might say overcorrection. Bank buying in the short and medium-range has kept interest rates relatively low in this sector but lagging enthusiasm of other investors for longer bonds has pushed yields up sharply at this end. While the result has been to transform the curves into the more traditional ski-slope pattern, it also has widened the yield spread between the short and long end of prime municipals to more than 100 points, easily the widest margin in three years. . . .[5]

Another saucer, somewhat shallower, was in the making in 1967–1968 as this chapter was written and as *The Bond Buyer Index* climbed 40 basis points higher than it had been at the height of the crunch in August 1966. The important point to be made, however, is that credit restraint, when short-term rates rise relative to longer-term rates, makes long-term tax-exempt bonds exceptionally difficult to sell, and thus contributes to the other pressures leading to very high yields for municipal bonds.

C. PRICE LEVELS FOR LOWER-QUALITY BONDS

Yield Differentials

Price fluctuations for lower-quality municipals are greater than for prime-quality bonds. Moreover, Robinson reported that the differential between grades of state and local government securities continued to be large, although yield differentials between grades of corporate securities shrank considerably during the first postwar decade. He investigated those

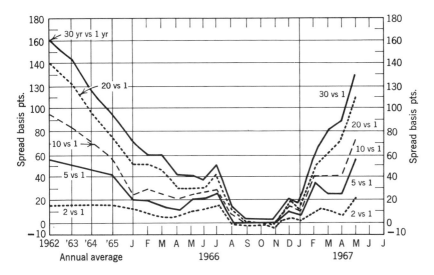

Figure 31 Yield spreads between maturity groups of prime municipals, by year, 1962–1965, and by month, 1966–1967.

[5] *Bond Buyer*, May 8, 1967.

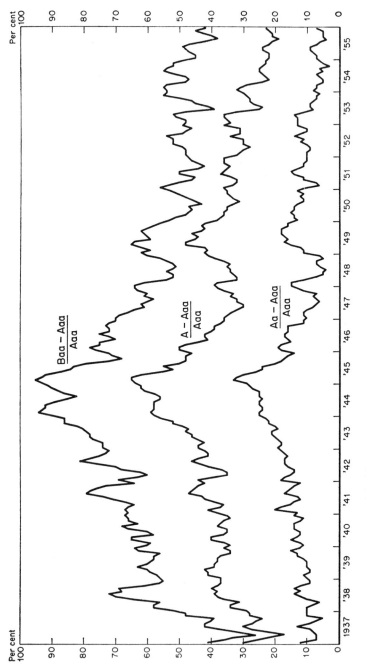

Figure 32 Municipal bond yield differentials by quality of issue in relative terms, 1937–1956.

214

differentials in two ways: (a) in absolute amounts of yield, the number of basic points between an Aaa-rated bond and a Baa-rated bond, for instance, and (b) in relative amounts, the number of basis points difference as a percentage of the Aaa yield. The results of the second, or relative, method can be seen for the 1937–1955 period in his chart, reproduced here as Figure 32, with the calculations based upon a comparison of Moody's data for the four top rating groups.

As soon as the commercial banks began buying tax-exempts in quantity in the early 1960's, however, these large yield differentials between quality grades largely disappeared and remain quite small at this writing. The story is nowhere better told than by Sidney Homer, who prepared Figure 33, which shows the differential between "prime" and "best medium-grade" bonds declining from a high of 50 in 1957 to the 1966 low of 15 basis points. Unfortunately, data comparable to his are not available for later years, but little has happened in the market to disturb Homer's conclusions:

It is apparent that the quality differential has declined almost steadily since 1957 and by 1965 almost vanished. The decline in the quality differential is, no doubt, attributable to two factors: (1) Long years of prosperity have caused investors to forget the financial problems which many communities suffered in earlier times. After all for several decades the debt payment record of mediocre credits has been exactly as good as the debt payment record of prime credits. (2) During the past four or five years there has been intensive competition between institutional investors, mostly commercial banks, for maximum yield in order to offset the high cost of deposit money. This has led portfolio managers to accept progressively lower yield differentials in order to improve their current income performance. . . .

In the depression years of the 1930's for example, there were times when the bonds of shaky cities sold to yield 6 per cent or more, while simultaneously the bonds of prime credits were selling to yield 3 per cent. At one time New York City (medium grade) long 4's were selling at 60, while simultaneously New York State (prime) long 4's were selling at twice that price, i.e., 120.

For the future, it seems probable that the differentials between prime and lower quality municipals will again widen. Furthermore, if municipal debt increases too rapidly in the years ahead, it is certain that at least a few municipalities will become dangerously overextended. In such an event, it would only take one large default to bring about a drastic revision of investor sentiment adverse to all types of lower quality municipals. This would quickly result in drastic repricing of lower and medium quality municipals to wider or perhaps very wide spreads from prime municipals. In this way the new issues of industrial bonds or risky revenue bonds could damage the market for a very wide range of general obligations.

Medium quality and low quality municipals will in the years ahead be importantly influenced by the fluctuations discussed above for prime municipals, but they will also be influenced by changes in the market's appraisal of the risk factor. Since at present the risk differential is at a minimum, it is apt to widen. This means that the market for medium grade and second grade municipals should do distinctly worse than the market for primes.[6]

[6] JEC—*Financing* (1), p. 289–291.

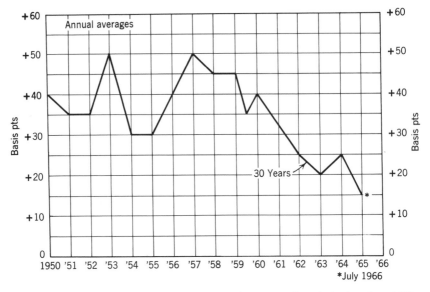

Figure 33   Municipal yield spreads—good grade versus prime, in basis points, 1950–1966.

Effect on Credit Ratings

One effect of the pressure for acceptable bonds created by the massive buying for commercial bank portfolios in recent years that is a corollary to the narrowing differentials for quality grades is the persistent upgrading of individual credit ratings. Thus a bond that might have been rated Baa in 1959 had a high probability of carrying an A rating in 1967. Similarly, this writer's analysis of White's Ratings, which measure the level at which a bond of one issuer tends to sell in relation to a bond of another issuer and whose numerical ratings tend to reflect the alphabetized credit ratings set by Moody's and Standard and Poor's, reveals a steady upward shift of ratings: whereas, in the late 1950's, ratings for a very large sample of general obligation bonds were distributed throughout the rating scale, from high to low, by 1965 these market ratings had demonstratably clustered in what might be called the A-rated bond range.

In any case, the theory behind the White's measurement is that, regardless of how a bond is rated in terms of credit, it tends to sell at a certain level in relation to similar bonds of other issuers. In the terminology of the market, a bond will sell "like a high-A" meaning that its yield is slightly lower than a "straight-A" but higher than a "double-A," and what has happened in recent years is that more and more issuers found their bonds priced a little higher than they might have expected whenever the commercial banks were aggressive buyers in the market. This effect, of course, would be missed by an analyst who only considered the differential between two grades of bonds at different dates but has become generally appreciated by dealers and investors. The extent to which more bonds now selling like A's will be reappraised by either the market or the rating agencies so that they begin selling like B's again is unknown, but it might well take place coordinately with the return to the larger differentials anticipated by Homer.

Bonds Issued by Small Municipalities

A companion study of the credit problems of small municipalities provides confirmation of the decline in differential. That study, by the National League of Cities, considered data provided by the Investment Bankers Association covering sales of new issues distributed by year of issue, size of issuer, and maturities and ratings of the bond. The comparisons were between groups of bonds with A ratings (Aaa-Aa-A), B ratings (Baa-Ba-B), and Unrated. The differential (in basis points) between A and B ratings for the average annual net interest costs fell from 34 points in 1961 to 17 points in 1965 for communities below 10,000 population and from 30 points in 1961 to 15 points in 1965 for communities between 10,000 and 250,000 population. The change in the differentials was smaller when Unrated bonds were compared to A-rated bonds, possibly because so many revenue issues that are not rated sell at prices that are comparable to well-rated bonds.[7]

Summary

There are many indications that the relative price level of tax-exempt municipal bonds will continue to fall over the decade ending in 1975. Yields on tax-exempts will therefore rise to a level closer to taxable corporate yields. Perhaps the most important cause of this condition is the drift of investible money into pension funds and other forms of nontaxable enterprise traditionally uninterested in municipal bonds, combined with an increase in the amounts of municipal bonds being issued.

The effects of persistent relative price declines are widely distributed. Portfolios of bonds currently outstanding depreciate in terms of market value. Wealthy investors and taxable institutions remain in a position to obtain high tax-sheltered income. Local government issuers, especially those of lower credit standing, receive increasingly smaller benefits in interest-cost savings from their tax-exempt privileges. These and other effects are inexorable consequences of the price system in the market combined with the fiscal and tax policies of the federal government and its state and local partners, but we shall have to leave to the next chapter an appraisal of the significance of these trends in municipal bond pricing.

[7] JEC—*Financing* (m).

Chapter XVI   Final Perspectives

Suppose that, in a hypothetical case, *United States versus The Municipal Bond,* one of the charges made against the present municipal bond system is that it represents an inefficient allocation of resources. The indictment reads that bonds are sold at the will of a given local body without reference to national priorities in the use of capital and labor. In addition, the issuance of bonds allows local governments unilaterally to confer federal tax exemption on institutions and individuals. Both these charges were made during the debates about the industrial revenue bond situation, but they apply to all municipal bond undertakings. However, until such time as the institutions of local government have withered away to be replaced by centrally controlled programming, an event that is as unlikely as it is undesirable, the nation will have to accept the possibility of such misallocation of resources.

On the other hand, the proponents of the present system by which local governments obtain long-term financing for capital projects do not claim that it is either efficient or equitable. They admit that many features of their multifaceted, interrelated, unregulated process require improvements, but they also assert that local government in the United States is unthinkable without maintenance of the ability of individual communities to determine and implement their own developmental programs, with or without tax exemption for interest on bonds.

On the Market

The market mechanism described in Part 1 has operated remarkably well in spite of unremitting pressures since the early 1960's. The steady increase in the interest costs on new bond issues has enabled the underwriters and dealers to find investors for an impressively large quantity of bonds, justifying in part the contention that high yields will bring new categories of buyers into the market for bonds. The spate of industrial revenue bonds, which may have been legislated out of existence as a factor in the future, was the proximate cause, however, of the current review of the pernicious effects attributable to the rising interest rate curve.

The market's attention has thus been riveted on a number of unfavorable conditions, including (a) the depreciation in the market value of outstanding portfolios (especially those held by the casualty insurance companies which were suffering other inroads on their reserves during the period); (b) the extreme risks incurred by underwriters in holding the essential inventories that are required to serve the market, a risk that was heightened by the willingness of commercial bank underwriters to work for smaller margins of profit than were deemed feasible by non-bank underwriters; and (c) the steady erosion in the cost saving theoretically received by local governments from tax exemption, plus the strong possibility that high interest costs systematically discriminate against those local communities least able to undertake long-term indebtedness.

On The Status Quo

In the light of these conditions, how would the system fare if no fundamental alterations were made to ease the pressure under which the market has been operating in recent years? The answer is not hard to find. Undoubtedly the same conditions would persist, since the only self-correcting feature is the decision on the part of an independent local government to defer indefinitely a capital program that relied on the issuance of tax-exempt bonds. Such deferrals would lighten the visible supply to some extent, but the stream of new bonds would still be heavy and yields would tend to continue rising until the market was cleared. Rising personal incomes and the possibility of higher tax rates would help bring some new customers into the market, but the flow of investible funds into nontaxable institutions might operate to reduce the number of potential buyers. As at present, the short-term market trends will be importantly determined by the collective investment policies of the commercial banks, and over the longer term it is improbable that either the commercial banks or the middle-income investors hopefully waiting in the wings will come forward in sufficient numbers until yields rise to still higher levels, perhaps even with those posted for taxable bonds of comparable quality.

However unbearable market conditions may seem to be, and however gloomy the prediction if fundamental improvements are not made, the nation will not be changing the rules of the game in order to stabilize the municipal bond market. The basic changes will come about in the pursuit of far more pressing items on the public agenda, with improvements in the municipal bond market coming as an extra set of benefits.

On Fiscal Policy

An example can be found in the question whether municipal bond interest should be exempt from federal taxes in the future. Although the statistical arguments advanced by the Treasury are quite unconvincing, as we saw in Chapter X, the maximum net dollar loss to the Treasury is not large enough to justify abandonment of the principle of reciprocal immunity even if appropriate Constitutional and statutory amendments were adopted. The loss is a small fraction of one per cent of federal revenues, and the potential dollar cost of additional federal support of important social programs affecting local governments is vastly greater than the loss of revenue possibly resulting from tax exemption. Thus the only way in which the elimination of tax exemption could be justified would be for the federal government to share its revenues with the states and their political subdivisions so that local governments could obtain funds for capital outlays without offering bonds to the market. Alternatively the federal government could expand its own purchases of local bonds at submarket interest rates.

At the same time as such alternative forms of financing were relieving pressure on the market and making the remaining bonds easier to sell as tax-exempts, a further increase in income tax rates to finance the broadened scope of federal assistance would tend to increase demand for bonds as a means of avoiding income tax. Thus paradoxically the very steps that would allow exemption to be given up would strengthen the ability of the municipal bond market to serve both issuer and investor and strengthen the arguments of those who would retain exemption on philosophic rather than economic grounds.

On Credit Analysis

There are other examples of how the municipal bond system will be improved by programs beyond its boundaries. The process of rating bonds, for instance, will remain a modest horse-and-buggy operation so long as the rating agencies serve only one master, the limited number of underwriters, dealers, and investors who pay for service. The conflicts inherent in trying to serve two masters, the issuing local governments and the financial community, suggest that little basic change in the rating business will occur without the intervention of higher levels of government, an event that would end up pleasing neither group. Yet the vast forces lining up to improve the functioning of local government in an urbanized America, with the Advisory Commission on Intergovernmental Relations providing leadership, may result in the availability of quantities of information of the type required by competent bond credit analysts. The purpose of governmental reform is to introduce such techniques as planning, programming, and budgeting systems, but the incidental effect will be to transfer much of the cost of improving bond ratings to governmental fact-finding and analytic agencies.

Yet when all the indirect benefits derived from the general attack on the problems of state and local government under the banner of creative federalism have accrued to the municipal bond field, there will remain two great areas for change that lie more directly within the province of the participants in the municipal bond market. The first area covers a number of changes in the market mechanism that might be implemented by the participants. The second area involves value judgments on the part of policy makers in government and finance.

On Selling Methods

Within the market itself substantial improvements could be made. For example, one speaker after another points to the need for broadening the market to include the small investor, but as the editors of *The Bond Buyer* can show, the eager individual who requests his stock broker to buy a single $1000 bond is in for a long and frustrating hassle. Thus the market is hardly serving the needs of small investors, except by means of the unwieldy but growing bond funds in which certificates of interest can be bought, and it currently suffers from lack of automated communication in serving the needs of large investing institutions in both the primary and secondary market (in much the same way as the Stock Exchange is currently unable to serve effectively the trading needs of holders of very large blocs of stocks). The subject of more efficient distribution of municipal bonds, together with improvements in the organization and operation of the bidding and underwriting functions, should claim the attention of issuers, underwriters, dealers, and investors alike for years to come.

On Banking Regulations

Finally we come to the great policy decisions to be made regarding the commercial banks and their right to underwrite bond issues that are not general obligations of local governments with unlimited powers of taxation. Econometric analysis (as presented to a subcommittee of the Senate Banking and Finance Committee and argued in behalf of the contesting commercial and investment bankers in conjunction with representatives of the Treasury, the Federal Reserve, and the Comptroller of the Currency) is indeterminate on this issue, largely because the basic data employed in the various analyses are so crude and because the geographic and operational dimensions are so extensive. The issue, as developed in Chapter VIII, is ultimately one of trust in the ability of commercial bankers to refrain from practices condemned after the debacle of the 1920's. The potential benefit to issuers is so problematic (and small in dollar terms), the potential damage to investment bankers so large, and the potential for profitable domination of the market mechanism on the part of commercial banks so clear, that allowing commercial banks unrestricted entry into the revenue bond underwriting business seems unwise and unnecessary, even though the care and feeding of commercial banks is important if they are to absorb the majority share of all tax-exempt bonds to be issued during the 1965–1975 decade as projected by the Joint Economic Committee.

On Differences of Opinion

The deepest sort of value judgments are involved in one man's desire to enhance the independence of local governments and in another man's insistence that local government prerogatives are subject to control in the name of the general welfare, especially in metropolitan areas, but resolving such great controversies not only is beyond the province of this book but can be handled on more practical grounds. With respect to the tax-exemption privilege, for instance, one can discount the Treasury's claimed loss of revenue with little difficulty, but the fact remains that certain wealthy individuals can avoid federal taxes on very large incomes by investing in local public securities. To some, this privilege of avoiding taxation is socially reprehensible, even though it is a necessary result of the tax code as written in conformity with the presumed Constitutional doctrine of reciprocal immunity between the federal government and the state and local governments.

Tax exemption, however, allows certain taxable institutions and individuals to hold the bonds local governments wish to sell. Tax-exempt institutions and pension funds have no interest in municipal tax-exempt bonds so long as the yield is below yields on corporate bonds. If wealthy individuals are penalized for buying tax-exempt bonds, demand for such bonds will fall, yields will rise further, and neither the Treasury nor local government may be measurably better off. Thus tax exemption remains an issue of surpassing complexity, with more to be said for retaining it and the apparatus of institutions that are based upon its existence than for converting to a more symmetrical but federally dominated system of taxation and local finance.

Taxable municipal bonds may come to play a role, especially with regard to the financing of local industrial development programs, but the heart and soul of the municipal bond market in all its glory are tied to the institution of tax exemption. The reader is therefore invited to join the writer in expressing a final value judgment to the effect that we have relatively little to gain and possibly much to lose by removing tax exemption from the municipal bond; instead we should direct attention to improvements in the market mechanism and in the vast arena of intergovernmental relations.

Bibliographic Notes

Citations in the text refer to the headings that have been alphabetized in the following pages. Each heading refers either to a group of related materials or to a cited author.

ACIR

Advisory Commission on Intergovernmental Relations, Washington, D. C. 20575

(a) *State Constitutional and Statutory Restrictions on Local Government Debt.* Report A-10. September 1961.
(b) *Industrial Development Bond Financing.* Report A-18. June 1963.
(c) *State Technical Assistance to Local Debt Management.* Report M-26. January 1965.
(d) *Factors Affecting Voter Reactions to Governmental Reorganization in Metropolitan Areas.* May 1962.
(e) *Metropolitan America: Challenge to Federalism,* a study submitted to the Intergovernmental Relations Subcommittee of the Committee on Government Operations and prepared by Professor Bernard J. Frieden. (U.S. Govt. Printing Office, Washington, D.C., October 1966.)
(f) *State Constitutional and Statutory Restrictions on Local Taxing Powers.* Report A-14. October 1962.
(g) *Measures of State and Local Fiscal Capacity and Tax Efforts* (Report M-16, October 1962), *The Role of Equalization in Federal Grants* (Report A-19, January 1964), *The Role of the States in Strengthening the Property Tax* (Report A-17, two volumes, June 1963), *Local Nonproperty Taxes and the Coordinating Role of the State* (Report A-9, September 1961), and, among others, *Tax Overlapping in The United States* (a supplement to Report M-23, selected tables updated, December 1966).
(h) *Fiscal Balance in the American Federal System,* Vol. 1, and *Metropolitan Fiscal Disparities,* Vol. 2, October 1967. These two are the Advisory Commission's most comprehensive treatments of the problem.

BOND BUYER

The Bond Buyer, 67 Pearl Street, New York City. Its daily and weekly editions are the leading journals of record and news for the municipal bond market.

(a) Data and quotations in Chapter I come from editions during the week of June 26–30, 1967. Other citations in the book give the edition date and on occasion the author.

(b) *Bond Buyer Statistics,* an annual handbook of market statistics published since February 1963 (Volume I).

(c) *Preparing a Bond Offering of a Local Government for the Market* (pamphlet), by Harry L. Severson and *The Bond Buyer* staff. 1962.

(d) See Internal Revenue Service statement of August 11, 1966, declining to issue rulings pending study, printed in *The Bond Buyer* of that date, and "Tax exempt status of local government bonds used in arbitrage transactions," *George Washington Law Review,* Vol. 35, March 1967, p. 574.

FEDERAL

(a) *Economic Report of the President,* as transmitted to the Congress in specified year, together with the annual report of the Council of Economic Advisors. Supt. of Documents, Washington, D.C., 20402.

(b) *Fiscal Planning for an Urban Community,* A Study of Public Finance in Pittsburgh and Allegheny County, Pennsylvania, sponsored by the U.S. Housing and Home Finance Agency, the Urban Redevelopment Authority of Pittsburgh, and the Redevelopment Authority of Allegheny County, Pittsburgh, Pa. 15219. November, 1965.

(c) *Our Cities, Their Role in the National Economy.* Report of the *Urbanism Committee* of the National Resources Committee. (U.S. Govt. Printing Office, Washington, D.C., 1937.)

(d) *Program Planning for State County City,* by Harry P. Hatry and John F. Cotton, State-Local Finances Project, George Washington University, Washington, D.C., January, 1967 (program structure taken from pp. 17–18). Another version of this report may be found in *Criteria for Evaluation in Planning State and Local Programs,* prepared for the Senate Committee on Government Operations. (U.S. Govt. Printing Office, Washington, D.C., July 21, 1967.) See also *Handbook for Local Officials,* Office of the Vice President, Washington, D.C., November 1, 1967. Appendix D, pp. 275–284.

(e) *The Effectiveness of Metropolitan Planning,* by the Joint Center for Urban Studies of the Massachusetts Institute of Technology and Harvard University in cooperation with the Subcommittee on Intergovernmental Relations, U.S. Senate, Committee on Government Operations, Washington, D.C., June 30, 1964. Especially Chapter 4-C and Appendix D.

(f) "Municipal Bonds: Major Source of State and Local Construction Funds," *Construction Review,* U.S. Department of Commerce, Vol. 13, No. 1, January 1967, p. 9.

(g) Bonds for housing are usually either "urban renewal notes" (short-term obligations to help finance projects under construction with long-term financings being arranged largely through the private sector) or "new housing authority bonds" to finance individual housing projects that are subsidized by the federal government. "New Housing Authority Bonds" are uniformly accorded the highest credit ratings available for tax-exempt municipal bonds, for they are considered to be backed by the credit of the United States. It has been customary for these issues to be sold in "Groups" with slight price differentials reflecting the character of the cities in the group, and variations in state tax exemptions. Coming in batches sometimes exceeding $100 million for sale at the same time, Group A might have $30 million bonds being sold by housing authorities of five cities across the Nation; Group B might have $63 million covering another eleven communities; and so forth.

An excellent source of information on the market characteristics of New Housing Authority Bonds, and also the many varieties of revenue bonds in the transportation and education field, is "*Of the People, By the People, For the People, An Informal Analysis of Tax-Free Public Bonds*," by E. H. Davis, Vice-President and Manager of Research, John Nuveen & Co., Inc. (a leading municipal bond house with offices in New York and Chicago), 1959. *The Bond Buyer*, however, suggests that the time may have come for "public authorities backed by the P.H.A. to sell the bonds singly instead of as part of a national package." (Editorial, September 19, 1966.)

(h) *The Census of Governments* constitutes a primary source of data concerning state and local government. The first such census was conducted immediately prior to World War II, but only selected portions were published. The next census was taken in 1957 and provides many of the important benchmarks. The 1962 Census was considerably more detailed than the earlier ones and was published in parts over the following years. Only the preliminary totals have been published from the Census of 1967, but no detailed reports are available at this writing. Citations have been made to the following: *Compendium of Government Finances*, Vol. IV of the 1962 Census—Table A. p. 3. Table 1, p. 27. Table 6, p. 30, Figure 10, p. 21.

HANSON-PERLOFF

State and Local Finance in the National Economy, by Alvin H. Hanson and Harvey S. Perloff, W. W. Norton and Company, New York, 1944, pages 11–12. At that time Hanson was a professor at Harvard University School of Public Affairs; both he and Perloff had been working as economists with the Federal Reserve System.

A valuable critique of the Hanson-Perloff hypothesis in the light of post-war developments is provided in Rafuse, R. W., Jr., "Cyclic Behavior of State-local Finance" in Musgrave, R. A., *Essays in Fiscal Federalism*, The Brookings Institution, Washington, D.C., 1966.

HEARINGS

(a) *Bank Underwriting of Revenue Bonds*, Hearings before the Subcommittee on Financial Institutions, Committee on Banking and Currency, U.S. Senate, 90th Congress, 1st Session, on S. 1306, August 28, 29, 30 and September 12, 1967. (U.S. Govt. Printing Office, Washington, D.C., 1967.)

For data on defaults, see information submitted by National League of Cities, pp. 137 ff. Readers may also refer to JEC—*Financing*, Chapter 15, prepared by Dun and Bradstreet, Inc. Similar data is found in *Ratings* (b) below.

(b) See recent hearings cited in *Ratings* (b) below

IBA

Investment Bankers Association of America, Washington, D.C.

(a) *Fundamentals of Municipal Bonds*, edited by Gordon L. Calvert, 1959 edition. Same quotation appears on p. 101, 4th Ed., May 1965.

(b) Annual Report of the Municipal Industrial Finance Committee of the IBA, printed in *The Bond Buyer*'s Convention Issue, December 13, 1967, p. 46.

(c) "Short Cycles in Interest Rates in the Municipal Bond Market," *IBA Statistical Bulletin*, No. 15, June 1960, p. 1.

ICMA

International City Managers Association, 1313 East 60th St., Chicago 37, Illinois.

(a) *Technique of Municipal Administration*, International City Managers' Association, Chicago, 4th Ed., 1958, pp. 120–122.
(b) *Municipal Finance Administration*, 1955. See MFOA (d) below.
(c) *Planning and Budgeting in Municipal Management*, by Joseph M. Heikoff, International City Managers' Association, Chicago, 1966.
(d) *Program Development and Administration*, the International City Managers' Association, Chicago, 1965, pp. 32–39. See also Edward Bacon's discussion of Philadelphia in *Journal of the American Institute of Planners*, Vol. 22, 1956, pp. 35–38.

JEC—*NEEDS* and *FINANCING*

State and Local Public Facility Needs and Financing is the full title of the two-volume study prepared for the Subcommittee on Economic Progress of the Joint Economic Committee, Congress of the United States. (U.S. Govt. Printing Office, Washington, D.C., December 1966.)

The *Needs* study in Volume 1 includes contributions from a score of professional groups and governmental agencies on the capital requirements for public facilities. *Financing*, Volume 2 of the study, is also a collection of submitted papers, analyzed by the Committee staff under the direction of Arnold H. Diamond, Consulting Economist. Citations to either *Needs* or *Financing* without identification of a chapter signifies a reference to the staff's summary and analysis. The papers specifically cited are listed below.

JEC—*NEEDS*

"State and Local Government Capital Expenditures in Relation to National Economic Activity With Projections for 1975," by Louis J. Paradiso and Mabel A. Smith, Office of Business Economics, Department of Commerce, in *Public Facility Needs*, Chapter 1, especially Tables 1 and 2, p. 54.

JEC—*FINANCING*

(a) "Municipal Bond Underwriting," prepared by John E. Walker, Research Director Investment Bankers Association of America, printed as Chapter 9.
(b) "The Secondary Market in Municipal Bonds," by John J. Kenny of J. J. Kenny Co., printed as Chapter 13.
(c) "Patterns of General Obligation Bonds," by John B. Dawson of Wood, King, Dawson & Logan, printed as Chapter 6.
(d) "Patterns of Revenue Bond Financing," by Frank E. Curley, of Hawkins, Delafield & Wood, printed as Chapter 7. See also his letter to *The Bond Buyer*, printed May 18, 1967.

(e) "Municipal Bond Counsel," by Joseph Guandolo of Mitchell, Pershing, Shetterly & Mitchell, printed as Chapter 11.

(f) "Municipal Financial Consultants," by Arthur R. Guastella of Wainwright & Ramsey, printed as Chapter 10

(g) "Municipal Bond Ratings," by James F. Reilly, of Goodbody & Co., printed as Chapter 14.

(h) "Patterns of Lease-Rental Financing," by James F. Reilly, of Goodbody & Co., printed as Chapter 8.

(i) "Comparison of the Interest Cost Saving and Revenue Loss on Tax-Exempt Securities," by the treasury Department, Office of the Secretary, printed as Chapter 20.

(j) "The Effect of Credit Conditions on State and Local Bond Sales and Capital Outlays Since World War II," by Paul F. McGouldrick, Division of Research and Statistics, Board of Governors of the Federal Reserve System, printed as Chapter 18.

(k) "State and Local Government Financing of Capital Outlays, 1946–65," by Allen D. Manvel, Bureau of the Census, Department of Commerce, printed as Chapter 1.

(l) "Factors Determining Municipal Bond Yields," by Sidney Homer, of Salomon Brothers & Hutzler, printed as Chapter 17.

(m) "Credit Problems of Small Municipalities," by David R. Berman and Lawrence A. Williams, National League of Cities, printed as Chapter 16.

LEASE-RENTALS

(a) Harry W. Clark, Executive Director, Texas Industrial Commission, American Industrial Development Council, special advertisement section, *New York Times,* May 1967, p. 26.

(b) Statement by Marquette deBary, Marquette deBary Co., New York City, before The Municipal Forum of New York in debate with John F. Thompson, April 11, 1968. See also his pamphlet, "Why Industrial Revenue Bonds Prevail," 1967.

(c) Letter from 21 investment banking firms to "the Governors of all States," July 20, 1966. Written by James F. Reilly, Goodbody & Co.

After months of pressure from the Treasury Department, the restrictions on the sale of industrial revenue bond issues with respect to tax exemption were included in the tax surcharge bill of June 1968 (see *Wall Street Journal,* June 27, 1968, p. 28) and were modified in supplemental legislation signed by President Johnson on October 25, 1968 (see "New Factory-Bond Rules Are Said to Pose Potential Problems to Firms, Communities," *Wall Street Journal,* October 30, 1968, p. 68).

MFOA

Municipal Finance Officers Association, 1313 East 60th St., Chicago 37, Illinois.

(a) *"Factors In Determining Municipal Utility Rates,"* by Melwood W. VanScoyoc, public utility consultant, in Special Bulletin 1965A, *Municipal Finance Officers Association,* Chicago, August 1, 1965.

(b) Lorens F. Logan, Partner, Wood, King, Dawson & Logan, bond attorneys of New York City, in letter printed in *The Daily Bond Buyer,* April 26, 1967, and reproduced by the Municipal Finance Officers Association for distribution to its members as Special Bulletin 1967C, May 16, 1967.

(c) "A Checklist for Determining Debt Policy," by Edward B. Mikrut, issued as Special

Bulletin 1961C, *Municipal Finance Officers Association of the United States and Canada*, 1313 East 60th Street, Chicago 37, Illinois, September 1, 1961.

(d) As recommended by ACIR: "For discussion of local planning and capital budgeting, see International City Managers' Association, *Municipal Finance Administration* (1955), pp. 339–340; Municipal Finance Officers Association of the United States and Canada, *Budgeting with Special Reference to Capital Budgeting* (1956); and Lennox L. Moak and Kathryn W. Killian, A Manual of Suggested Practice for the Preparation and Adoption of Capital Programs and Capital Budget, Municipal Finance Officers Association of the United States and Canada (1964)."

(e) "Some Guideposts Toward Stronger Local Governments," by David M. Ellinwood, in Proceeds of the National Conference on Local Government Fiscal Policy, Washington, D.C. (November 16–19, 1966), reported in *Municipal Finance* (Official Magazine of The Municipal Finance Officers Association of the United States and Canada), Vol. 39, No. 3, February, 1967, pp. 118–122.

OTT-MELTZER

Federal Tax Treatment of State and Local Securities, by David J. Ott and Allan H. Meltzer, Studies in Government Finance, The Brookings Institute, Washington, D.C., March 1963, p. 3. (Referred to hereafter as Ott-Meltzer.)

RATINGS

(a) *"A Municipal Credit Rating Scale,"* by James E. McCabe, Maxwell Graduate School, Syracuse University, May 1941. See also "Text of Award Winning Paper Analyzing Ratings of Municipals," by Thomas E. McCabe in *The Bond Buyer*, December 14, 1966, p. 1.

(b) *Financing Municipal Facilities*, Subcommittee on Economic Progress of Joint Economic Committee, December 5, 6, and 7, 1967 (USGPO, 1968). Those hearings largely provided an update of JEC-*Financing* and an opportunity to review the rating problem. Some of the same materials, with additional comments are found in two issues of *Financial Analysts Journal*, Vol. 24, No. 3, May–June 1968, pp. 59–73, and No. 4, July–August 1968, pp. 93–97. Included are articles by Roy M. Goodman of New York City, James Reilly of Goodbody & Co., Brenton W. Harries of Standard and Poor's, Robert C. Riehle of Moody's, and Stephen B. Packer.

READINGS

(a) For useful discussions of Dillon's *Commentaries on the Law of Municipal Corporations*, see Herbert Kaufman, *Politics and Policies in State and Local Governments*, Prentice-Hall, Englewood Cliffs, N.J., 1963, pp. 30–31; and Jule I. Bogen, *Financial Handbook*, 3rd Ed., Ronald Press, New York, 1952.

(b) See also: (1) Review of *Economic Behavior of the Affluent*, by Robin Barlow, Harvey E. Brazer, and James N. Morgan, Brookings Institute-University of Michigan Research Center, 1966, in *The Weekly Bond Buyer*, November 28, 1966; and (2) *The Great Treasury Raid*, by Philip M. Stern, Random House, New York, 1964, Chapter 10.

(c) ACIR noted that its historical summary relied heavily on the following: A. M. Hillhouse, *Municipal Bonds, A Century of Experience*, Prentice-Hall, New York, 1936;

B.U. Ratchford, *American State Debts*, Duke University Press, Durham, N.C., 1941; and Harry L. Severson, "The Formative Century in the Evaluation of Today's State and Local Bonds," *The Daily Bond Buyer*, May 22 and June 5, 1961.

(d) Harold S. Thomson, October 1964, now Vice-President, Austin Tobin & Company, Inc., New York.

(e) "Federal Income Taxation and Immunity of Municipal Bond Interest," by Dean S. Eiteman and Ronald M. Copeland, *MSU Business Topics*, Michigan State University, East Lansing, Vol. 15, No. 1., Winter 1967, p. 54.

(f) *Revenue Sharing and the City*, by Harvey S. Perloff and Richard P. Nathan, based on a conference sponsored by the Committee on Urban Economics of Resources for the Future, Inc. (with papers by Walter W. Heller, Richard Ruggles, Lyle C. Fitch, Carl S. Shoup, and Harvey E. Brazer), Johns Hopkins Press, Baltimore, Md., 1968.

(g) See: (1) *Intergovernmental Fiscal Relations*, by George F. Break, Brookings Institution, Washington, D.C., 1967; and (2) see *ACIR (h)*, *Fiscal Balance in the American Federal System*.

(h) The following are a few useful references in the developing professional literature on urban economics that the author has used and recommends.

Metropolitan America, a selected bibliography with annotations prepared for the Subcommittee on Intergovernmental Relations of the Committee on Government Operations of the United States Senate, dated August 7, 1964. U.S. Government Printing Office, Washington, D.C., 1964.

Wilbur R. Thompson, *A Preface to Urban Economics*, published for Resources for the Future, Inc., Johns Hopkins Press, Baltimore, Md., 1965.

Public Expenditure Decisions in the Urban Community (edited by Howard G. Schaller, 1963) and *The Public Economy of Urban Communities* (edited by Julius Margolis, 1965), both containing important papers presented at conferences under the sponsorship of the Committee on Urban Economics of Resources for the Future, Inc., Johns Hopkins Press, Baltimore, Md., 1963 and 1965.

Public Finances: Needs, Sources and Utilization, National Bureau of Economic Research, Princeton University Press, Princeton, N.J., 1961. An excellent collection of essays.

Three unpublished Ph.D. dissertations: (1) Kee, W.S., *City Expenditures and Metropolitan Areas: Analysis of Intergovernmental Fiscal Systems*, Syracuse University, 1964; (2) Pidot, G.B., Jr., *The Public Finances of Local Government in the Metropolitan United States*, Harvard University, July, 1965; (3) Whitelaw, W. E., *An Econometric Analysis of A Municipal Budgeting Process Based on Time-Series Data*, Massachusetts Institute of Technology, 1968.

And a useful bibliography: Knox, V.H., *Public Finance Information Sources*, Gale Research Co., Detroit, Michigan, 1964.

(i) "The Structure and Determinants of Local Public Investment Expenditures" by Niles M. Hansen, *Review of Economics and Statistics*, Vol. 47, No. 2, May 1965, p. 150.

(j) "Spatial and Locational Aspects of Local Government Expenditures" by Seymour Sacks in *Public Expenditure Decisions*, p. 181. See Readings (h).

(k) *The Question of Government Spending Public Needs and Private Wants*, by Francis M. Bator, Harper & Row, New York, 1960, especially Chapters 7 (The Allocation of Scarce Resources—Inefficient Markets versus Inefficient Government) and 8 (Notes in Economics, Politics, and Freedom).

(l) See *The Intellectual versus The City, from Thomas Jefferson to Frank Lloyd*

Wright, by Morton and Lucia White, Harvard University Press, Cambridge, 1962.
(m) See also: (1) *A Data Processing System for State and Local Government*, a Rand Corporation Study, Prentice-Hall, Englewood Cliffs, N.J., 1963; (2) *Computer Challenge to Urban Planners and State Administrators*, by Harry H. Fite, American University, Spartan Books, 1965; (3) *The Role of Budgeting in Government* by Grover W. Ensley, The Tax Foundation, New York, 1941; and (4) *Governmental Budgeting* by Jesse Birkhead, John Wiley & Sons, New York, 1956.
(n) The two other studies are:
(1) A study on national goals prepared by the Center for Priority Analysis of the National Planning Association and published as *Goals, Priorities and Dollars*, by Leonard A. Lecht, The Free Press, New York, 1966.
(2) "Project '70," a study of the state and local government sector based on material developed for the Federal Inter-agency Study on Economic Growth and Employment Opportunities. See the summary report published by the *Council of State Governments*, "State and Local Government Capital Outlays: Projections to 1970," by Selma Mushkin and E. McLoone, August 1966, and the series of detailed Research Memoranda on expenditures in connection with higher education, transportation, local schools, water supply and sanitation, and health and hospitals.

ROBINSON

Postwar Market for State and Local Government Securities, by Roland I. Robinson, National Bureau of Economic Research, Princeton University Press, Princeton, N.J., 1960.

SPIEGEL

Based on testimony before the Federal Power Commission by the Comptroller of the Florida Power Corporation, introduced February 8, 1967 related to Docket E-7257, pages 751–758. Furnished to the author through the courtesy of George Spiegel, attorney-at-law, Washington, D.C. See also: *Municipal Monopolies*, edited by Edward W. Bemis, Thomas Y. Crowell & Co., N.Y., 1899.

STAATS

"Commercial Banks and the Municipal Bond Market," by William F. Staats, *Federal Reserve Bank of Philadelphia Business Review*, February 1967. See also: "The Move to Municipals," by Jack C. Rothwell, *Federal Reserve Bank of Philadelphia Business Review*, September 1966.

VERNON

The Myth and Reality of Our Urban Problems, by Raymond Vernon, Harvard University Press, Cambridge, Massachusetts, 1962.

Appendix A   New Issues of Tax Exempt Bonds, 1957-1965

Table 1 New Issues of Municipal Bonds by Type Offering and Issue, 1957–1965

[Dollar amounts in millions]

Year and type issue	Competitive		Negotiated		Total	
	Amount	Number	Amount	Number	Amount	Number
1957:						
General obligation	$4,525	4,983	$210	869	$4,808	6,104
Revenue	1,267	444	644	259	1,976	721
Public Housing Authority	66	10	----------	----------	66	10
Total	5,858	5,437	855	1,128	6,850	6,835
1958:						
General obligation	5,247	5,023	198	874	5,515	6,089
Revenue	1,207	534	434	328	1,693	893
Public Housing Authority	185	44	----------	----------	185	44
Total	6,639	5,601	633	1,202	7,394	7,026
1959:						
General obligation	4,592	4,866	197	652	4,817	5,682
Revenue	1,283	515	1,127	295	2,430	836
Public Housing Authority	335	76	----------	----------	335	76
Total	6,209	5,457	1,324	947	7,581	6,594
1960:						
General obligation	4,629	4,961	136	565	4,775	5,626
Revenue	1,242	550	838	315	2,095	881
Public Housing Authority	281	68	----------	----------	302	69
Total	6,153	5,579	973	880	7,712	6,576
1961:						
General obligation	5,601	5,132	126	487	5,739	5,705
Revenue	1,458	655	962	292	2,444	954
Public Housing Authority	315	116	----------	----------	315	116
Total	7,374	5,902	1,088	79	8,498	6,775
1962:						
General obligation	5,437	5,238	121	277	5,590	5,526
Revenue	1,912	821	774	242	2,711	1,069
Public Housing Authority	437	122	----------	----------	437	122
Total	7,786	6,181	895	519	8,737	6,717
1963:						
General obligations	5,527	4,609	264	663	5,831	5,333
Revenue	2,362	904	1,783	572	4,246	1,500
Public Housing Authority	254	64	----------	----------	254	64
Total	8,143	5,577	2,047	1,235	10,331	6,897
1964:						
General obligations	6,194	4,592	195	470	6,402	5,136
Revenue	2,181	789	1,377	468	3,608	1,274
Public Housing Authority	637	163	----------	----------	637	163
Total	9,012	5,544	1,571	938	10,646	6,573
1965:						
General obligation	6,989	4,438	167	360	7,266	4,915
Revenue	2,410	767	1,025	455	3,521	1,267
Public Housing Authority	478	129	----------	----------	478	129
Total	9,877	5,334	1,192	815	11,265	6,311

NOTE.—Subtotals may not add to totals due to rounding and inclusion in the total of small amounts not classifiable as competitive or negotiated.

Source: Investment Bankers Association of America.

Table 2 New Issues of Municipal Bonds by Average Maturity and Type Issue, 1957–1965

[Dollars in millions]

Type issue	1 through 4 Amount	Number	5 through 9 Amount	Number	10 through 14 Amount	Number	15 through 19 Amount	Number	20 through 29 Amount	Number	30— Amount	Number	No record Amount	Number	Total Amount	Number
1957:																
General obligation	$104	422	$795	1,601	$2,490	2,056	$812	694	$190	137	$4	10	$412	1,184	$4,808	6,104
Revenue	2	9	247	64	235	159	285	132	300	112	519	29	389	216	1,976	721
Public Housing Authority		1											66	9	66	10
Total	106	432	1,043	1,665	2,725	2,215	1,098	826	489	249	522	39	868	1,409	6,850	6,835
1958:																
General obligation	134	446	962	1,639	2,506	1,969	1,140	638	265	127	145	15	363	1,255	5,515	6,069
Revenue	2	13	181	73	334	150	324	140	222	127	243	60	386	330	1,693	893
Public Housing Authority													185	44	185	44
Total	136	459	1,143	1,712	2,841	2,119	1,464	778	487	254	388	75	935	1,629	7,394	7,026
1959:																
General obligation	81	412	801	1,536	1,951	1,763	1,182	638	241	124	4	11	554	1,198	4,817	5,682
Revenue	8	13	66	53	345	136	280	127	322	107	978	81	430	319	2,430	836
Public Housing Authority													335	76	335	76
Total	90	425	868	1,589	2,296	1,899	1,462	765	564	231	982	92	1,320	1,563	7,581	6,594
1960:																
General obligation	91	373	598	1,464	2,171	1,892	1,073	602	158	126	55	8	630	1,161	4,775	5,626
Revenue	5	8	40	59	307	149	276	139	309	125	706	81	453	320	2,095	881
Public Housing Authority													302	69	302	69
Total	95	381	638	1,522	2,477	2,041	1,349	741	467	251	761	89	1,384	1,550	7,172	6,576

236

[Dollars in millions]

Type issue	Average maturity														Total	
	1 through 4		5 through 9		10 through 14		15 through 19		20 through 29		30—		No record			
	Amount	Number	Amount	Number	Amount	Number	Amount	Number	Amount	Number	Amount	Number	Amount	Number	Amount	Number
1961:																
General obligation	$149	343	$690	1,448	$2,612	1,955	$1,469	608	$312	137	$35	12	$472	1,202	$5,739	5,705
Revenue	8	12	90	55	255	144	432	126	399	131	646	64	613	422	2,444	954
Public Housing Authority	22	3			17	3	3	1	104	4			170	105	315	116
Total	179	358	780	1,503	2,884	2,102	1,903	735	815	272	681	76	1,255	1,729	8,498	6,775
1962:																
General obligation	165	270	649	988	2,037	1,461	852	440	282	76	1	1	1,604	2,300	5,590	5,526
Revenue	2	5	26	31	112	66	365	89	157	67	522	44	1,526	767	2,711	1,069
Public Housing Authority													437	122	437	122
Total	166	275	675	1,019	2,149	1,617	1,217	529	439	143	523	45	3,567	3,189	8,737	6,717
1963:																
General obligation	235	274	736	1,191	2,639	1,732	1,239	592	375	150	12	5	595	1,389	5,831	5,333
Revenue	11	14	99	68	401	182	657	195	621	174	727	72	1,730	795	4,246	1,500
Public Housing Authority													254	64	254	64
Total	246	288	835	1,259	3,040	1,914	1,896	787	996	324	739	77	2,579	2,248	10,331	6,897
1964:																
General obligation	191	196	755	1,040	2,547	1,715	1,372	600	296	123	298	7	943	1,455	6,402	5,136
Revenue	2	5	96	72	377	157	801	192	551	161	770	60	1,010	627	3,608	1,274
Public Housing Authority							81	20					556	143	637	163
Total	193	201	851	1,112	2,924	1,872	2,254	812	847	284	1,068	67	2,509	2,225	10,646	6,573
1965:																
General obligation	337	183	1,127	1,055	3,097	1,748	1,278	567	468	135	235	12	727	1,215	7,266	4,915
Revenue	10	9	160	68	366	154	811	202	858	196	219	37	1,096	601	3,521	1,267
Public Housing Authority							2	1	31	4			445	124	478	129
Total	347	192	1,285	1,123	3,463	1,902	2,091	770	1,357	335	454	49	2,268	1,940	11,265	6,311

Table 3 *New Issues of Municipal Bonds by Use of Proceeds and Type Issuer, 1957–1965*

[Dollars in millions]

Type issuer	Use of proceeds													
	Education		Transportation		Utilities and conservation		Social welfare		Miscellaneous		Refunding		Total	
	Amount	Number	Amount	Number	Amount	Number	Amount	Number	Amount	Number	Amount	Number	Amount	Number
1957:														
State	$249	34	$558	36	$14	5	$84	6	$499	44	$2	1	$1,407	126
City, etc.	482	468	355	661	950	1,335	153	258	590	946	34	78	2,665	3,746
School district	1,584	2,390	0	0	0	0	0	0	0	0	14	28	1,598	2,418
Special district	116	76	349	95	543	230	96	53	176	88	1	3	1,281	545
Total	2,432	2,968	1,263	792	1,508	1,570	333	317	1,265	1,078	51	110	6,850	6,835
1958:														
State	406	95	681	45	12	7	168	13	636	60	8	2	1,910	222
City, etc.	509	408	396	696	875	1,363	165	287	684	934	43	125	2,073	3,813
School district	1,456	2,281	0	0	0	0	0	0	7	1	8	34	1,471	2,316
Special district	152	128	349	79	411	287	224	85	177	85	25	10	1,339	674
Total	2,523	2,912	1,428	821	1,299	1,657	557	385	1,503	1,060	84	171	7,394	7,026
1959:														
State	334	64	384	36	59	17	93	5	647	53	38	2	1,554	177
City, etc.	395	358	440	632	858	1,257	231	279	603	978	33	71	2,560	3,575
School district	1,349	2,222	0	0	0	1	0	0	1	1	5	13	1,354	2,237
Special district	119	99	410	73	1,013	269	265	83	273	75	33	6	2,113	605
Total	2,196	2,743	1,234	741	1,931	1,544	589	367	1,522	1,107	109	92	7,681	6,594
1960:														
State	234	43	246	24	9	5	15	7	508	42	0	0	1,012	121
City, etc.	340	336	437	598	819	1,249	407	270	663	912	24	76	2,690	3,441
School district	1,477	2,141	0	0	0	0	0	1	0	0	17	24	1,495	2,168
Special district	253	187	710	103	420	330	170	64	418	160	4	4	1,975	846
Total	2,304	2,707	1,394	725	1,247	1,584	593	342	1,589	1,114	45	104	7,172	6,676

[Dollars in millions]

Type issuer	Education Amount	Education Number	Transportation Amount	Transportation Number	Utilities and conservation Amount	Utilities and conservation Number	Social welfare Amount	Social welfare Number	Miscellaneous Amount	Miscellaneous Number	Refunding Amount	Refunding Number	Total Amount	Total Number
1961:														
State	$434	64	$369	36	$51	10	$105	15	$869	41	$2	1	$1,829	167
City, etc.	485	434	509	669	1,033	1,336	290	291	745	941	24	69	3,085	3,740
School district	1,417	1,982	0	0	0	0	0	0	1	2	7	12	1,425	1,996
Special district	394	174	687	112	537	328	239	114	231	135	71	9	2,160	872
Total	2,729	2,654	1,565	817	1,621	1,674	634	420	1,846	1,119	103	91	8,498	6,775
1962:														
State	371	103	315	24	26	4	223	17	356	34	16	2	1,307	184
City, etc.	460	405	449	595	989	1,193	247	241	987	934	109	113	3,242	3,481
School district	1,562	2,041	0	0	0	0	0	0	2	4	15	27	1,578	2,072
Special district	477	210	826	118	519	312	347	148	300	139	141	53	2,609	980
Total	2,870	2,759	1,591	737	1,534	1,509	817	406	1,644	1,111	280	195	8,737	6,717
1963:														
State	442	101	267	30	13	4	186	14	401	49	142	10	1,450	208
City, etc.	513	420	466	526	1,121	1,371	242	260	1,032	917	353	234	3,727	3,728
School district	1,429	1,683	0	0	0	0	------	1	------	1	140	119	1,669	1,804
Special district	461	301	625	109	915	408	494	124	316	121	775	94	3,586	1,157
Total	2,844	2,506	1,358	665	2,048	1,783	922	399	1,749	1,067	1,409	457	10,331	6,897
1964:														
State	462	93	202	22	259	10	67	13	476	52	49	6	1,496	196
City, etc.	383	307	277	455	1,139	1,231	192	234	1,474	869	208	154	3,674	3,250
School district	1,610	1,694	0	0	0	0	0	0	------	2	84	99	1,694	1,795
Special district	809	299	684	138	901	457	783	236	301	128	304	74	3,783	1,332
Total	3,265	2,393	1,163	615	2,299	1,698	1,043	483	2,231	1,051	646	333	10,646	6,573
1965:														
State	560	91	360	23	203	5	85	12	1,060	69	15	3	2,283	203
City, etc.	458	365	410	412	984	1,054	223	253	1,030	916	219	164	3,371	3,186
School district	1,721	1,596	0	0	0	0	0	0	0	0	60	69	1,840	1,703
Special district	757	278	568	125	621	354	671	185	695	201	292	64	3,772	1,219
Total	3,497	2,330	1,338	560	1,809	1,413	979	450	2,785	1,186	585	300	11,265	6,311

Source: Investment Bankers Association of America.

Note.—Subtotals may not add to totals due to rounding.

Table 4 New Issues of Municipal Bonds by Type Issue and Issuer, 1957–1965

[Dollar amounts in millions]

Type issuer	General obligation		Revenue		Public Housing Authority		Total	
	Amount	Number	Amount	Number	Amount	Number	Amount	Number
1957:								
State	$993	89	$413	37	0	0	$1,407	126
City, etc	1,891	3,240	673	506	0	0	2,565	3,746
School districts	1,594	2,411	4	7	0	0	1,598	2,418
Special districts	329	364	885	171	$66	10	1,281	545
Total	4,808	6,104	1,976	721	66	10	6,850	6,835
1958:								
State	1,524	148	386	74	0	0	1,910	222
City, etc	2,099	3,244	574	569	0	0	2,673	3,813
School districts	1,471	2,314			0	0	1,471	2,316
Special districts	421	382	733	248	185	44	1,339	674
Total	5,515	6,089	1,693	893	185	44	7,394	7,026
1959:								
State	1,229	123	325	54	0	0	1,554	177
City, etc	1,821	3,011	633	530	105	34	2,560	3,575
School district	1,345	2,221	9	16	0	0	1,354	2,237
Special district	421	327	1,462	236	229	42	2,113	605
Total	4,817	5,682	2,430	836	335	76	7,581	6,594
1960:								
State	857	93	156	28	0	0	1,012	121
City etc	1,836	2,870	573	503	281	68	2,690	3,441
School districts	1,491	2,160	3	6	0	0	1,495	2,166
Special district	591	503	1,364	344	20	1	1,975	848
Total	4,775	5,626	2,095	881	302	69	7,172	6,576
1961:								
State	1,510	113	256	52	63	2	1,829	167
City, etc	2,333	3,110	692	585	60	45	3,085	3,740
School district	1,404	1,987	21	9	0	0	1,425	1,996
Special district	493	495	1,475	308	192	69	2,160	872
Total	5,739	5,705	2,444	954	316	116	8,498	6,775
1962:								
State	985	90	267	92	55	2	1,307	184
City, etc	2,437	2,887	725	572	80	22	3,242	3,481
School district	1,578	2,070		2	0	0	1,578	2,072
Special district	589	479	1,718	403	302	98	2,609	980
Total	5,590	5,526	2,711	1,069	437	122	8,737	6,717
1963:								
State	1,090	121	360	87	0	0	1,450	208
City, etc	2,618	2,921	1,109	807	0	0	3,727	3,728
School district	1,567	1,797	2	7	0	0	1,569	1,804
Special district	556	494	2,776	599	254	64	3,586	1,157
Total	5,831	5,333	4,246	1,500	254	64	10,331	6,897
1964:								
State	1,298	126	198	70	0	0	1,496	196
City, etc	2,602	2,602	1,072	648	0	0	3,674	3,250
School district	1,693	1,793	1	2	0	0	1,694	1,795
Special district	809	615	2,336	554	637	163	3,783	1,332
Total	6,402	5,136	3,608	1,274	637	163	10,646	6,573
1965:								
State	2,053	125	230	78	0	0	2,283	203
City, etc	2,406	2,578	964	608	0	0	3,371	3,186
School district	1,838	1,700	1	3	0	0	1,840	1,703
Special district	968	512	2,325	578	478	129	3,772	1,219
Total	7,266	4,915	3,521	1,267	478	129	11,265	6,311

NOTE.—Subtotals may not add to totals due to rounding.
Source: Investment Bankers Association of America.

Table 5 New Issues of Municipal Bonds by Size and Type Issuer, 1957–1965

[Dollars in millions]

Year and size of issuer	Type issuer								Total	
	States		Cities, etc.		School districts		Special districts and Public Authority			
	Amount	Number	Amount	Number	Amount	Number	Amount	Number	Amount	Number
1957										
Less than 10,000	0	0	$171	859	$322	643	$22	65	$514	1,567
10,000 to 24,999	0	0	220	564	260	301	72	40	552	905
25,000 to 49,999	0	0	211	388	171	132	276	24	658	544
50,000 to 99,999	0	0	248	265	167	87	26	19	441	371
100,000 to 249,999	$41	13	369	259	97	42	104	21	570	322
250,000 to 499,999	73	12	272	146	74	17	53	13	441	189
500,000 to 999,999	1,262	86	326	153	57	9	33	13	490	187
1,000,000 and larger	30	15	464	112	91	7	324	27	2,142	232
Population not recorded			284	1,000	359	1,180	370	323	1,042	2,518
Total	1,407	126	2,565	3,746	1,598	2,418	1,281	545	6,850	6,835
1958										
Less than 10,000	0	0	236	1,381	379	936	26	132	642	2,452
10,000 to 24,999	0	0	216	692	261	324	24	33	501	949
25,000 to 49,999	0	0	293	444	244	196	21	21	558	661
50,000 to 99,999	2	3	269	293	117	82	33	20	419	395
100,000 to 249,999	50	15	332	290	111	49	57	30	503	373
250,000 to 499,999	82	27	251	149	49	10	34	8	383	182
500,000 to 999,999	1,711	149	436	170	43	7	27	7	589	211
1,000,000 and larger	65	28	568	87	75	5	193	23	2,546	264
Population not recorded			72	407	192	707	924	400	1,255	1,542
Total	1,910	222	2,673	3,813	1,471	2,316	1,339	674	7,394	7,026
1959										
Less than 10,000	0	0	253	1,493	431	1,370	58	181	742	3,044
10,000 to 24,999	0	0	236	571	308	376	22	35	566	982
25,000 to 49,999	0	0	276	434	183	178	225	42	684	654
50,000 to 99,999	0	0	233	301	125	106	25	24	383	431
100,000 to 249,999	48	13	275	237	110	55	40	29	426	321
250,000 to 499,999	69	16	220	123	32	11	74	16	374	163
500,000 to 999,999	1,363	111	380	162	49	6	42	11	540	195
1,000,000 and larger	73	37	617	95	64	7	228	21	2,272	233
Population not recorded			69	159	53	128	1,399	246	1,595	570
Total	1,554	177	2,560	3,575	1,354	2,237	2,113	605	7,581	6,594

241

Table 5 New Issues of Municipal Bonds by Size and Type Issuer, 1957–1965—Continued

1960

Less than 10,000	0	0	177	705	196	448	19	65	392	1,308
10,000 to 24,999	0	0	200	508	278	296	21	32	499	836
25,000 to 49,999	0	0	238	325	160	145	8	19	406	490
50,000 to 99,999	0	0	203	266	129	89	17	15	349	370
100,000 to 249,999	0	0	340	211	89	45	42	23	471	279
250,000 to 499,999	17	5	193	100	40	10	50	14	300	129
500,000 to 999,999	17	5	295	130	41	5	78	18	430	158
1,000,000 and larger	770	76	479	77	20	2	189	25	1,457	180
Population not recorded	209	35	556	1,029	542	1,126	1,551	637	2,868	2,827
Total	1,012	121	2,690	3,441	1,495	2,166	1,975	848	7,172	6,576

1961

Less than 10,000	0	0	238	1,097	226	481	103	86	567	1,664
10,000 to 24,999	0	0	260	634	296	344	52	66	608	1,044
25,000 to 49,999	0	0	317	447	172	158	49	37	38	642
50,000 to 99,999	0	0	257	324	118	83	29	20	404	427
100,000 to 249,999	0	0	307	209	95	50	76	34	477	293
250,000 to 499,999	30	11	344	184	30	10	30	16	435	221
500,000 to 999,999	60	13	398	160	51	6	73	22	581	201
1,000,000 and larger	1,577	107	701	114	115	7	180	20	2,573	248
Population not recorded	161	36	262	571	323	857	1,569	571	2,316	2,035
Total	1,829	167	3,085	3,740	1,425	1,996	2,160	872	8,498	6,775

1962

Less than 10,000	0	0	289	1,165	250	505	30	48	549	1,719
10,000 to 24,999	0	0	296	647	325	368	54	41	675	1,056
25,000 to 49,999	0	0	294	444	214	193	21	17	572	654
50,000 to 99,999	0	0	282	309	152	100	37	27	455	436
100,000 to 249,999	7	5	400	242	110	38	31	22	553	307
250,000 to 499,999	48	20	424	165	32	10	21	12	525	207
500,000 to 999,999	37	14	363	122	38	4	132	22	570	162
1,000,000 and larger	1,076	111	650	106	103	9	208	28	2,036	254
Population not recorded	139	34	263	281	355	845	2,043	763	2,801	1,923
Total	1,307	184	3,242	3,481	1,578	2,072	2,609	980	8,737	6,717

1963

Less than 10,000	0	0	351	1,199	162	346	62	84	576	1,629
10,000 to 24,999	0	0	334	589	222	251	136	80	691	920
25,000 to 49,999	0	0	392	461	205	163	272	51	869	675
50,000 to 99,999	0	4	293	294	200	97	51	15	544	406
100,000 to 249,999	8	11	446	242	176	44	72	21	702	311
250,000 to 499,999	27	45	457	165	67	13	115	11	664	200
500,000 to 999,999	168	120	416	123	47	5	65	10	696	183
1,000,000 and larger	1,060	28	717	93	50	3	256	14	2,083	230
Population not recorded	187		323	562	440	882	2,556	871	3,506	2,343
Total	1,450	208	3,727	3,728	1,569	1,804	3,586	1,157	10,331	6,897

[Dollars in millions]

Year and size of issuer	Type issuer									
	States		Cities, etc.		School districts		Special districts and Public Authority		Total	
	Amount	Number	Amount	Number	Amount	Number	Amount	Number	Amount	Number
1964										
Less than 10,000	0	0	$366	1,125	$256	410	$39	76	$662	1,611
10,000 to 24,999	0	0	402	600	305	275	64	78	771	951
25,000 to 49,999	0	0	359	443	237	174	49	38	644	655
50,000 to 99,999	0	0	305	305	172	99	56	21	533	425
100,000 to 249,999	$8	1	427	193	133	45	44	21	611	260
250,000 to 499,999	105	31	337	140	45	8	45	10	532	189
500,000 to 999,999	76	30	485	133	42	4	61	17	663	184
1,000,000 and larger	1,267	107	815	71	25	1	90	12	2,196	191
Population not recorded	40	27	178	240	478	779	3,336	1,059	4,013	2,105
Total	1,496	196	3,674	3,250	1,694	1,795	3,783	1,332	10,646	6,573
1965										
Less than 10,000	0	0	336	1,049	220	232	55	68	611	1,349
10,000 to 24,999	0	0	435	616	297	256	116	75	847	947
25,000 to 49,999	0	0	494	447	207	166	60	36	762	649
50,000 to 99,999	0	0	385	293	198	97	65	30	648	420
100,000 to 249,999	0	0	404	214	191	56	41	16	636	286
250,000 to 499,999	45	6	491	160	55	7	58	12	649	185
500,000 to 999,999	194	41	241	84	34	4	190	19	659	148
1,000,000 and larger	1,830	128	384	59	84	4	367	18	2,664	209
Population not recorded	215	28	200	264	554	881	2,821	945	3,790	2,118
Total	2,283	203	3,371	3,186	1,840	1,703	3,772	1,219	11,265	6,311

NOTE.—Subtotals may not add to totals due to rounding and miscellaneous issuers not given in subtotals.

Source: Investment Bankers Association of America.

Table 6   The Volume of New Issues, by State of Origin and Type Issuer, 1957–1965

[In millions of dollars]

State and type issuer	1957	1958	1959	1960	1961	1962	1963	1964	1965
Alabama	77	77	138	161	147	118	120	228	369
State		21	2	4		9	3	10	
Cities and counties	43	51	61	49	91	52	46	94	83
School districts	4		1	1			1	1	
Special districts, public authorities	31	5	74	108	55	57	69	122	285
Alaska	2	20	16	18	36	29	34	26	12
State		2			14	7	8	8	
Cities and counties	2	15	11	10	16	11	15	2	12
School districts		3	4	7	5	10	2	17	1
Special districts, public authorities				1	2	1	10		
Arizona	51	26	65	65	58	96	50	86	100
State				2		1	1	2	3
Cities and counties	26	10	30	17	28	58	32	23	41
School districts	20	16	15	27	28	21	11	22	26
Special districts, public authorities	5		20	19	2	18	6	39	34
Arkansas	15	11	19	15	21	18	51	101	49
State							1		
Cities and counties	14	11	14	10	6	11	29	76	19
School districts	1		4	4	11	5	9	9	11
Special districts, public authorities					4	2	12	16	19
California	888	1,081	953	1,081	1,317	877	1,103	1,349	1,642
State	300	400	250	393	591	207	200	644	535
Cities and counties	208	242	188	216	212	225	205	177	236
School districts	289	239	240	232	316	251	209	254	249
Special districts, public authorities	92	199	275	241	198	194	489	273	622
Canada									
State									
Cities and counties									
School districts									
Special districts, public authorities									
Colorado	67	73	41	36	47	70	204	151	137
State	16	5	6				28	6	1
Cities and counties	32	43	20	21	20	30	47	53	57
School districts	18	24	15	12	26	35	107	46	48
Special districts, public authorities				2	1	6	22	45	31
Connecticut	263	232	209	132	185	205	117	187	189
State	149	127	140	64	95	102	49	94	91
Cities and counties	77	96	62	56	81	95	61	81	94
School districts		5	1	7	1	2			
Special districts, public authorities	37	4	6	4	8	7	8	12	4
Delaware	41	56	42	32	23	74	21	170	59
State	32	38	29	16	11	38	12	49	3
Cities and counties	5	6	11	16	5	1	7	6	1
School districts	4	12	1		7	4	1	12	8
Special districts, public authorities						32	1	104	3
District of Columbia	1	185	110	35	3			14	8
State									
Cities and counties			6						
School districts									
Special districts, public authorities	1	185	104	35	3			14	8
Florida	267	167	159	240	320	248	297	499	364
State		20	19	18	8	10			
Cities and counties	132	101	74	119	94	122	193	171	169
School districts	54	12	21	14	34	13	23	57	48
Special districts, public authorities	80	33	45	89	184	104	81	271	147
Georgia	120	108	56	49	183	212	137	171	204
State					30				
Cities and counties	55	45	36	44	40	66	68	46	65
School districts	14	7	18	3	10	11	28	8	7
Special districts, public authorities	51	56	2	2	104	135	41	116	132

Table 6 The Volume of New Issues, by State of Origin and Type Issuer, 1957-1965—Continued

[In millions of dollars]

State and type issuer	1957	1958	1959	1960	1961	1962	1963	1964	1965
Hawaii	48	36	65	23	32	29	76	55	58
State	34	21	53	7	10	10	66	30	32
Cities and counties	15	15	12	16	22	18	11	20	10
School districts									
Special districts, public authorities						1		5	16
Idaho	4	11	10	10	11	11	10	8	11
State			1				1		2
Cities and counties	1	7	1	2	5	2	2	2	4
School districts	2	4	3	8	6	8	7	4	4
Special districts, public authorities			4			1		3	1
Illinois	336	379	425	324	424	426	564	344	354
State	4	3	8	18	124	106	183	24	8
Cities and counties	206	183	281	182	143	130	70	83	90
School districts	98	78	77	75	61	75	109	82	110
Special districts, public authorities	28	115	59	49	96	115	202	155	146
Indiana	71	145	133	78	119	143	107	137	187
State		43	7	6	8	10	8		2
Cities and counties	33	50	40	31	52	71	33	25	40
School districts	15	8	17	14	15	8	8	2	5
Special districts, public authorities	24	45	69	26	43	54	58	110	140
Iowa	38	68	49	48	50	59	52	53	58
State		25							7
Cities and counties	16	22	20	23	32	27	14	17	29
School districts	21	21	28	25	19	28	21	15	21
Special districts, public authorities						4	17	21	1
Kansas	133	56	42	55	52	69	62	64	104
State		1	1	1	1	1			
Cities and counties	76	33	21	32	28	42	22	35	71
School districts	16	21	20	20	19	15	9	7	8
Special districts, public authorities	41	1		2	4	11	31	23	25
Kentucky	72	60	37	102	415	138	228	147	155
State	35	35	3	41	169	42	85	56	21
Cities and counties	29	25	34	50	79	55	122	65	87
School districts									
Special districts, public authorities	8			10	166	40	21	25	47
Louisiana	151	140	123	140	105	288	306	190	299
State	12	21	31	52			61		2
Cities and counties	47	35	35	48	49	94	116	59	104
School districts	50	66	40	21	14	30	22	41	44
Special districts, public authorities	43	18	17	19	42	165	107	90	149
Maine	5	16	21	17	24	19	28	20	17
State		6	10	7	10	3	18	12	5
Cities and counties	3	4	7	6	6	12	5	6	7
School districts	1		2	2	4	2	1	1	4
Special districts, public authorities	1	7	3	2	4	2	3	2	1
Maryland	120	175	137	124	189	247	263	223	228
State	24	41	12	37	37	34	64	37	69
Cities and counties	68	87	86	30	96	97	135	106	99
School districts									
Special districts, public authorities	28	47	39	57	55	116	63	80	61
Massachusetts	256	308	324	172	231	383	219	447	251
State	129	159	84	35	109	40	76	62	93
Cities and counties	108	122	97	104	102	134	117	206	111
School districts	5	17	11	10	11	2	3	8	17
Special districts, public authorities	13	11	133	23	9	207	24	171	31
Michigan	267	350	373	349	397	349	288	392	380
State	52	103	75	93	102	86	8	6	5
Cities and counties	80	103	135	95	147	124	147	180	133
School districts	135	123	141	140	103	121	111	150	185
Special districts, public authorities		21	22	21	45	19	22	56	57

245

[In millions of dollars]

State and type issuer	1957	1958	1959	1960	1961	1962	1963	1964	1965
Minnesota	155	154	165	180	118	142	296	233	283
State	12	47	38	49			123	7	68
Cities and counties	56	57	67	66	67	75	93	81	95
School districts	60	50	56	56	45	59	63	104	109
Special districts, public authorities	27		4	9	6	7	17	42	11
Mississippi	49	75	103	79	81	81	77	113	119
State	18	30	56	15	17	22	14	30	23
Cities and counties	20	27	24	35	39	37	41	56	47
School districts	9	15	14	8	11	10	12	14	13
Special districts, public authorities	1	3	9	21	14	10	9	13	36
Missouri	140	154	73	81	89	125	140	121	137
State	23	55			1		1	3	
Cities and counties	67	58	45	49	48	72	57	66	81
School districts	31	40	28	31	37	38	43	24	30
Special districts, public authorities	19	1		1	4	15	39	28	26
Montana	17	18	11	18	12	20	19	8	22
State		6							9
Cities and counties	10	6	5	4	4	5	9	2	4
School districts	7	6	6	11	6	13	6	2	7
Special districts, public authorities		1		2	1	2	4	4	2
Nebraska	23	34	45	22	40	62	60	62	45
State			5			10			
Cities and counties	13	8	6	9	12	19	14	13	18
School districts	2	9	10	8	8	22	40	4	6
Special districts, public authorities	8	16	25	5	20	12	6	46	21
Nevada	9	18	6	17	26	16	59	50	47
State							2		6
Cities and counties	4	6	2	3	6	3	21	18	11
School districts	4	11	1	12	5	10	23	27	23
Special districts, public authorities			3	3	15	3	12	4	7
New Hampshire	7	34	28	10	28	14	40	20	55
State		29	12		16		23		25
Cities and counties	5	4	12	7	7	9	8	9	16
School districts	2	2	3	2	5	3	7	9	10
Special districts, public authorities						2	1	2	4
New Jersey	149	198	219	203	239	329	292	201	345
State			92		21	42	58		45
Cities and counties	65	88	42	115	107	91	102	76	184
School districts	74	94	55	76	84	95	75	73	57
Special districts, public authorities	9	16	31	11	26	101	56	51	59
New Mexico	17	22	17	42	32	37	65	121	81
State	4	3		1	14	5	21	49	22
Cities and counties	8	10	9	27	9	20	28	32	7
School districts	5	8	7	13	8	12	14	17	11
Special districts, public authorities					2		3	23	41
New York	711	950	1,176	998	1,078	1,281	1,483	1,569	1,416
State	92	227	165		63	275	117	135	646
Cities and counties	240	319	224	259	455	465	681	647	153
School districts	234	235	144	238	204	204	129	215	189
Special districts, public authorities	145	169	644	500	355	337	556	572	428
North Carolina	58	83	66	91	93	59	94	87	149
State		25	3	22	27		22		28
Cities and counties	56	58	52	66	61	52	67	74	85
School districts			6	1			1	1	
Special districts, public authorities	2		6	2	5	7	3	11	35
North Dakota	16	8	6	20	13	16	7	9	17
State	9							1	1
Cities and counties	5	7	2	12	6	6	1	3	9
School districts	1	1	4	7	7	11	5	3	6
Special districts, public authorities								2	2

[In millions of dollars]

State and type issuer	1957	1958	1959	1960	1961	1962	1963	1964	1965
Ohio	472	396	306	305	312	281	318	345	416
State	220	155	65	17	70	7	3	2	90
Cities and counties	139	139	132	125	130	127	178	102	148
School districts	114	102	100	153	100	116	103	117	124
Special districts, public authorities			8	10	12	31	35	124	54
Oklahoma	48	69	42	98	204	82	182	89	150
State					36	2	6	1	15
Cities and counties	26	18	25	16	45	44	58	49	74
School districts	18	23	17	16	11	24	28	34	26
Special districts, public authorities	3	27		66	113	13	90	6	34
Oregon	91	55	95	59	136	79	101	125	57
State	52	24	63	1	81	30	11	61	
Cities and counties	15	12	11	39	18	18	53	18	19
School districts	19	14	16	15	21	23	24	25	31
Special districts, public authorities	5	6	5	5	17	11	12	22	7
Pennsylvania	298	384	485	395	406	588	768	649	675
State	11	24	131			27	22		27
Cities and counties	74	91	105	139	72	71	102	109	105
School districts	32	38	34	31	11	32	29	27	74
Special districts, public authorities	181	232	215	225	323	458	615	514	469
Puerto Rico	37	69	102	94	95	147	101	122	155
State	10	27	55	17	40	25	30	53	54
Cities and counties	5	1	14	35	7	38	27	17	11
School districts									
Special districts, public authorities	22	40	33	43	49	84	43	53	90
Rhode Island	43	44	15	10	29	40	59	49	84
State	27	19		2	11	19	38	23	24
Cities and counties	16	24	13	7	14	20	21	22	30
School districts		1	1	1					2
Special districts, public authorities		1			4			4	28
South Carolina	44	63	44	27	36	32	46	23	63
State	21	46	17	5	6	5	5		17
Cities and counties	14	11	15	10	15	12	21	13	30
School districts	2	1	9	5	7	5	18	5	8
Special districts, public authorities	6	4	3	8	8	9	3	5	8
South Dakota	10	6	8	5	7	3	7	13	12
State									
Cities and counties	2	4	4	3	4	1	2	3	4
School districts	7	1	4	2	3	2	5	8	7
Special districts, public authorities								2	
Tennessee	59	92	91	106	125	156	301	157	149
State	10	15	15	15	16	14	25	18	25
Cities and counties	48	74	76	84	106	122	156	121	103
School districts				2					
Special districts, public authorities	1	3		5	3	20	120	18	21
Texas	387	360	345	308	422	444	440	471	657
State	16	67	30	1	79	10	1	3	3
Cities and counties	192	160	179	158	197	217	201	244	227
School districts	132	103	101	102	97	136	169	141	208
Special districts, public authorities	47	30	36	47	49	81	70	82	218
Utah	8	26	16	19	21	48	21	43	102
State							2	5	79
Cities and counties	1	5	4	5	8	19	3	19	3
School districts		10	12	9	7	27	15	18	18
Special districts, public authorities	7	10	1	5	7	2		1	3

Table 6 The Volume of New Issues, by State of Origin and Type Issuer, 1957–1965 — Continued

[In millions of dollars]

State and type issuer	1957	1958	1959	1960	1961	1962	1963	1964	1965
Vermont	16	15	15	17	8	12	16	20	22
State	9	12	13	14	5	10	6	17	10
Cities and counties	4	1	1	1	2	1	7	----	4
School districts	3	2	1	3	1	1	3	2	7
Special districts, public authorities	----	----	----	----	----	----	----	----	----
Virginia	71	53	67	308	119	128	114	110	166
State	----	----	----	----	•1	7	2	2	34
Cities and counties	69	47	62	58	82	98	96	77	65
School districts	2	----	3	----	----	----	----	3	1
Special districts, public authorities	----	7	1	250	36	23	17	27	66
Virgin Islands	----	----	----	2	----	7	----	----	9
State	----	----	----	----	----	----	----	----	5
Cities and counties	----	----	----	----	----	----	----	----	----
School districts	----	----	----	----	----	----	----	----	----
Special districts, public authorities	----	----	----	2	----	7	----	----	4
Washington	481	104	320	211	111	203	723	540	269
State	85	13	38	47	3	64	37	23	56
Cities and counties	33	51	27	85	64	35	75	149	125
School districts	54	25	41	40	26	34	26	35	53
Special districts, public authorities	309	15	215	39	18	70	584	333	36
West Virginia	4	23	56	17	24	27	16	61	84
State	----	19	18	10	3	14	4	21	63
Cities and counties	4	4	35	1	12	7	10	14	9
School districts	----	----	3	1	----	----	----	5	----
Special districts, public authorities	----	----	----	4	9	6	1	21	12
Wisconsin	128	100	92	113	182	164	133	160	222
State	----	----	----	----	----	15	----	----	----
Cities and counties	93	74	78	91	122	83	90	103	124
School districts	31	17	14	422	24	56	42	41	22
Special districts, public authorities	4	8	----	----	36	10	1	16	77
Wyoming	7	8	17	13	21	4	16	10	16
State	----	----	9	3	----	----	6	----	----
Cities and counties	3	1	----	----	11	2	----	5	2
School districts	3	7	6	8	9	2	5	4	2
Special districts, public authorities	1	----	----	1	----	----	----	2	12

NOTE.—Subtotals may not add to totals due to rounding.

Source: Investment Bankers Association of America.

Table 7   New Issues of Municipal Bonds, by Region [1] of Issue

Year	Region							
	Northeast		South		North-central		West	
	Amount [2]	Number	Amount [2]	Number	Amount [2]	Number	Amount [2]	Number
1957	$1,749	1,511	$1,584	1,692	$1,789	2,438	$1,691	1,184
1958	2,181	1,594	1,798	1,863	1,849	2,363	1,496	1,177
1959	2,493	1,347	1,636	1,832	1,717	2,262	1,633	1,144
1960	1,953	1,459	1,932	1,698	1,579	2,145	1,611	1,253
1961	2,229	1,418	2,510	1,821	1,804	2,323	1,860	1,203
1962	2,870	1,454	2,350	1,903	1,840	2,211	1,520	1,137
1963	3,022	1,529	2,694	2,153	2,035	2,024	2,480	1,176
1964	3,162	1,461	2,854	1,979	1,935	1,954	2,573	1,166
1965	3,053	1,380	3,271	1,991	2,216	1,789	2,559	1,137

[1] Bureau of the Census, census region.
[2] Millions omitted.

Source: Investment Bankers Association of America.

Appendix B Critical Factors Affecting Demand by Bank, Insurance Company and Individual Investors

This is the text of the Joint Economic Committee's summary of investor characteristics, as further discussed in Chapter V above. See also: *JEC-Financing*, pp. 16–20.

COMMERCIAL BANKS

"During the past four years, 1962–65, commercial banks materially stepped up their acquisitions of municipal securities (to a large extent attributable to the effects of the Federal Reserve amendments to Regulation Q in 1961, 1963, and 1964, that raised the maximum interest rate that may be paid on commercial bank time deposits) so that they accounted for 74.9 per cent of the net expansion of municipal debt holdings in these years. Owing to the dominant role played by commercial banks as a buyer of municipal securities during 1962–65, the share of the market accounted for by "individuals and others" dropped to 3.7 per cent, and the share of fire and casualty insurance companies declined to 9 per cent. On the other hand, personal trust funds accounted for 13.4 per cent of the net increase in municipal debt outstanding during 1962–65.

"Over the past two decades commercial banks have experienced a steady increase in the proportions of loans and investments represented by holdings in municipal securities, with the ratio rising from 3.8 per cent in 1946 to 12.1 per cent in 1964. Analysis of the municipal security investments by commercial banks finds (a) a growing interest in revenue bonds, (b) a rising trend (especially in recent years) in investments in long-term (maturities over 10 years) municipal securities, and (c) a decline since 1960 in the proportion of municipal security holdings represented by holdings of speculative issues or issues in default. . . .

"Commercial banks must necessarily consider their liquidity requirements, the demand for loans from business and consumer borrowers and their legal needs to hold Government securities as collateral for Government accounts. Funds that remain after these needs have been accommodated are then invested in 'bonds', with municipal security investments depending upon a comparison of the tax-exempt yields with the bank's particular tax situation (income subject to tax). During periods of credit tightness, since commercial banks generally seek to accommodate their business and consumer customers first, their net expansion in municipal security investments tends to diminish."

FIRE AND CASUALTY COMPANIES

". . . Municipal security investments have become increasingly important, accounting for 30 per cent of their assets in 1962. . . . Analysis of municipal security investments by fire and casualty insurance companies finds (a) a rising proportion of such investments in revenue bonds (almost 50 per cent in 1965), (b) a tendency to purchase longer maturities (over 10 years), (c) that, while bond ratings are considered by some, many companies prefer to perform their own credit analysis of municipal borrowers, and (d) that intended use of bond proceeds does influence purchases, but geographical location of borrower has little effect. . . .

"Fire and casualty insurance companies similarly have to review their cash flows and income picture as well as comparative yields in determining whether to buy municipals. These companies necessarily consider whether their insurance underwriting is at a profit (or loss) and the amount of their taxable portfolio income before seeking municipal securities that yield a tax-free income. When, as in recent years, underwriting losses are heavy, many of the companies have less need for tax-exempt income and their purchases of municipals have fallen off correspondingly. . . ."

Commercial banks and the fire and casualty companies together are the buyers for almost three-quarters of the municipal securities being offered. The bulk of the remaining customers are to be found among individuals and their alter egos, the personal trust funds they have access to in various forms, and it is noteworthy that individual investment is increasingly institutionalized in the form of such trusts. Reference to sources for Figure 14 shows that in the first postwar decade, individuals added twice as many municipals to their portfolios as did the personal trusts, in the second decade (1956–65) only half again as much, and, in the projection for 1966–75, additions to individual portfolios will be only a little more than a third of comparable additions to personal trusts. In addition, individuals will be investors in the new municipal bond investment funds.

INVESTMENT BY AND FOR PERSONS

"A recent innovation in municipal security financing has been the development of municipal investment funds. These are registered investment companies, the assets of which are invested in municipal securities. The tax exemption of the interest income on the municipal securities is 'passed through' to the holders of the shares in these bond funds, which by the end of 1965 aggregated $249 million.

"While personal trust funds have expanded their holdings of municipal securities over the past two decades, municipal securities as a percentage of assets have varied little, rising from 10.4 per cent in 1946 to 13.2 per cent in 1955 and to 13.7 per cent in 1965. However, in recent years many of the commercial banks (that administer these personal trusts) have established common trust funds for investments in municipal securities, with the number of such 'tax-exempt' funds rising from 24 in 1962 to 104 in 1965. Analysis of personal trust holdings of municipal securities finds (a) an increasing trend in revenue bond investments, (b) considerable investments in maturities over 20 years, (c) while there is some reliance upon bond ratings, most trust departments prefer to do their own credit analysis, and (d) neither intended use of proceeds nor geographical location of borrower have much influence on municipal security investment decisions. . . .

"In the case of personal trusts (and, as appropriate, individual investors), comparative yields as contrasted to marginal tax rates is the principal determination governing investments in municipal securities, after due allowance has been made for the expenditure requirements of the income beneficiary (or individual). The higher the tax bracket of the personal trust (or individual investor), the greater is the need for tax exempt income."

OTHER INVESTORS

"Many nonfinancial business corporations, after considering their cash flow requirements, invest a portion of their cash balances in municipals so long as the tax-exempt yield compares favorably to the after tax returns on alternative short-term investments. For institutional investors such as life insurance companies or mutual savings banks (which have appreciably lower marginal tax rates than high income individuals, most nonfinancial corporations, commercial banks or fire and casualty insurance companies), the prime consideration is a comparison of tax-exempt municipal yields with taxable investment yields. Generally, these institutions have less immediate liquidity or expenditure requirements. In the case of life insurance companies. . . . , investments in municipals take place if their yields are from 60 to 90 per cent of taxable yields (mainly if the ratio is over 80 per cent) or if the tax-exempt yield is 50 to 100 basis points lower than the taxable yield."

See also "The Tax-Exempt Bond Funds Are Designed to Lure New Investor Cash into Municipals," by Fred Golden, *The Weekly Bond Buyer,* December 12, 1966, p. 3.

Index